Comments

From Sir, With ⌒⌒⌒⌒

If this book's effect is anything like Mr Edgecombe's classes or assemblies, you will not only come away from reading it entertained and intellectually stimulated but also with a new drive to become a better person. Which is the effect Mr Edgecombe has had on myself and the majority of Queen Margaret College students.

Erinn Aspell
Queen Margaret College Head Girl, 2021

... a great record of education and learning and of a faith in practice. And of a teacher's journey.

Michael Keith
Wellington writer and editor

... jam-packed with colour and literary appeal and wonderful wisdom coming through in every paragraph. ... full of quite profound insights into Christian communication to audiences of varied backgrounds, as well as being thoroughly entertaining.

Tom Slater
former National Director of the Australian Evangelical Alliance

Every generation worries about the values and beliefs of the next. From his experience at a private girls' school, Ken Edgecombe gives us a fascinating glimpse of how young people view — and experience — faith.

Philip Yancey
author of *What's so Amazing about Grace?*

... whimsical style and understated quips had me hooked ... I would enthusiastically recommend the book ...

Peter Lineham MNZM
Professor Emeritus of History, Massey University

I listened happily in many Chaplain's Assemblies, one of approximately 700 people present who felt like Ken was talking just with them. The chapters of this book give me the same feeling that the two of us are engaged in conversation, and showcase Ken's profound skill as a storyteller.

Jacqui Brown
Principal, New Plymouth Girls' High School

Ken Edgecombe's teaching style and ability to connect with students was exactly what the College needed. Students were safe in his classes to express themselves without fear ... they knew that he cared about them as people, whether or not they believed the same as he did.

Jayne-Ann Young
Principal, Queen Margaret College

This book is written from experience. As a result, it is honest, raw, funny – and doesn't offer formulaic answers to life's big questions. It will leave you wondering: What do I believe? What might I have said?

Wendy Strachan
Australia, Scripture Union International Children's Ministry Coordinator, 2000-2017

I have appreciated Ken Edgecombe's writing for many years. What a treat to now have it bundled up in a book. Ken offers us insight into a different world with his usual mix of wry, humorous, and shrewd reflections. Here is a writer on top of his craft with a story to entertain and inspire.

Tim Cooper
Professor of Church History,
Theology Programme, University of Otago

Not everyone felt an immediate connection to Religious Education at first glance, but through Mr Edgecombe's warming presence, intellectual, interactive, and inclusive lessons, it became a subject we all loved. Now, we have a book with more of the same. The blessing to Queen Margaret College faculty and to students' lives may go further abroad.

Lilly Taulelei
Queen Margaret College Head Girl, 2022

From Sir, With Love

Glimpses of Faith Through a Classroom Window

Ken Edgecombe

Ark House Press
arkhousepress.com

Cataloguing in Publication Data:
Title: From Sir With Love
ISBN: 978-0-6455947-6-8 (pbk)
Subjects: Memoirs; Education; Christian Living;
Other Authors/Contributors: Edgecombe, Ken; Kennedy, Sharon; Galloway, Hamish.

Design by initiateagency.com
With illustrations by Sharon Kennedy.

For the girls I taught, and the women they became.

Beyond Mathematics, English, History,
We talked of faith, of ethics, mystery,
Considered things beyond the square
And took our thinking everywhere.

Contents

Foreword...xiii

Introduction

Introduction.. xvii

1 New Shades of Teaching 1

2 Good Reasons to Stay 13

3 Hearing the Voice 23

Year 7

4 Groundwork in Year 7 33

5 Year 7 Meet the Prophets 41

Year 8
(And The Bible)

6 Reading for Meaning: Year 8...53

7 The Bible: Resilient, Not a Checklist.............................64

8 Chaplain's Assembly...75

9   Science and Faith:
    No Cause for Conflict...85

10 What About God? 95

11 God, Truth and Practice...109

12 What You See Depends on Where You Stand................117

13 Points Not Too Strident 126

14 Holding a Light Touch 134

Year 9
(And Other Faiths)

15 The Theory of Edgecombe and Other Conversations 145

16 Only One of You 155

17 Islam, Narnia and Israel: Year 9.............................163

18 The Level of Discourse...173

Year 10
(And Big Issues In General)

19 "Other Religions" 183

20 Beatitudes, Buddhism and Barbarism: Year 10 192

21 For Love or Money 203

Year 11
(And Current Affairs)

22 History, Choices, and the Unseen Outlooks: Year 11 215

Years 12/13
(And Current Affairs)

23 To Forgive or to Fester 227

24 Where Did We Get To? Years 12 and 13 235

25 Faith and Life 247

26 Current Affairs...257

27 Parables in Lockdown 264

Conclusion

28 Good People to Be Around...279

29 A QM Sort of Place 287

Notes: Sources and Quotes..301

Acknowledgements...319

Foreword

School chaplaincy and RE teaching is a calling that is often misunderstood in the church and outside the church. And yet it is a wonderful opportunity for engagement with young people about life, meaning, God, spirituality … The things Ken writes about in this book are so familiar to me as I was the chaplain at St Andrew's College in Christchurch for 21 years. I certainly think this is a story worth telling!

Religion and spirituality are a huge dimension of the human story. Art, music, literature and history are so much more difficult to understand without a religious education. Engagement with the growing cultural and religious diversity of our nation is prone to stereotyping and prejudice without a deeper knowledge of the values and beliefs that people genuinely hold. Current political issues so often have a religious dimension that needs unpacking. And given the continual human search for meaning and fulfilment, to ignore the answers of religious faith is to exclude a major and abiding player in this search. For all these reasons, religious education in our schools has huge merit. Other countries see this — I think of the religious education programme in the schools in the UK. Yet in New Zealand it is left to the church schools, and I personally think that is a shame. It may be that the story Ken's told here will awaken some in our land to the potential for this dimension of good education?

An interesting dimension of Chaplaincy in schools is the spiritual depth that one comes across. The cohort of young people basically reflects the general population in terms of faith — most of them are not church-going, and nor would they call themselves Christian. And yet there is a spiritual interest that leads to deep engagement. This book brought back lots of good memories of meaningful interactions that came as the result of wondering and questioning from students I taught. I thought the bit at the end of the chapter on 'New Shades of Teaching' where the students ponder Jonah, 'where did he have left to run to?' 'inside himself', 'maybe hell', 'maybe they are the same place' was really profound. I can remember moments like that, and the reflective, Spirit-filled silence that followed. Special moments. Memorable moments.

And there is so much more to reflect on in this book…

For instance, the chapter that deals with other religions models good RE teaching in a Presbyterian school — respectful of others but not shying away from the Christian perspective, and presented without being dogmatic. And the chapter where Ken reflects on the school's special character is gold — well said, and so appropriate to the context. A view honed by years of working well in that space.

Hamish Galloway
Moderator
Presbyterian Church of Aotearoa NZ
March 2022

Introduction

Introduction

In 2001, I was sucked into the vortex of Queen Margaret College. I didn't get out for 21 years. Queen Margaret is a private girls' school in Wellington, owned and operated by the Presbyterian Church, and I was siphoned in to teach Religious Education. The school might be Presbyterian, but the students of its intake are not Presbyterians. Nor are they necessarily members of any other church, Christian or otherwise. Some are, of course, but by the process of random selection, they are a pretty standard cross-section of the New Zealand religious landscape.

"So how did you get on?" my friends have often asked me. "Are they happy to receive compulsory religion?"

Well, they'd signed on for it. But it's not actually religion I was teaching. It's "Religious Education" — academic, teaching "about", not faith practice. But the answer to the question is, of course, "It varied." Some were. Some weren't. But my experience over those 21 years was overwhelmingly positive. Girls have often voiced or written deep appreciation at the time they have left, some have emailed after they have gone, parents have made their comments. Not in their hundreds, obviously, but enough to convince me that an interest in religious or spiritual issues is very much alive in the present age.

These pages are an attempt to capture some of the flavour of the years. What did we do, and why? How did it look? How did it go down? The approach is more anecdotal than analytical, more of a window than a survey, but something of the flavour is here. The stories, of course, are not mine — or, they are not mine alone. They belong to the girls I taught, who provided them or received them, and I have not asked them all for permission to pass them on to you. Consequently, their identity is vague — first names only, or perhaps "Someone..." When it is "Someone..." it means either that I can't remember who she was, or maybe I think she might not want to be identified. But the names that are here are real. I have not fictionalised them, and if anyone thinks she sees herself here, she probably does. If that's the case, thank you for helping, whoever you are.

New Shades of Teaching

It was my first day as a brand-new teacher of Religious Education at Queen Margaret College. I was not only new to the school, but I'd never taught RE before. I was sensitive to the vibes the class might give me over it. It's a sensitive area, after all.

I did have a couple of guidelines to operate on. One of them had come from the school principal, Ann Mildenhall, when she employed me. "I don't want them preached at," she'd said.

That suited me. I had no wish to become a classroom preacher. It's not a good way to run a class. It's not the best way to consider religion.

I did have some clear religious views, and I had been employed as a person of faith. I was also an experienced teacher in fields other than RE. I figured I'd be able to work out how to do it as I went along, if I was careful enough.

On day one, Year 10 were looking at the Beatitudes — "Blessed are the poor in spirit, for theirs is the kingdom of heaven" and so on. And a girl called Lauren, I can see her now, asked me, "Does this mean that good people go to heaven and bad people go to hell?"

I obviously didn't know it then, but the question was to be bookended many years later, on my third-to-last day at the school, when Laura — how close could she be? — asked me, "What's Jesus doing now?" It was a much more straightforward question to answer: "Representing you and me to God." But all that was ahead.

Preaching a sermon for Lauren would have been comparatively simple. A percentage of my audience would have known me, for one thing. And I would not have chosen a question quite like this, for another. But I didn't have a sermon. I had Lauren's question hanging in the air and I had a roomful of teenaged girls wondering not just "What's he going to say?" but also "Who is this guy, anyway?"

In the mini-seconds that followed, a clutch of impressions came to mind with lightning speed. The distortion of the text; don't preach at them; how much detail for an answer? And the biggest revelation: when a key question is asked, you have seconds to say something pertinent or to be publicly exposed as someone without the good stuff close at hand.

It's a different thing from teaching English. And Lauren's waiting for an answer, and all the spectators are too, and we begin to unpack the term "heaven" as Jesus used it, and then how it's not about being good but about having the right attitudes to God, and the role of forgiveness, and then what about those who are very good but just don't believe in God, and a long time later we're nearly ready to move on. And I have learned already to be very wary of that word "just", which will rear its head many times in the years to come. One of the hatful of lessons I was about to learn.

I'd already learned one of them earlier in the day, about the tenor of the school climate. I taught my lessons in a small room on the school's boundary, a bit of a walk from anywhere, and at the end of my first two classes I returned to the staffroom carrying about a dozen blazers I had salvaged after the lesson, from the backs of girls' chairs. "What's with all the blazers?" someone asked. "You doing a production of some kind?"

"No," I said. "They've all been left in my room. They'll get stolen."

"They won't get stolen," my adviser told me. "Everybody's got their own blazer. Take them back — the girls will *think* they've been stolen." So I staggered back with all these stripey coats: first lesson learned about my new surrounds. I had sometimes been in schools with quite different sorts of approaches to unattended property.

My last school, in fact, had been a long time before. Apart from three terms relief teaching a couple of years earlier, I had been out of the profession for over 10 years, spending most of them as National Director of a Christian organisation, Scripture Union. I had been happy before that as an English teacher, and then as a deputy principal, but it was kind of historical by now.

My move to Queen Margaret had begun when the phone rang one evening a few months earlier. I was at home alone, just preparing dinner and minding my own business. The caller was Ann Mildenhall. I had met Ann numerous times because my wife, Felicia, was the Head of Music at Queen Margaret College. But Ann didn't casually ring me, and nor was I prepared for her first comment after the pleasantries.

"My RE teacher's leaving," she said. "Will you come and do the job? I know you're a teacher who's not teaching."

Well, she was right about that. Having finished with Scripture Union, I was working for myself as a writer and editor-for-hire. It was supporting me, just, but it looked like it might grow. Did I want to go and teach again? Religious Education? In a private girls' school?

Actually, it was more than "Did I want to?" Pretty close to the surface was, "Could I?" Any early-career success would cut no ice now, and I would need to start again as a classroom teacher, and a teacher of RE at that. I suspected that RE might not be top of the popularity scale, and things in schools change in 10 years, among the pupils and in me. I didn't know if it was possible to go back to where I'd come from, and the three terms' relief teaching that couple of years before Ann rang hadn't gone well. So I stalled a bit, and arranged to meet her at the school and talk about it.

We agreed on a few things. I'd go for a term, and then we'd review it. No preaching, Ann said. No problem. I'm a teacher. I understand about compulsory attendance and delicate territory. Ann suggested she could omit Year 12 from the course if it made it easier for me to accept it: I said, "Keep them in." She said, "I want them to engage with the big things of life. And put some rigour into it." I assumed that meant that she wanted them to do more than colour in pictures of Jesus at Lake Galilee. That suited me too. And so I began at the start of 2001. And on my first day they leave their blazers all over my chairs and Lauren asks me black and white questions about heaven and hell. On a faulty premise.

But it's a good day. And then I'm at the railway station on my way home and I meet a friend who says, "What are you doing now?" and when I mention Queen Margaret College, he asks, "What are they like up there?" More considered answers to a simplistic question.

The years that followed, more than 20 of them, were mostly about questions. One day not long after I started, a group of senior girls gave me a list of written questions and I provided them with written answers. There were a lot of questions so the answers were necessarily brief, but at the end of the exercise Jaimie-May said to me, "You've really thought about this, haven't you?"

I had, and I wanted her to think about it as well. Rigour, after all. There were people in my life who saw my role as proselytising, and were either suspicious or enthusiastic about it depending on their own standpoint. Others feared I might be inoculating a generation of schoolgirls against Christian faith or spiritual awareness, and the dangers of that were never too far from my own mind. But if I could model, and seek to encourage, a little bit of engagement with the wider issues of life, I would consider that I was doing an honest job.

Because the questions that Jaimie-May and her friends gave me were significant questions, and they demanded a deal of thought. They asked enough to occupy the ponderings of many better theologians or philosophers than I am. But I had a shot at them. I prefaced my remarks by saying, "Note that any attempt to address these questions has to presuppose a starting point. Mine is the teaching of the Bible as I understand it. Other people will have other starting points and I mean them no disrespect, but this is mine."

Before I started in the classroom, I read the syllabus they gave me. There were about two-thirds of a year's work in any class level's course, and I worried about inventing the other third. But I found that any given lesson can be blown out of the water by some girl saying, "I was wondering about ..." and before you know it the bell's ringing and your planned lesson is still available for another day.

Which was one of the blessings of teaching a course not held to ransom by a tight assessment system. Here's a point of interest: let's follow it. It has made for reality of education at every level, and sometimes you lose out by not having an external lever to apply. But much more often the learning has been real, because when you engage with the issue someone has chosen to raise, you don't need the external lever anyway. I have never been kept so honest.

I had a student teacher once. That's not common in RE, because of course the state schools don't teach it. But a young woman turned up one year to observe some classes, and there was a morning when we were about to begin a Year 11 lesson. As the girls unpacked their books one of them said, "I've been meaning to ask about …" and someone else said, "Yes. What about that?" I can't remember now what the actual question was, but I do recall that the interest it generated was very wide, and one thing led to another so that just as I was finally saying, "What I want to do today is …", the bell rang for the end of the lesson. As they filed out, my student teacher looked at me and said in a voice of wonder, "Well, I've heard of flexible teaching, but that's insane." It has often been like that, albeit not usually so extreme.

You had to keep an eye on it, of course. There was a day many years later when I was introducing a Year 8 class to some thoughts from the Book of Revelation. "It was written by John," I said. "He had been condemned to exile." And I gave them a quick explanation about the nature of exile. A girl at the back raised her hand and I gestured toward her, and she launched into a lengthy dissertation about an uncle of hers who had been held for questioning on some sort of drugs charge. I listened intently so I could follow the link, but it beat me completely and I finally said, "Is this to do with being an exile?" She looked at me patiently, a bit puzzled, and then said, "No, no. John. His name is John."

The questions came from everywhere. Some of them were deeply perceptive, and profound in their implications. Some were entirely away from any related topic. Some were superficial and some were simply dumb, although of course you never said that — "the only dumb question is the one you didn't ask." Many began with "This is maybe off the subject, but …" and not a few began "Mr Edgecombe, I don't mean to be offensive, but …" Such questions invariably led us to rich fields of mutual thought.

Actually, there are only two kinds of question in an RE classroom. One is the cooperative sort represented by "I don't mean to be offensive", and such questions never are offensive. The other sort accompanies a belligerent thrust of the jaw and an approach that might begin with "What about" and often includes the word "just", used dismissively as a rejection of whatever you may think as "just your opinion" and therefore beneath consideration, although interestingly enough their opinions are never beneath consideration. Those sorts of questions, of course, are not really questions — and I have to say, were not nearly as common as I thought they might have been. In later years, in fact, they were very rare indeed.

Which was good. When I first went there, I imagined all sorts of resistance from reluctant consumers of a compulsory course covering sensitive ground; typically, it wasn't like that. But one of the Gospel writers said about Jesus, "He looked on the crowds and had compassion on them, because they were like sheep without a shepherd" and I figured that if compassion was good enough for him, then maybe I could try and find some too. So I told God that I wouldn't run away from any question fairly asked, and although I was sometimes led into areas I would rather have avoided, I rarely did.

I did run one day. It wasn't from a belligerent question, nor was the topic too innately delicate. But it was in a Year 7 class, and I'd forgotten how young they were. I was in full flight telling them the Bible story of Joseph, dramatic in its detail and more so with embellishment, and I got to the fuss over his boss's wife, who tried to seduce him. Smart man that he was, he wasn't having any of that. Rejected and furious, she thrust her head out the window and bellowed into the street, "Rape!" And at the height of the drama a little voice in front of me said, "What's rape?" I came back from Joseph and Potiphar's wife to rejoin Year 7, blinked, thought fast and said, "Ask your father."

The whole question of the use of the Bible has had its subtleties. Unashamedly I used it to reinforce a point as much as to introduce one. The approach generated a sympathy and a broad consideration of the issues of life: a search for the principles above chapter and verse. I was asked one day, "Do you believe all the Bible is literally true?" and recognised another occasion of being caught in the micro-second. Say "yes" and spend the next week defending everyone's challenges about every obscure fetish they can think of; say "no" and rob the Bible of credibility of any kind; spend too long thinking about it and create the impression that it's a new idea, and lose your own lingering vestiges of credibility in the process.

It was one of those moments when I believe God himself came to my rescue. Inside the allowable microscopic timeframe I heard myself saying, "I believe it all has authority." And in the time thus bought we found it possible to explore the word "literally" and for me to say that no, I did not believe all the Bible was literally true, and to defend that response while still holding to the integrity of scripture. For the record, the example I chose had nothing to do with six days of creation or the universality of the flood or people surviving being swallowed by a fish. I chose a line from Revelation where John wrote, "There was silence in heaven for about half an hour" and I said that heaven was a place beyond time, so the half an hour had to represent impact rather than passing minutes on a clock. From there, we went on to other, bigger, issues.

I was writing at the time an article for a conservative Christian magazine, and I used this question to base it on. It drew some fire from several people who chose to write letters to the editor. "Where are we," someone demanded, "when we can't give a straight answer to a little girl's question on a topic like that?" Well, I thought I had. And if I had to do it again, I would say something very similar. Someone else helpfully suggested that if we left out the word "literally" it would ease the whole question, but the whole point of it was that I hadn't phrased the question in the first place and the girl who did phrase it had included the word, presumably deliberately. On balance, I have to say that I found my classroom more discerning than my correspondents.

Which has been a joy through the years. A combined Year 12 and 13 class in 2019 looked at the story of Cain and Abel. Their responses were exhilarating.

There are more than a few imponderables in the Cain and Abel story. The two sons of Adam and Eve, who bring a sacrifice each to God. Cain's sacrifice, from his harvest, is unacceptable; Abel's, from his flock, is good. No reason is given for either response. I have heard preachers through the years speculate that it might show God's preference for a blood sacrifice, but the story is not explicit about it.

My girls went straight to a far more immediate question. "Why does he kill his brother over it?" one wondered. "I mean — he's obviously jealous, but ... *that* jealous?"

"Maybe he had a history of jealousy," said someone else. "And here it all boils over."

And a third person said, "Yes — look at the end of it all. God says, 'Sin is crouching at your door, but you must overcome it.' Sounds to me like something he's faced for a while, and he finally doesn't overcome it." And another voice said, "Maybe it's his mean spirit that wipes out his sacrifice." No platitudes here based on assumptions brought from somewhere else. Rather, a pondering on character and human responsibility, leading away from suggestions of non-understood or arbitrary laws. Classic human possibilities, nothing arcane about them, as up-to-date as Starbucks.

Then they wondered about how one of only four people in the world gets on after he has murdered one of the other three, and before long the obvious question emerged. "If he and the dead brother are the only people around except for Adam and Eve, who is he worried about when he says to God, 'Don't send me there — the people will kill me'?" It's a good question, and I don't know the answer to it. And neither does anybody else. So you say that. About the only suggestion I know that makes any sense is that the Bible is not telling us all that is going on, only what we need to know so we can learn what we need to learn. Once you accept that, there is room for all kinds of good understanding.

The Cain and Abel lesson was a great reminder that honest people will often tangle with real issues. I recall another Year 12 lesson in about 2010, when I wanted to talk about Jonah. I can't remember why I wanted to talk about Jonah, but I do recall being nervous about it. Jonah, of course, is the man who was swallowed by a fish and returned to convert a city. I braced myself for a grilling about whether such a story is or can be credible and all the associated thrusting out of jaws and demands about my own naiveté and was it all going to be as much as my real goals were worth. I needn't have worried.

We read the story, and the opening comment came from a girl in the back row: "Why did God choose Jonah to be his prophet?"

"Where are you coming from?" I asked.

"Well, look at him — he's hopeless. He's running away from God at the start and arguing with him at the end. What sort of a prophet is that?"

It's a good question. "What do you think?" I asked the rest of them. Someone said, "Maybe that's the only kind of person God had available. Everyone likes to do it their own way."

"Still like that," I suggested. Someone else said, "Well, he does learn. He finally goes where he's told to, and they all respond to his preaching." And someone else said, "Maybe it's more about learning than about knowing it all in the first place." I don't know if I've ever heard Jonah unpacked as well anywhere.

Nor had they finished. "Look," someone said, "it says here that he told the sailors he followed the God of the earth and the sea and the heavens. Where is there left for him to run to?"

Two voices, in quick succession, gave their response. One said, "Inside himself?" Another said, "Maybe to hell?" And in the silence that followed another voice said that maybe "inside yourself" and "hell" were the same place, if you had run away from God comprehensively enough.

There is a story, source of it long forgotten, about a man talking to God about heaven and hell. "I will show you hell," said God. And they went into a room which had a large pot of stew in the middle. The smell was delicious, and around the pot sat people who were famished and desperate. All were holding spoons with very long handles which reached to the pot, but because the handles of the spoons were longer than their arms, it was impossible to get the stew into their mouths. Their suffering was terrible.

"Now I will show you heaven," said God, and they went into an identical room. There was a similar pot of stew and the people had the same identical spoons, but they were well nourished, talking and happy. At first the man did not understand.

"It is simple," said God. "You see, these ones have learned to feed each other." When our focus shifts away from ourself, we may discover an entirely new perspective.

On another day, another class was reflecting on what heaven might be like. One girl suggested, "It could be a reflection of how you lived on earth. Your experience in the afterlife may be the aftermath of your actions before your death, and will therefore be either a lesson, a punishment, or a reward." That's not a bad way of saying that whatever we walk into later might be shaped by what we are grooming in ourselves now: that what we get is what we really want. It's a challenging thought.

The principal had said she didn't want them preached at. I hadn't expressed any of those thoughts. But I've pinched them many times since, in sermons for other people who did want to be preached at.

Good Reasons to Stay

I told Ann Mildenhall, in 2001, that I would commit to a term and review it again before the end of the year. At the end of that year, I committed to a second. At the end of the third year — when Ann left — I stayed on. Eighteen years after that, I was still there. So, what was the secret?

I once heard Jerry Seinfeld (on YouTube!) asked why he had stayed in stand-up comedy, and he said, "I fell in love with the work, which was joyful and difficult and interesting." I wish I'd thought of that line; he speaks for me. There are two main reasons why I stayed. One is that I liked it, and the other is that I believed it to be worthwhile. On its own, neither might have been enough. Together, they became compelling.

I am a teacher. I was given my first timetable, at Tawa College, in 1969. For over half a century, with a ten-year break, I was allowed to involve myself in the lives of other people's kids. Perhaps I can hope, in all that time, to have taught some of them something. But I can say with full assurance that they have taught me about as much.

There is nothing treacly about that comment. I share the contempt of all right-thinking people for the sort of mushy sentiment that says "I really care about the youth": patronisation at its worst and usually with a deal of self-deception. I have not forgotten those days when a class finally leaves the room after a lesson you know has been a nightmare. You know it because you've spent the last 20 minutes furtively looking at the clock and marvelling that it still has all that time to go. What's more, you know whose fault the nightmare is, and it's nearly always yours.

Rose-tinted spectacles are a wonderful thing. But when you take them off and remember all those days when you wondered why you had not followed some other pathway, *any* other pathway, you realise that it really has been a privilege to spend your days among people who hold you to account and see through your own screens of self-delusion from 40 paces and make you answer the queries that every honest person ought to have. On one of the days when I asked a class to write down their immediate questions and give them to me their responses included, among all the "How do you know there's a God?" and "Why doesn't God wipe out poverty?" questions, one that was a whole lot closer to home. It was, "Does teaching RE ever make you examine your own beliefs?" Quite simply the answer was, "Every week." Sometimes it was every day. And if the core beliefs have remained intact, the implications around them certainly have not.

I cannot say that my time at QMC was unalleviated joy. The first few weeks were quite literally fearful. I was trying to remember what a teacher did, and find out what an RE teacher did, and who all these people were and who among them I was, and the day I was walking down a corridor and a girl approaching said quite naturally "Hello, Mr Edgecombe" I was so delighted that I nearly put the whole thing at risk by embracing her on the spot. I was arriving, and it was wonderful to discover. Two years later I was walking with an easy swagger, but it took that long to find it.

And always, the lessons were a gamble. Well, not quite a gamble — I was an experienced professional, after all — but you never knew if this was going to strike oil or just be boring. You had a theme, you found a story, you had a vision of engaged debate, and then when you got to the classroom someone sighed and said "I suppose she gets it wrong" or, worse, no one said anything. But the days when someone else began a chain of rich discussion out of nowhere came to far surpass them, and always there was the chance of real gold, for you and them.

It was the stories that unlocked it all. The stories, and the questions. Some philosopher wrote that the shortest route between truth and the human heart passes through a story, and I can say that's true. I said that Jesus looked on the people with compassion and I tried to do the same. Mixed success. But the other thing that Jesus did was that he taught them in parables. I figured I could have a go at that too.

How many times does someone ask Jesus a question, often a tricky question, and he says, "A certain man ..."? That opening, "a certain man", is the ancestor of the classic modern joke: "There was this ..." It might be followed by anything — Irishman, blonde, old man — anything at all, but the ground is established. The subject is no one in particular, some kind of cliché is about to be exploited, I hope you like the story. And then Jesus went on to complete his parable before, often, hitting them between the eyes with a penetrating, and often personal, question or remark.

Well, I reckoned I could do that. I've always liked swapping jokes, and even if I did learn years ago to never tell a stock joke in the classroom and risk the common groan, I thought there must be times to tell a story and let the message seep out of the lining when it wanted to. So I gathered stories, from everywhere — conversations, family stories, Bible stories, personal stories, from friends, from books and films and the internet — anywhere a story gathered, maybe you could do something with it. Some you wrote out and filed and never used; some you rediscovered after three years; some became stock features. Many of them came back to mind on the spur of the moment, unpremeditated — "That reminds me ..." Very often when a story ended a girl would ask "Is that a true story?", and I learned to say, "Do you mean did it happen, or has it got truth?" And we all learned that a thing is not a lie just because it never happened, and indeed it might be deceptive even when it did.

You learned to get a feel for a story, and you'd be prepared to say, "I don't know if that story happened or not. But it feels like it should have, doesn't it?" Something about the detail would suggest its authenticity. Sometimes you were wrong. I found a great little story somewhere, web I suppose, about an African American lady who was rescued from torrential rain by a passing white man, a truck driver, sometime in the 1960s, in Alabama. Unusually, he went to a lot of trouble to help her out, getting himself soaked in the process. She was in a great hurry to go to the hospital and visit her husband, so she just thanked the man quickly and took his address. A week later, a giant console colour TV is delivered to his door with a note to thank him for his efforts, signed by Mrs Nat King Cole.

The story suggests various good things and I used it accordingly, assuming it to be historical as well as true. But it wasn't. Reading about it somewhere one day I came across a by-line, "This story is an urban legend." Not history: still true, but my instincts were astray. Another lesson in not being too adamant when you're light on information.

There was a similar experience with a story called "The Cab Ride I'll Never Forget". A taxi driver picks up a fare late at night, an old lady on her way to a hospice and leaving behind her home and her life. When she asks him to take her through the city, he turns off his meter and spends the early hours of the morning visiting all the haunts of her young womanhood. Then, when he's dropped her off without charging her for the ride, he goes off alone to reflect that he has rarely done anything as significant. It's a story an RE teacher can use, and I did, under the initial impression that it was an autobiographical piece. Then I read that it wasn't: it was a story written to make the sort of point that I and my girls had been inferring from it. Then, later again, I read that it was historical after all. Whatever. It made no difference to its power.

Jesus' parables are like that. I could have used them, if I had wanted to, in answering the girl who asked me if I thought that all the Bible was literally true. The parables are literally invented, on the spot, by a storyteller who wanted to convey a truth that was bigger than the story. These are stories you might describe as metaphorically true. Truth is bigger than mathematics.

Which is something that came to mind every time, and there have been many times, that I have been asked, "Can you really prove God?" The short answer, of course, is "No." The slightly longer answer is, "No, and no one else can disprove him." But the real question is around the word "prove", especially if we widen the discussion to include the word "evidence".

A typical conversation on the "prove God" lines would begin with someone asking if you could prove there is a God, and my giving a no-both-ways response and going on to say, "That's if you mean, by 'proof', some sort of a formula that doesn't allow any more wondering. But then, you can't prove many things that far."

"What sorts of things can't you prove?"

"Just about everything. I mean, you can prove mathematical things, and scientific things, and measurable things. But even then, you have to agree on a few things as a basis. Say you've got a metre ruler. Now, is a metre *really* a 'metre', or do we just invent a term to agree on? Like, 'this far' is always 'this far'. Then we can move on to say something that really matters."

"You mean like, when I see blue, you might see red?"

"Well, yeah, maybe I do. We can't 'prove' red is red or blue is blue. But as long as we're both consistent, it might not matter if we're not using the same words about it. Who here plays an instrument, or sings?"

Always a few. "Well, can we prove music?"

"What do you mean by prove?"

"That's the question. Do we know there *is* music?"

"There is if I'm playing it."

"That's what I'd say, too. But if someone said they didn't think music really existed and we were all just deceiving ourselves, what would we say then?"

"We'd probably tell them to go away while we got on with it. Their loss."

"That's pretty much what I'm tempted to say about people who go on about 'proving' God. But it's not a loss I'd want anyone to have." We'd be getting fairly well into it by now, and I'd be likely to go on along the lines of, "What about beauty, or even truth?"

By now, we're not really talking about God at all. We're talking about proof. I remember once saying, "I doubt if I could prove myself. I mean I'm here, and I have an effect, but if you wanted to argue that I wasn't and I didn't, I don't know what I could do to 'prove' it. I guess I might walk on your foot and ask you if you noticed, but if you said, 'Well, I did feel something, but I think it was just a twinge of arthritis happening at the same time,' I'm not sure we'd be any further ahead. And I'm not sure I would be bothered trying to convince you." I once trod on the foot of a girl in the front row to illustrate this shaft of brilliance, but I'm not sure if it helped.

"So where are we in the proving? I'm here, you say I'm not, I'll leave you alone till you want to talk to me. I wouldn't be surprised if God feels the same way. He might be waiting for us to react to the evidence."

"What sort of evidence?"

"Well, would the world do for a start? Very delicate, and complex, and it's here. It seems to me that someone probably put it here."

"But you can't prove that."

"No. That's my point. We can prove certain facts such as whether it's raining or not, but it's a lot more involved when things are a bit subtler. What about proving guilt in a court room? They have a magic phrase: 'beyond reasonable doubt.' I might believe on very strong evidence that he shot the milkman, and you can ask, 'Who saw him pull the trigger?' And unless that witness is absolutely reliable and the person who vouches for him is too, there will still be a margin of possible doubt. Strong evidence, but case only proven beyond reasonable doubt. The man in prison might still claim he is innocent."

I got carried away on this theme one day with Year 10, arguing that, if it came to it, you couldn't prove to a sceptic that there was such a person as Queen Elizabeth. You can't "prove" any event or person of history if you're prepared to dismiss all the witnesses. "How do you know Queen Elizabeth is real?" I asked.

"But we've seen her on television!" they protested.

"Seen someone," I said. "How do you know it's her? What if it's an elaborate deception backed up by a cast of gifted actors?"

"But everyone talks about her all the time," they insisted.

"That's just people talking. How do we know they're telling the truth?" And as I began to hit my straps, after another couple of these enlightened sallies, some voice in the front row asked me, very seriously, "Mr Edgecombe, don't you believe in Queen Elizabeth?"

It was kind of deflating, I have to say. So much for parallel arguments. But evidence, proof and faith still seem to me to belong in the same bag, and it's good to know which stops where and to allow the next one to enter the picture.

So I long ago gave up trying to "prove" God, and I also gave up feeling insecure about it. I came to believe that the things that can be measured, observed and put in a bottle, proven beyond argument, are actually on a secondary level of importance behind things that can't be, like love or beauty, and awe. I used to say that, and at least some of my people understood it. They knew about things that were beyond words, never mind beyond measuring.

"Who likes Beethoven?" I once asked a class. Most of them had heard of him. "Who likes the Beatles?" They all did, even though they really ought not to have heard of the Beatles, given their age. "Which is better?" Personal taste.

Different tastes, but everyone knew there is power in music. Is Mozart bigger than Marley? Is the Rolling Stones a better band than the Lumsden Fire Brigade social group? All right, now, who can prove it? Yeah, sure, more people like one more than the other, but that's not the same thing. And yet we know there is a scale of quality, even if we can't quite measure it.

I told a class about a fantail I saw once when I was on a tramp. It was about half a tree away, and my tramping mate and I just stood, silently, and watched it. They all understood what I was talking about. We considered wonder, and awe. I never asked a class what looking up at the sky on a clear night did to them and failed to get a 100 percent response to the idea of awe. Siobhan once described it as "being gobsmacked". I put the line on the classroom wall right next to a comment from Lucy, who said "Awe makes you jealous without the negative connotations." Powerful, universal. And not measurable.

The sky at night, a sunrise or a waterfall, and we stand still in wonder. Same with a baby's fingers. Or a master craftsman or a musician or a masterpiece of creativity or beauty. Something deep inside us moves. First we stop, then we stand in respect, then we want to show it to someone else.

Those things are bigger than I am, and bigger than anyone else is, and we all understood it. I talked to a girl who had seen the Grand Canyon during the school holidays and was full of it. When I made a remark about a hole in the ground, she all but spat on the floor. She knew, and so do I, that you are short of a soul if that's all you want to call it. Stay with the mud on your boots.

Like ethics, awe is beyond measuring. You might ask why, when the moonlight shines in her hair and he is all choked up and she wants to laugh and cry at the same time, no one describes molecular changes. You might reflect that no sight in the world is more common than a newborn baby, but every mother looks at her baby and knows, deep in her heart, that this has never happened before.

The girls go all quiet when you talk about this. Awe, one pace removed. When art absorbs your attention and you look into the distance and ponder, and come back to it and see something a little different; when music catches your soul and leaves a lingering peace, or maybe an ache, that you can never quite describe; when poetry says for you exactly what you couldn't say for yourself and does it with words that only suggest things and do not fully spell them out, you pause. You have little to say, for nothing can capture quite the impact on your soul. You see a person playing a flute, or using a cricket bat as delicately as if it were a scalpel, or soothing a dog by talking to it, and you recognise the transcendent. Something is going on that you cannot capture, and your soul responds.

These things are good. They enrich us. They do more than that. They put us in touch with something bigger than we are, and bigger than the world is, that seems somehow to represent the essence of the universe. They stop us in our tracks, and we feel moved to wonder. And we can't "prove" any of them.

Mostly, the girls haven't wanted to argue about all that. They have certainly wanted to discuss it, and to question it, and to add qualifying ideas, and how healthy that has always been. No wonder I found it work that was joyful and difficult and interesting. Why did I stay all that time? I was happy, and privileged, to stay in my classroom through the years because the richness of dialogue meant that I hadn't wanted to go anywhere else.

Hearing the Voice

So, apart from matters of awe and wonder, what sorts of things did we consider in a Religious Education class? At first glance, any question about RE topics seems like a pathway to the obvious. Religion, surely.

Well, yes, of course. But "religion" is a chewy sort of a word. Queen Margaret College is a Presbyterian school (I was once asked by a girl in Year 7 if QMC was "a Christian school or an Anglican one", and had great pleasure in relaying the question to my Anglican principal) and I am a Christian, but we did not spend our time singing hymns. A departing Year 12 girl once bemoaned that fact. The founders might have been Presbyterian, but the clients most decidedly are not.

Over the years the student body included girls whom I personally knew to be Muslim, Jewish, Sikh, Hindu, Buddhist, and every stripe of Christian from Catholic to Pentecostal including maybe 10 or a dozen card-carrying Presbyterians, and you can chuck in the odd Mormon and a Christadelphian or two. Most of them, appropriately, I had no idea what they were. But there were many who arrived prepared to state, "I'm not religious", often with the incipient suggestion, "Therefore I can't be expected to do any work around here." I learned to define "religion" as that which shapes your life at the deepest level, be it God or golf. Formal religions take a more corporate form and a recognisable pattern of behaviour, but all of us live for something. That for which we live, we may call our religion. So you can certainly do a bit of work around here, starting from whatever platform the day might offer.

The platforms varied, depending on the desired outcome. I often liked to work up to the outcome, rather than tabling it up front and working back. Year 11 classes often considered the story of Henri Charrière, the French prison inmate who escaped from Devil's Island in French Guiana. The world knew him better as Papillon, from the butterfly tattoo on his chest. He published his story, *Papillon*, in 1970 and followed it in 1974 with a sequel, *Banco*. It's not a book that looks initially like a religious text.

It's the story of a desperate man. Convicted of murder in 1931, Charrière strenuously maintained his innocence and clung to the belief that he had been deliberately framed through 30 years of imprisonment, escape and criminal adventuring over half of South America. Through it all, he was completely driven by a wish for revenge. Revenge, he said, had kept him going for years in the cells, and it was his "one religion". And religion was something you must never give up.

He doesn't look at first glance like a religious man, not if you define religion in conventional terms. But he didn't define it in conventional terms, and nor did we. There was many a profitable conversation as Year 11 considered his claim about revenge, and what it signifies.

He'd have justified his inclusion in our course if that had been all he said, but he doesn't leave it there. He goes on. He reflected on his life, and he wondered if God had been looking after him. He spent some time in a safe-blowing gang where the motto of his mates had been, "Each for himself and God for all." Things had become decidedly dicey and he had thought that if his escape from disaster had really been God's protection, then God had been magnificent for him. But he didn't think it could have been God, because he had tried to talk to God once, as he was being released from El Dorado prison. Grateful for his good fortune, he had said to the "God of the Catholics" that he would like to do something to show gratitude for God's kindness, and he had heard a voice, almost audible, inviting him to give up his revenge, and he had refused. Anything else, but not that. And so he was left with the conviction that it could not have been God looking after him later. He put it down to luck. Surely God had nothing to do with things like he had been doing.

So we set about probing the question, might God have been involved? Or would a man like Charrière have been outside God's orbit? The common opinion in Year 11 was that God is probably ready to talk to anyone who is ready to listen, and if Charrière is indeed ready, then he's probably not beyond God's attention. It's a pretty good line of logic, really, and it places responsibility for hearing God on both God and me.

Later on, Charrière's new wife Rita becomes a spokesman for God. She lines her husband up and in the name of love, renewal and a new life, challenges his passion for revenge. She tells him that her view of "revenge" is that he and his family should free themselves of his whole shoddy past and become honest people. A reputation for integrity, she says, would be a negation of all that was behind, and might count as revenge indeed. It would prove to all those who had wronged him, that they were wrong. Let them get used to that. Such an outcome would be worthy of her love and trust. My girls at Queen Margaret didn't have much trouble with recognising Rita as a voice for love and thus an agent of change, and many of them could see in her a voice from God as well.

Those understandings led us well to the point in Charrière's story when French civil proceedings against him lapsed, in June of 1966. He did return to France, for the publication of his memoir in 1969, and by then he was free from the driven passion of the past. He met his sisters and their families as a long-lost uncle and not as a desperate killer. He credited the change to the love of Rita.

His story ends on another note, about the fourth, that would have been enough on its own to attract our attention. He went to the street where the courthouse had been at the time of his original trial, the place he had once dreamed of dynamiting. He sat on a bench in the street, for eight days in a row, once on each day he spent in Paris. Each time he relived his trial, and each time he told himself he had given up his revenge. And each time he asked God that as a reward for doing so, the same kind of thing should never happen to anyone else.

He went away each day a little less bowed down than he had been the day before, and on the last day he felt as straight and supple as a man in his youth. He told himself to give up the people of the past. He told himself he had won. He told himself he was a miracle, and that God did not work a miracle every day.

Of course, for the girls in Year 11, the next questions are going to be, what about a miracle? Is he one? Does God work such miracles every day? Charrière may not look like a conventional priest, but his memoir takes us close to the heart of religious thinking.

There is a key phrase in Charrière's statement here that never escaped attention. It comes when he is talking about a reward for giving up his revenge. It is that the same kind of thing should never happen "to anyone else." There was a general agreement that when a person begins to think about other people after a lifetime of thinking about themselves, the suggestion of a miracle just might have been strengthened.

I always believed that anyone completing an RE course at Queen Margaret College should leave with a clear understanding of what Christian faith is all about. To that end, we returned often to basic Christian tenets — after all, about a third of the world's population claims some allegiance to them. Henri Charrière was one way to get there.

Then, when we'd done with considering whether God might have talked to him, we might go on to ask, "How might God talk to any one of us, if he were going to do so?" And their answers were perceptive and encouraging.

"When we're ready to listen," was one suggestion. "Through a friend, or someone we trust," was another. "By an inner conviction?" "By something we might read?" "When I especially need to hear him." No one wanted to tie God down to green smoke from the wardrobe and a booming voice from the sky. For logic and reason, they led the field.

On the subject of whether God might speak to you and how it might happen, there is a wonderful story told by the American sociologist and preacher, Tony Campolo. It was rare for me to present American preachers in RE lessons. Wrong style, and often too much other baggage. But if you are going to make an exception, Campolo is a good one. He is not only free of redneck politics, but as a dramatic storyteller he would take a lot of beating; had he not dedicated his life to greater callings, he could probably have made it in the entertainment field. And he is a vigorous thinker with a refreshing outlook. And I had him on a DVD.

He recounts being invited to preach at a Pentecostal college somewhere in the United States. He said he liked going there because they took him into a little room and prayed for him. And in the Pentecostal tradition, they prayed long; all good, he said, because he needed a lot of prayer. But on this one occasion, "they prayed so long, *they* got tired …

"And one of them's not praying for me! He's praying for some guy called Charlie Stoltzfus. That's not right. You lean on my head, you pray for me!" Campolo developed his story: the man prayed repeatedly — "You know who I mean, Lord. Charlie Stoltzfus…" with our narrator interjecting his own commentary as he recounts it ("He's God. He knows who the guy is!"), and the man's story unfolds. He is leaving his wife and three children, and the intercessor wants God to stop him from doing so — "*Send* someone! Send an angel!" — while Campolo waits and they all lean on his head. The man is specific — "You know who I mean, Lord. He lives in the silver house trailer, about a mile down here on the right…" and Campolo refrains from suggesting "He's God. He knows where the guy lives!" He tells it all in a practised flourish, and my classes were very happy to be listening to an American preacher. My biggest problem was to do with humility: this man did my job better than I did.

Well, the men finish praying for Campolo and he delivers his address and then he begins his drive home, toward the motorway. He stops on the way there to pick up a hitch-hiker, and he introduces himself — "Hi. I'm Tony Campolo." The man looks at him and nods, and says, "I'm Charlie Stoltzfus."

Campolo nods back at him and says nothing in particular, but at the next off-ramp he leaves the motorway and begins heading back the way they have come. His passenger is alarmed — "Where are you taking me?" and he is stunned by the response, "I am taking you … home! Because you have just left your wife and three kids — right?" And as Campolo pulls up outside the silver house trailer the man, completely freaked out, asks "How do you know I live here?" and hears his driver reply, with all the drama of a considerable performer, "God told me!"

For Year 11 the question was, "Well, did God tell him?" The answers were fascinating. A few usually wanted to say, spontaneously and without introspection or doubt, "Obviously." A few others wanted to say "No," and probably a few more would have liked to but didn't want to be rude about it, or were maybe forced to a re-think by the fact of the question. And a lot wanted to say something along the lines of "Well, maybe."

But one day one of the answers went in a tantalisingly different direction. "No, it couldn't have been God," one person said, "because I don't believe in him."

I needed, quickly, to find a way to demonstrate all respect to the person who said it while suggesting that this is an outstanding example of reverse logic. The message here is that if I don't believe it, then any evidence for it has to be reshaped. Usually we would say, if the evidence suggests something, then my beliefs will be shaped. I've never been to Siberia, but I think it's a cold place. Someone comes home from there and says they were warm. I might say, "That's a new thought," and I might think about it and find there was some reason for it that I hadn't known about. But I might not say, "They couldn't have been, because I don't believe it." Suddenly, the topic has moved from "How might God speak?" and has become "Does my belief make anything true, or does not believing it stop it from being true?" This is going to be another day when the bell will ring too early.

Year 7

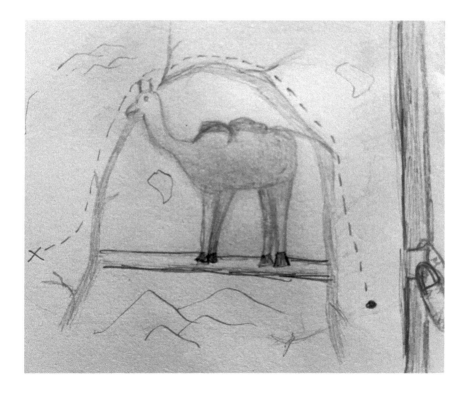

Groundwork in Year 7

I have to say that, when I started teaching at Queen Margaret, Year 7 filled me with more anticipatory dread than almost anyone else. They were followed pretty closely by Year 8, but if it were a straight-track race I think Year 7 would have won it.

The reason is not too obscure. I was an out-of-practice teacher and that was bad enough, but I was an out-of-practice *secondary* teacher, and the most junior I had ever gone before, or ever wanted to go, was Year 9. I knew that intermediate school-aged girls were another planet, and I had always been glad enough to leave that planet unexplored. I felt I was being called where angels feared to tread, and that they feared rightly.

To be fair, the fears were not all groundless. On any given day, about four of my new charges wanted to know the date and none of them seemed satisfied to hear, "Oh, some time in March, I think." They all wanted to put the date in the margins of their books and then ask me if they should use pen or pencil or underline their headings or was black all right instead of blue. I understood that they were following excellent and well-ingrained practices from a former age and that I would have to learn how to conform, but I still had to do it. It never did come naturally.

The question of what to teach them was another issue. I stood back a pace and thought about it. Religious Education, from Year 7 to 13, ground floor. OK: religions of the world.

All of them? Well, in a way, yes. Well, give or take. We might as well have a big picture. We could make a sort of backdrop, and elaborate on the details we chose to put in front of it in the years ahead. Start with an overall view and then zoom in.

So we did. I mean, we never set out to consider *all* of the world's faiths. How many are there, for a start? (The answer is that no one knows, but one source suggested 4,300, and I have no doubt that questions of definition and practice and interpretation might well double the number.) In fact, I suspect there might be as many "religions" in the world as there are citizens, plus a couple, but Year 7 might not want to visit all of them.

So I chose a few of the biggest, or the most obvious, or the ones Year 7 might recognise. I found an initial list of Christianity, Islam, Judaism, Hinduism, Buddhism and Taoism and made it up to about ten by adding Sikhism, Animism including Egyptian/Roman/Greek beliefs, and Materialism. Someone asked me once why I had left out atheism: I told her to have a closer look at materialism. Someone else wanted to know why there was no witchcraft and I said that no cookery book included poisonous mushrooms. Also, we only had so many weeks in the year, and also, Year 7 were generally getting a bit sick of the ones we did have by the time we got to the end of them. Also, all of life's a compromise.

We began by asking what religion was. Some people think it means a defined set of worship practices, and I think it is the way we live out our answers to the implicit questions about the big things of life. So we talked about that, and came down with a working definition that religion began where your beliefs about God and other people and the universe intersected near enough with the way you lived to put a shape on your practices. That is, the distinction between religion and philosophy might be said to be that when you believed something it was a philosophy, but when you lived it, it became a religion. I am sure that enough doctors of philosophy — or theology — could be found to cavil at such a line, but I was the man who was talking to Year 7, and they weren't.

In order to codify a view of religion and lay a foundation, I invented my own taxonomy. It was very simple: God; god; many-gods; no-god. God with upper-case "G" represented a supreme power with a personality who could be named and related to; god with lower-case "g" suggested a life force without personality, such as fate or destiny; the last two explain themselves. I maintained that all faiths and any individual corruptions of them could be fitted in there somewhere. I still think that.

Having got that far, Year 7 and I then did a wide-ranging survey. It was a high-altitude flight over the landscape to be sure, and it was pretty general, but it was wide-ranging. We looked at Christianity first, as the biggest religion — by numbers of adherents — in the world. We noted that estimates of numbers with religion were so wildly variable as to be misleading, but relativities might still mean something. After Christianity, Islam as the second biggest. Judaism next, not because it's the next biggest but because it is the parent religion of the first two. Then Hinduism and the rest, ending with humanism and materialism.

We drew a little symbol for each one – a cross for Christianity, star and crescent for Islam and so on, and my major task was preventing them from creating a multi-coloured artwork of precision and beauty and covering half a page for each one. I remember being mildly nonplussed when a girl asked what symbol she might draw for materialism. I probably suggested a ten-dollar bill.

It was also necessary to explain the difference between varying religions on the one hand, and internal branches of a given religion on the other — that is, that Buddhism and Christianity are different religions, but Anglicans and Catholics are both Christian; different branches. Sometimes this was pretty straightforward; sometimes it wasn't. I remember a day when I was exemplifying Christian branches — Anglican, Presbyterian, Lutheran, Brethren, Methodist — and when I got to Salvation Army, a voice said, "Is Salvation Army a religion? I thought it was a chain of shops." Someone should tell the Brigadier.

The questions appeared as we went along. "Are all religions the same? Why are they different? How are they different? Can you believe in more than one at the same time? If you can't, do you have to disapprove of the others?" Some of the answers became self-evident, others we stopped and discussed. In terms of disapproving, there was a line to be drawn between not accepting a set of teachings, and disrespecting its adherents. Also, it was possible to point out that there is often overlap of detail among faiths which are fundamentally different.

We addressed this overlap issue by considering the Olympic rings, and many a Year 7 RE book no doubt lies around to this day decorated accordingly. As an irrelevant side issue, it was always interesting to see how many girls knew how many rings there were, in what pattern and colours and what they all symbolised. Very few knew that the top three rings did not interlock with each other and the bottom two didn't either. Most knew that there was some interlocking going on. In fact, three of them are linked to two others, and two are linked to one: none is linked to more than two. They all knew there was a variety of colours, a few knew what the colours were, no one could put them in the right sequence. I couldn't either. (To remove any frustration or furtive Googling here, I can record that the colours across the top are blue, black, red, for Europe, Africa, the Americas, with yellow and green below for Asia and Oceania.)

All very religious, of course. Well, give us a minute. Once I had scribbled a facsimile on the whiteboard and the girls had produced a thing of beauty in their books, we said, "Now, say these circles represent different religions. We can see here an area of overlap, and another one here. Here, we can see there is none. So these three religions might agree on some things, but they disagree on other things. So they are not the same and we must not insult them by suggesting that they are, but they are not so entirely different that they have to be totally divorced from mutual respect."

So far, so good. But the underlying question, which is "Are they therefore equally credible?" would sometimes be made explicit, and it would need addressing with care. The best answer was along the lines of, "Well, no one who belongs to one faith accepts that some other faith is of equal merit because they all talk about truth, and if A thinks truth is black and B thinks it's white, they can't both be right. Nor is the problem solved by C suggesting they are both wrong and truth is actually grey, because that view does not remove either the first or the second belief, it simply adds a third." And the groundwork is laid for the next seven years of religious exploration.

Once we finished the world religion survey we were generally ready to go to Easter, as we did with every class level at the appropriate time every year. Christian school: Easter and Christmas were de rigueur.

Then in Term 2 we went to the Bible. We went to the Bible because it is the foundation document of the Christian faith that had established the school in which we were learning. There are times to consider exotic beliefs pursued by "them", and those times are best approached after one has covered the indigenous ground occupied by "us".

I began that approach early in my career, with the notion that we would proceed through the Bible during the year and emerge at the end of it. We never did emerge at the end of it. In fact, by the end of the year, we had generally got to about the start of the New Testament. That is, Christmas. Very appropriate for the end of a school year, and it left us the New Testament for Year 8. That was pretty much how it worked out for many years.

We began the Old Testament with the story of Abraham. The earlier story of creation we would get to sooner or later, Noah and the ark we might get to or we might not and most of the girls had heard the story anyway, albeit in some colourful forms, and Abraham offered us the opportunity to begin our narrative on a man whose date could be fairly decently approximated and whose recognition in history as the "first Jew" made him pivotal.

The style was simple. I told the story, they responded as they wanted to, we made a book entry and moved on to the next individual.

In round figures, Abraham's story dates from about 2000 BC. He was the man who followed God to the Promised Land. He did this without knowing where he was going — that is, he trusted God, having first learned what it was to relate to God. The questions were predictable enough.

"How did he know it was God?"

"What if he was wrong?"

"Why did God pick him?"

"Why did he go?"

And similar. I did point out that I wasn't there and was therefore speculating, but I speculated that if God was serious about leading Abraham then perhaps he would make himself understandable; that if Abraham was wrong he would be a big-time loser; that he went because he did in fact trust God. The one about why God picked him I generally threw back at them: "Why do you think?"

They were pretty good. Maybe, they thought, he and God had a thing going before this dramatic call to leave home. I think they were right. I doubt that God would look up one day and call some rando of doubtful allegiance. It was a two-way deal, after all, and God would have wanted a person he could trust.

The story is that Abraham followed God to the Promised Land: the lesson is that anyone following God must exercise faith: the activity was to create a sliding camel.

This sliding camel was a major engineering and geographical feat, not to mention the history and theology involved. You drew a sketch map to include the Persian Gulf, the Mediterranean coast and the Mesopotamian Fertile Crescent skirting the north of the region. That's the route that Abraham followed. You included the Arabian Desert, a straight line through which took you from Abraham's origin to his destination and was the route that he did not follow, for the simple reason that it was desert and he was cunningly following the oases and streams of the Fertile Crescent.

You explained to the girls that we were now cheating, and you took a craft knife and cut twin incisions, close together, in their book pages from A to B – Persian Gulf to Mediterranean coast, through the Arabian Desert. Elaborately, they attached a small picture of a camel to a piece of string thoughtfully coated with Sellotape, and inserted it into the cuts so it could be pushed from Abraham's old home to his new one, along the route he never actually took. (You had to cheat because the mechanics of causing this camel to travel around the curve of the Mesopotamian

Crescent were insurmountable.) No girl ever forgot it: many of them happily displayed their camel to me in quite senior years. Whether the message about faith being a prerequisite for following God stuck as well was less clear, but I guess God and the girls would know that better than I could.

So we got Abraham to the Promised Land, and then we waited with him for the birth of his promised heir, and we agonised with his servant over finding a wife for the heir and watched agog as the heir's twin sons, Jacob and Esau, competed for favour until the expected order of inheritance had been reversed in favour of Jacob who then exiled himself back to Abraham's old home town before emerging 25 years later with four wives and twelve sons. And a daughter. The girls always wanted to know about the daughter. And you had to explain about polygamy, not to mention inheritance patterns and the roles of women. Concubines too, given that two of the four wives were not technically wives after all. It all helped to illustrate that the Bible is set in a real time among local customs, and its talking in the terms of those times does not necessarily mean it is promoting their customs.

It took some weeks to cover all this ground. After all, Abraham, Isaac and Jacob are dramatic citizens who occupy some 25 chapters of the Book of Genesis even before you get to Joseph, Jacob's eleventh son and the one that all the girls knew about. But if you are going to understand Christianity it helps to know about Judaism, and if you are going to get a handle on Judaism you can hardly go past the patriarchs.

Year 7 Meet the Prophets

The girls always enjoyed the narrative through Abraham, Isaac and Jacob, with its attendant by-ways and inherent adventures. But the character who really brought a light to the eye was Joseph. It might take a sentence or two but sooner or later someone would say, "Was he the one with the coat?"

It would be a sad commentary on our times to suggest that this recognition owed more to Andrew Lloyd Webber than to Genesis so we won't suggest that, but yes, he was the one with the coat. The amazing technicolour dreamcoat, if you will. Not a girl but was horrified by the fact that it represented the extraordinary favouritism of the brothers' father, and we often explored the fact that everyone God relates to is a person of frailty or sometimes worse. Nor does the relating to God excuse the frailty or the sometimes worse.

Anyway, Joseph's coat gets him banished as a slave to Egypt while the boys go home and tell their heartbroken father of his untimely death at the hands of some desert predator. The years pass and the brothers no doubt forget him to all intents and purposes, although the father never does. The brothers likely come to believe their own fiction.

Joseph is, of course, far from dead and he is in fact the subject of many an exotic adventure in Egypt, the details of which engross Year 7 for weeks, until he emerges as the Prime Minister and the Minister of Agriculture of Egypt and in a unique position to relate to these same brothers when famine and drought drive them to Egypt to plead with him for food.

The food exists in Egypt only because of Joseph's acuity in causing people to save it up before the time of short supply, and that same acuity now enables him to ensure the brothers bring their father down to Egypt to meet him and to wait out the drought. I have always rued the absence from the Bible of the scene where they have to tell their father they have found their long-dead brother – it seems to me there's half a feature film in that missing dialogue and it's hardly fair that I had to invent it every year for myself, but I gave it my best shot. And after the girls had manufactured a multicoloured coat to mount on paper springs in their books, we summarised the whole saga in about five sentences and prepared to move on from Genesis to Exodus.

There is a 430-year gap between the end of Genesis and the start of Exodus. During this time the Hebrews move from guests of the king to abject slavery, and the Bible has nothing to say about it at all. Frankly, I wonder if some of the Bible writers knew their job. Anyway, we covered it by taking a complete half-page and writing on it, in large and coloured letters which the girls loved, "430 years pass!" I wanted them to have some sense of time scale.

And then we could move on to Moses. Again, they all had some view of Moses and again, that view sometimes owed more to popular media than to the source documents, but some view was better than no view. Moses was a lot like Joseph in that he was a Hebrew in favour with the palace, but he was a lot unlike Joseph in that the Hebrews he represented were slaves and victims of genocide whereas Joseph's had been honoured guests with royal patronage.

One feature of the life of Moses that was popular among Year 7 was the resilience of the women who surrounded him in his early years. They were a remarkable lot.

We might begin with the midwives of the day, who had been instructed by the king to stifle the Hebrew boy babies at birth, but who resisted these orders. So Moses survived. Then his mother, the narrator casually says, "hid the baby for three months."

Anyone with a baby in the house, or even in the neighbour's house, knows that to hide a baby for three hours is a pretty mean feat. Year 7 and I covered some wonderfully fanciful theories in discussing how she might have achieved it for three months. The most common agreement was that, since baby girls were legal, Moses became an honorary girl and his mother engaged in fast talk whenever any helpful visitor offered to change his naps.

Given that such a setup would have had limited currency, the famous baby-in-the-bullrushes scene takes place. The view that the baby was left to float down the river was near-universal, and it is possible that some film studio is responsible for it, but the Bible story simply says "among the reeds along the bank of the Nile." Whatever, it's his mother who hides him, his sister who watches him, a servant girl who discovers him, and the Egyptian princess herself who salvages him, all in the face of the king's instruction that he ought to die. I hope he treated his wife well in the years ahead.

After a lot of happy speculation about how these various women explained their actions, we got Moses through his life story as far as the burning bush. Incidentally, I had a little faux pas of my own over this bullrushes scene one year when I had a Muslim girl in the class. I had invited them to draw the baby in the basket and was wandering around looking at their efforts when I became aware of an anxious voice at my elbow saying very courteously, "Mr Edgecombe, is it all right if I don't draw the prophet?" Obviously it was all right, but I hadn't thought about the subtlety before this little girl had to ask me.

So we got Moses through his career, including the plagues, the parting of the Red Sea and his receipt of the Ten Commandments, and we moved on from him into the Promised Land and talked about the judges, using Gideon and Samson as representative examples. And let me tell you that a classful of 11-year-old girls shouting, "A sword for the Lord, and for Gideon!" in their most bellicose voices is an electrifying thing.

After the judges, the kings. David was capable of using half a school term on his own if you let him, starting well before he met Goliath, and his dealings with Bathsheba required tact and discretion with Year 7. David's date was always useful: at 1000 BC, he was symmetrically placed between Abraham and Jesus, and if you wanted to you could always mention William the Conqueror as further symmetry between Jesus and our own good selves. Not that Year 7 cared.

The motley lot who were the kings after David we mostly gave a miss, except that we did look at Ahab and his wife Jezebel alongside the prophet of their day, Elijah. For sheer drama, their story would take a power of beating. We represented it in a single-page drawing of a bearded man in a cave with a stream and a minimum of two ravens, and a verse that read:

> Elijah was a prophet and he told the wicked king,
> "Your idol worship means the rain won't fall on anything
> Until I say so: God has said you're just an evil man

Get ready for the drought that's gonna dry out all the land."
Then Ahab told Elijah, "You be gone, and quit my sight!"
So he went down to the stream, and there the ravens saw
him right.

He came back from his exile and he knew he wouldn't fail,
He said, "Ahab, you bring with you all the priests of Baal.
We'll build an altar on the hill, and give a mighty shout,
And the one who draws the fire will surely drive the
others out."

With Elijah thus commemorated we moved on to Jonah, about a hundred years on into the eighth century BC. Jonah, he of the fish, whose story everyone wants to call "Jonah and the Whale". It's understandable too, but not ideal — it really should be titled "Jonah and God", because that's where the real action is. The whale, or more correctly the big fish, is "provided by God" according to the narrative, and as such is one of a list of about nine items similarly provided by God with the single aim of sorting Jonah out.

Consider the story in summary. God calls Jonah to go to Nineveh, and he runs away to Tarshish. God provides a storm. The sailors throw him overboard, and God provides the fish. Jonah, understandably, prays while inside the fish, and God provides a vomiting for the fish and a new message for Jonah: back to Nineveh. He goes, he preaches, they repent, and Jonah complains to God about it, taking up a viewing station to watch the city judged. God provides a leafy vine to shield him from the sun, then a worm to chew out the roots of the vine, and a scorching east wind to blow on Jonah and assist him to pay attention. Small wonder that a senior girl said to me one year, "God stalks Jonah, doesn't he?"

Year 7 made a paper feature with a folding fish face, and we moved on to Daniel. About 300 years after Jonah, he was captured by the Babylonians when they conquered Jerusalem in 587 BC. Daniel is at the centre of a remarkable narrative.

Even if you were to leave out anything miraculous, the narrative would be remarkable. For one thing, Daniel is at or around the royal court for so long that he must have been little more than a boy when he went there and he was an old man at the end. He was selected for royal training, he refused to compromise his own people's dietary laws, he interpreted dreams for the Babylonian king and became the "third ruler in the kingdom". He instructed one king to turn from his pride and hubris and rebuked a second for the same thing in the famous writing-on-the-wall incident, and he then became the trusted counsellor of a third. If you add in the miraculous events, he watches his three mates emerge unscathed from a fiery furnace and survives a night in a den full of hungry lions, after interpreting dreams and visions for a couple of different kings. In it all, the narrator is at pains to remind us, he stays true to his God and to his convictions, which is where his value is for a modern reader.

Clearly, the girls' questions were related to the role of God in his life — how did he survive, why did he risk it, how could he interpret the dreams, why did he follow God so purposefully, how come the lions didn't eat him, how could his friends survive the furnace, and many another. The simple and only safe answer is to reference the power of God who, while not always doing so, is able to manipulate any circumstances if he chooses to. Daniel's companions explicitly spell this out, in fact, when they are threatened with the furnace — "Our God is able to save us from the furnace, O King. But even if he doesn't, we decline your Majesty's invitation to worship your heathen idol."

The concomitant question then, of course, is "Why does God choose to adjust one set of circumstances and not another?" To that question, there is no watertight answer. "Only God knows that" is the only comment you can really make, but the Year 7 girl never existed in my classroom who found such an answer deeply satisfying. I'm not sure I do either, but it happens to be true.

Exit Daniel, and if we had enough of the year left, we moved on to Esther. It was always good to get to Esther if we could, because she represents one of the women who became a Biblical hero. In a girls' school in the first fifth of the 21st century, female Biblical heroes were a very good thing to offer.

She is the centre of a complex story. She lived around say 470 BC as one of the Jewish minority in the Persian Empire, a colossal enterprise stretching from Israel to India. The day comes when the emperor sacks his queen and then rounds up all the virgins his harem officials can find so he can conduct enough field tests to select a new one. His favour falls on the reluctant Esther.

She turns for help to her uncle, a court official named Mordecai. His advice is kind but brutal: "Nothing we can do. Make the most of it — it might come in handy. Don't tell them you're a Jew." Mordecai himself is under threat from a court rival by the name of Haman.

Things simmer. Mordecai passes on to Esther news of an assassination plot against the king, and she is able to alert him and gain further favour. Meanwhile, Mordecai gets further offside with Haman by refusing to bow to him and Haman, pursuing a positively Trump-like sense of grievance, erects a gallows for the hanging of Mordecai.

Haman is further enraged when the king requires him to publicly pay obeisance to Mordecai, and he engineers a royal edict for the people to attack, not only Mordecai, but every Jew in the empire on a day to be observed in the near future, after due preparation.

Mordecai recognises the occasion to play his, as it were, court card. Though they both know it is at the risk of her life, he engages Esther to intervene with the king, and she does so. It's an elaborate cloak-and-dagger denouement, but by the end of it Haman is hanged on the gallows he has had built for Mordecai, and Mordecai has become a highly honoured cabinet minister.

And here's the real sting. The king says to Esther, "What reward can we give you for services rendered? Name your fee." Esther eschews personal aggrandisement and says, "You know that day when everyone is going to attack the Jews? The edict you said you couldn't change? Well, how about a pre-emptive strike? The day before it falls due, you could allow the Jews to attack everyone else first."

In a truly breath-taking display of statesmanship the king accedes to this, and when it all happens to the great satisfaction of the Jews he asks Esther, "Anything else?" and she says, "Yes. What about an encore tomorrow?"

It's not hard to see why a people with a history like the Jews' would find such a story gratifying. For thrust and counter-thrust and sheer drama, it would take a lot of equalling. The annual Jewish feast of Purim still celebrates Esther. The feast is observed to listen to the story and to hear every word, along with a lot of dressing up and a noisemaker, engaged every time Haman's name is mentioned, to keep the command to blot out his name. The holiday also includes giving gifts to the poor, along with a tradition of performing a satirical show either to dramatise the story, or just for the sake of it.

It's a powerful story, and Year 7 loved it, even without all the Purim observances. it brought the year to a suitable end (except for Christmas in the last couple of lessons), and it laid a foundation for the contrasts of the teaching of Jesus to come in the New Testament. When he said so famously, "Love your enemies", he was speaking to a culture of doing with your enemies anything but. Year 7 could take that understanding with them into Year 8, when the narrative moved forward.

Year 8

(AND THE BIBLE)

Reading for Meaning: Year 8

Children are great observers but poor interpreters. So said Ian Grant, well-known parenting and relationship expert, who once voiced that belief in my company. That is, he explained, children don't miss much of what goes on around them, but they may miss a lot of its significance by attaching a faulty meaning to what they see.

I'm sure he's right. Even if he's not, I'm in no position to argue with him. But I will say that I thought it was helpful to encourage my Year 8 classes to interpret some of the things that they observed in the Bible.

For one thing, it is not a single, cohesive book. They usually thought it was. It is actually a series of writings, set down by very different people over vastly long periods of time in a great variety of circumstances, and collated later because of the consistent thread of theme. The cohesion emerges, but not because any one person — or, worse, a committee of them — looked up one wet Sunday afternoon and said, "I know! Let's write the Bible."

It helped Year 8 if you told them this. It helped them even more if you told them that the writings collected are of different sorts. I used to invent a number of arbitrary exercises to try and illustrate it. "All writing is shaped by its purpose," I would say. They would understand that. If you wanted to sell books, then a line like "Six dollars, available here" is pretty good prose, whereas if you wanted to excite suspense, you would need something else. No one really had any problem with that.

The centrality of audience, while equally important, was a little subtler. You might have the same message for different people, but how you would say it depended on who they were. I used to illustrate this by telling them that they have just dramatically and unexpectedly discovered a dead horse on their front lawn and inviting some of them to write down the first thing they would say about it to their mother, others what they would say to their 11-year-old brother, and others to their science teacher. I also tried suggesting that they were walking on a footpath when they saw fresh dog droppings in the pathway of their mother, their brother and the mayor. When many of them thought they might not say anything to the brother at all, my point was made.

But the Bible, I reminded them, was not written to 21st-century New Zealanders. Certainly, it applies to us, but how it does that is a matter of subtlety and discretion. We are smart when we learn how to do the applying.

There are two groups of people who deliberately seek not to apply subtlety or discretion. They both do the Bible a disservice. They do themselves a disservice as well. And they often extend the disservice to other people.

Both of these groups have an approach that lacks academic subtlety. A lot of them are critical of those who see things differently. One group takes pride in a literal approach that would regard everything in the Bible as stated, applicable, final, and basically simple. On this basis, some of their number are happy to assume moral superiority, and to find quick and sometimes unkind judgement on those who disagree with them. They often use Bible verses as an opportunity to shut a conversation down, rather than to open one up.

The second group have a lot in common with them, in that they also want to read the Bible very literally, but then they use that stance as an excuse to pour scorn on the whole lot of it and abandon the wealth that they might be mining. The approach of both groups tends to be unyielding, and their attitudes often are too.

Some writer I once read described excessive literalism as a form of insanity. I think it may have been the British intellectual Terry Eagleton, but whether it was or not, he opens up subtler approaches than a quick response based on uncritical reading habits. In terms of Biblical understanding, to be too literal is not only unnecessary, it is likely to shut out genuine understanding. I suspect that a lot of it derives from a sense of insecurity felt by people who subconsciously fear that the other side might get them if they don't get the jump and claim unarguable authority at the earliest opportunity.

Quite a lot of it goes back to the first chapter of Genesis, which tells of the creation of the world and talks of seven days. Anyone with a passing acquaintance with any theory of origins developed in the last hundred years is going to find a problem with a view of seven days and a 168-hour week.

Personally, I am intrigued by a line in the narrative which talks about the "fourth day". That's the "day" on which the sun and the moon are created. And I want to know, given that we define a literal day by the links between earth and sun, how we are meant to measure the first three days before the sun is created. So I am sceptical about any lobby in the church that wants to dig in and complain about godless science on the basis of that particular issue, but nor do I have much sympathy with any opposition lobby that simply dismisses the literal days theory and the rest of the Bible with it.

I thought that Year 8 could do better than that. I used to start their year's course with a line from TS Eliot's poem, "The Love Song of J Alfred Prufrock". We never bothered with the whole poem — it's a challenging poem, after all. One line was enough to open the thinking: "The yellow fog that rubs its back upon the window-panes." I used to put it on the board and ask, "What's wrong with that?" There are three things, and within minutes they had isolated them all — fog is not yellow, it has no back, it could not rub it if it did.

"So … we can discount the poem then, and write off Eliot at the same time?"

"Well, no — it's a poem."

"So we'll cut the writer some slack so he can tell us what he really wants us to know?"

"Obviously. How else can we get anything out of it?" They're onto it, Year 8.

"Well, we should apply the same system to the writer of Genesis and the Creation story." Especially we might like to do that if we allow (a) he might be writing other than literally (b) he will have written a long time after the events he is talking about (c) whatever his level of scientific knowledge was, it will be a lot less than ours (d) his real aim is nothing to do with the process of creation, and everything to do with the agent of it.

Seven "days" of creation. If the writing is poetic, you may let the days stand for a possibility or two other than 24-hour periods. In fact, it is not vital to the understanding of the text to require them to be anything. What our writer is saying is that once there was nothing and then there was something, *because someone put it there.* Actually, the whole theory of a Big Bang is so close to "God spoke and it happened" that the wonder is that there should be any lack of sympathy over it.

To do that, though, you need to read the text as literature rather than literalism and that will mean paying some attention to subtler things, whether you want to follow God or dismiss him. That is, work. We will need to read with questions in our minds.

The Swiss theologian Karl Barth took this approach to the well-known Bible story of the fall of Adam and Eve, a few pages after the creation. Responding to the criticism that a snake can't talk but the story says that the devil spoke through one, Barth said, "It doesn't matter whether the serpent spoke. What matters, is what he said." If we want a window into what the serpent said, which was all about the destructiveness of doing my own thing ahead of the ultimate good, we need look no further than the tyrants and oppressors who have corrupted civilisation through the ages and into the present day.

TS Eliot and Year 8 were all about an approach to the Bible. We read bits of Genesis 1, and decided that whatever else it was, it was a long way short of science. "Two great lights" to rule the sky? Year 8 know the moon is not a light.

But the writer of Genesis wouldn't have. He was using his observation to say something a little more foundational than the composition of moon rock. If we want to hear what he is saying, we will need to do the Eliot thing and go past the words to the meaning.

When we were ready, we'd move on from there. A little while after Genesis, you get to Leviticus. Laws. Swags of them. Laws about everything: worship, food, purification after childbirth, sex, land transfer, cleansing from mildew, protecting the worker... Basically, a legal and moral code for a people beginning a society, and not a few of them the basis for the legal code by which we live in this country, still. Year 8 did not spend time among the laws, but if they had, they would have noted that it would not be smart to adopt the whole lot of them as is, and it would not be smart either to abandon the whole lot of them, as is. But they would have also noticed a different kind of writing from the narratives that had come earlier.

Moving on from the laws, you come to history. Different writing again — and like all history, written from the viewpoint of the writer, who is so often the winner and who in this case is the Jews. And the Bible continues: after the history, the poetry; after the poetry, the prophecy; after the prophecy, more history; after the more history, the letters; after the letters, the vision. After the vision, the end. We didn't read it all. But we read enough, and enough variety, to notice that you had to read it variously if you were to get the point intended.

We had finished Year 7 at a point where we could turn our attention from the Old Testament of the Bible to the New, or the coming of Jesus. Christmas told us how he came and Easter told us why. We did a little unit called "Seven Sayings of Jesus" to tell us some of what he said in between. We rarely completed all seven: I re-named the topic "Up to Seven Sayings of Jesus", because it allowed us to stop at the end of the term at wherever we had got up to. For the record, the "sayings" we chose from were:

Whatever you wish that others would do to you, do also to them.

Whoever wants to save their life will lose it, but whoever loses their life for my sake and the gospel's will save it. For what good is it for someone to gain the whole world and lose their own soul?

Whatever you did for the least of these my children, you did for me.

Do not judge, or you too will be judged. For in the same way that you judge others, you too will also be judged.

Whoever wants to be great among you must be your servant, and whoever wants to be first must be the slave of all.

You cannot serve God and money.

I am the way, the truth and the life. No one comes to the Father except through me.

By their fruit you will recognise them. Do people pick grapes from thornbushes, or figs from thistles?

And if you just counted eight in that list, well, I told you we never did them all.

In another unit we explored Harry Potter, who is a saviour figure with many parallels to Jesus. By no stretch of the imagination could I be called a Harry Potter expert, nor even a genuine enthusiast, but there was a day sometime around 2010 when a colleague in the English Department challenged my ignorance and lent me the first of Harry's books. I subsequently read three of them, and then extracts from the ones after they became tome-like (I think Rowling sacked her editor after about three books. Bad move.) So I read around the Potter themes, and I found a lengthy interview with Rowling by Max Wyman of the *Vancouver Sun,* from 2000.

In the course of the interview Rowling said, "Every time I've been asked if I believe in God, I've said, 'yes,' because I do. But no one has ever really gone any more deeply into it than that, and I have to say that does suit me, because if I talk too freely about that, I think the intelligent reader will be able to guess what's coming in the books."

In 2000 she was about halfway through writing the seven books that became the Harry Potter sensation, and her comment about guessing the sequence from an insight into her Christian faith is intriguing, to say the least. What might she mean by Christian faith?

She unpacked that in the same interview. "When a person states that they are a Christian, they may mean one of several things – 'I believe in God,' 'I'm not an atheist or some other religion,' 'I go to church sometimes,' or 'I believe that Jesus Christ was the incarnate God who died to redeem the world of their sins, and I have a personal relationship with him as my Lord and Saviour.'" She goes on to present a Harry Potter who looks a lot more like a redeemer than a passing nod to God.

I kept on digging, and I found an article by an American writer by the name of Abigail BeauSeigneur, who explored the Harry/Jesus parallels with a lot more detail than I needed, and a lot more rigour too. She became the basis of an approach to Harry Potter that took us through much of Term 2. BeauSeigneur said, and we were careful to acknowledge, "There is no mention of God in Harry Potter, or of gods, or heaven or hell. There's no prayer. Not all of Harry Potter has parallels in the Bible, but a lot does. There are many suggestions that Harry Potter is a modern-day adaptation of the life of Christ."

And even when he didn't look like a shadow of Jesus, his series explored and illustrated life's big issues: power, family, friendship, loyalty, love, courage, sacrifice, the journey from child to adult, the fight between good and evil, and the choice between what's right and what's easy. Those issues are valuable in any classroom seeking an approach to life that goes past the pragmatic.

The field of religion offers a huge variety of subject matter, and when we finished with Harry we were able to go anywhere. We looked at Māori spirituality. We noted that Māori understandings of creation began with the atua, or gods, moving in the void (te kore), then the night (te pō) and the world of light (te ao mārama). We observed certain overlaps with the Biblical creation narrative, and also differences from it, and then took our attention to the children of Papatūānuku and Ranginui (earth mother and sky father) including Tāne, god of forests, Tangaroa, god of the sea, Rongo, god of cultivated food, and Tūmatauenga, god of war.

The unit was broad enough to allow a look into various aspects of concept, history and politics. The sacred features of the tohunga and of tapu and mana took us to wairua, or the spirit, and we acknowledged the belief that the departed spirits left New Zealand at Spirits Bay, east of Cape Reinga, for the ancestral resting place. We noted the early acceptance of Christianity, especially in its Anglican form, and the later impact upon that of the land disputes. The King movement and the development of Ringatū and the resistance of Te Whiti and the events at Parihaka took us into a whole historical series of political events. The New Zealand government's formal apology for Parihaka came only in 2017, one of the actions of then Prime Minister Bill English being to go there to apologise for the actions of the Crown.

There was a lot of historical and social significance that we didn't look at, but a glimpse is a glimpse. By Term 3 we were ready for a production of our own. We developed a modest goal to present the New Testament as a children's book, in six pages.

We called it "The Church and the Empire", noting that the church meant the people who followed Jesus and not some kind of a building, and observing that those people were initially outlawed by the Roman Empire. Our title was thus rich in implication.

Our first scene in the book was the resurrection, central in Christian history then and to its doctrines since. True to children's book style, we represented our story in verse, and on this page we put:

> When Mary and the women went down to the tomb
> The stone was rolled back: they looked into the room
> No body was there. From out of his prison

The body of Jesus had certainly risen.

An elaborate, sliding tomb-opening feature and a lot of coloured picture captured the spirit of it all, and then we went on to the coming of the Holy Spirit, or Pentecost. That event 50 days after the resurrection transformed the early church from a cowering remnant into an evangelising force that has shaped the face of the world ever since. Pentecost, presented on a red page with a flame feature and a little dove, became:

> Jesus' people were all in one room
> And flames lit upon them — but there were no fumes.
> A strong wind suddenly blew all around
> They spoke in the dialects of all foreign towns.
> The Holy Spirit had arrived.

Continuing to select key events from the development of the church, we moved on to the vision given to Peter to cause him to take the gospel to the whole world, not just to the Jews. His vision of "unclean" animals lowered from heaven:

> Peter slept. In his dream was a wonderful sight.
> Animals lowered from a very great height.
> A voice said, "Kill yourself something to eat."
> But Peter said, "Nothing unclean is a treat."
> God said, "The rules have changed."

We took a while on the picture with its various animals and colours before we moved on, this time into the life of Paul. Paul has a modest claim to have done more to change the history of the world than any other individual apart from Jesus himself. (If this suggestion seems to be excessive, let me remind you of the number of people in the world today with some nodding acquaintance with Christian faith and then remind you of who wrote half the New Testament.) From the book of Acts, Paul's experience in Philippi:

> Silas and Paul were thrown into a cell.
> Where in spite of the darkness, their wounds and the smell
> They praised God anyway, sang hymns aloud
> And round about midnight, with screaming, the crowd
> Were hit by an earthquake that shook the walls down
> They all could have taken off into the town.
> But they stayed, and talked to the jailer of God.

And if you think the poet has been excessive here, check it out in Acts 16. Most of it's there. We had a largely grey picture on this page, but when we got to John's vision of heaven, taken from Revelation, we went into purple and gold:

> The River of Life flowed from God's very own throne
> On both sides of it full-fruiting trees had all grown
> Twelve months of the year, and the leaves of the tree
> Were healing the nations, and all were now free.
> Everyone was very happy.

It's the end of the Bible, the end of our children's book and if I had timed it right, near enough to the end of the term and the year. A couple of lessons on Christmas, and back for Year 9, which we would begin with a unit on Individuality.

The Bible: Resilient,
Not a Checklist

I have a friend who has been principal of three state secondary schools and who went on to advise and mentor newly appointed principals in other schools. He told me once that his career has been littered with professional development courses of every sort.

I would believe that. Mine was too, albeit I imagine at a less elevated level than his. I would also believe his next comment, when he went on to say, "And the major themes of the whole lot of them might as well have been taken directly from the Sermon on the Mount."

I am sure that's true. What are all the directors of teachers' courses trying to promote? Care for kids, that's what. And what was Jesus telling his listeners, on the Mount? Love your neighbour. It's about as close as you can get.

No one in a professional seminar in New Zealand is going to say that out loud, of course, because it's not fashionable in the opening years of the 21st century. But the difference between caring for kids and loving your neighbour is so fine that if it were represented on an archery target you'd need to be Robin Hood himself to land an arrow in the zone, while standing up close on a good day.

I have talked a little bit about how literally we might read the Bible. I have also offered some glimpses of how I used it. But the nature of the Bible wants a little more attention than that, and on any day in the classroom it was liable to get it.

Christians regard the Bible as the place to find the revelations of God to man. That is, people. But they do not look upon it as a rule book, and their view of it is subtler than a lot of people imagine. Their understanding of the Bible is different, for example, from that which the Muslim has of the Koran.

Muslims believe the Koran to be, word for word and punctuation point for punctuation point, the exact and unvarying wording of Allah to his prophet Mohammed. As such, it is not open to adjustment of any kind, not by translation nor by interpretation. The result is that a translation into any language other than Arabic, while tolerated, is always seen as less than the real thing. I have seen a group of Iranian Muslims whose first language was Persian bring in an Arabic-speaking imam to read to them in Arabic, because devotion takes precedence over comprehension. The view comes directly from the belief about the book's origins, which is that it was dictated directly to Mohammed, who transcribed the words and gave the world the word of Allah, as is.

That is not the Christian view of the Bible. I have met individual Christians who seem to think it is, but I am bold enough to say they have got it wrong. For Christians, the understanding is that the many writers who compiled the Bible wrote what they were inspired to write, but they did so as partners, not as conduits. Therefore, the words are words to be taken respectfully and reverently, but the search is for overall meaning, not individual details from isolated phrases. Consequently, the Bible has been richly translated into many languages and in some of them, including English, it has been many times updated. The aim is to try to convey its meaning in the current context.

This brings its own challenges. Literalism is one, but so is the discovery of style and of what that means for our reading and understanding. Year 8, after their fog-on-the-window-panes exercise, had a page on which I thoughtfully reproduced five extracts from the Bible. One was from the Genesis creation account, one came from the Psalms, one from an historical narrative of one of the kings, one from the New Testament letters and one from the apocalyptic book of Revelation.

"Which one's a poem?" I would ask. "Which one's historical? Or a letter? And what would you call this?" And Year 8 would get most of it right most of the time. Then we could talk about why you wouldn't read one sort of writing with the same expectations as you would have from another sort.

For a modern reader, the poetry of the Psalms will hold a different significance from that which can be seen in the letters of a first century missionary. Similarly, the passages of genuine history will be viewed differently from those of apocalyptic vision or morality pieces. The Bible has all of these genres, and others. Furthermore, none of them is directly written to our day, although all of them are written for it. Some of the worst sermons I have heard have come from some preacher's attempt to apply a single set of responses to different kinds of writing, believing that it's all the Bible so it must get the same wash. Not all Christians draw their distinctions in the same way, of course, and the resultant variances have led to debate not always seemly. But there is possible a resilience that allows faith to be subtle and living, adjusting, removed from a paint-by-numbers approach and a legalistic outlook.

Christians are required to not be legalistic. When Jesus responded to the question about what was the greatest law with his famous "Love God; love your neighbour" comment, he was really saying "You cannot do it by ticking 500 boxes. Get the essence of it, and let it shape your soul."

I understood the truth of this every time I put any general law in front of any class at all. It didn't matter what it was — biblical, political, ancient, modern, general, local — whenever you said "It's not to be like this," someone asked, "But what if"? And the what if was always, *always*, a suggestion that the rule must have a loophole. Speed limit is 100kph? What if your child is sick and you have to get him to the hospital? Muslims fast during Ramadan? But what if you're pregnant, or very old? Or could you do it in a cooler country, with shorter days, and would it still count? No stealing, you say? What if you are starving?

We all do it, of course. All of us. It's human nature — surely this can't apply to me, or to all of us, or in this way, or without exception. We all think that way. No one lives by rules. Which I guess is why St Paul wrote, in his letter to the Ephesians, "It is by grace you are saved, through faith, not by works. Then, no one can boast." It means God may spend his time working with people who want to work with him, I suppose, not hearing court cases mounted by bush lawyers who want to worship themselves but claim his advantages.

About halfway through my years at Queen Margaret College I was given my very own parable on this theme and I have retold it in many a class since, always with total understanding from every girl present.

We were approaching Christmas with a group of, I think, Year 9 girls who said, "Can we make a Christmas card?" Well, why not? But I wanted

Christmas, not commercial myths — a distinction, I used to say, between the story and the stuff. So on this day I said, "Give me the story. Draw a manger, or some wise men, or a shepherd or two. Mary, Joseph, a baby. Maybe a star." All good so far. And then I made my mistake. "No holly or snow. No gilt-wrapped gift boxes. No Christmas trees."

"No Christmas trees?" The indrawn breath was audible; the dismay was palpable. There was disbelief, there was outrage. They were aghast and appalled. I was firm. "No Christmas trees." When the muttering subsided, they carried on.

As was my practice when the girls were working individually, I wandered around the room looking over a shoulder here and there and making casual comments. Then I came to Caroline Hill. Caroline barely looked up. She was putting the finishing touches to an enormous and colourful tree, full of greenery and red decorations and at first glance in flagrant defiance of the clear instructions everyone had complained about. I stood taller. "Caroline Hill!" I said, in a voice of awful dignity.

She turned upon me a face of sweetness and innocence, surrounded by flaxen hair and split with a smile of purest charm. "Yes?" she said.

"Caroline," I said, gesturing to the artwork in front of her, "what is this?"

"This?" In a voice as of one who has just noticed a major tourist attraction for the first time. "Oh yes — this. Oh, but — it's not a Christmas tree, Mr Edgecombe."

"Forgive me," I said. "I thought for a passing moment there it just might have been. Tell me, Gorgeous — what is it?" Her beaming smile was a beautiful thing. "This," she said, "is a Christmas bush!"

Game, set and match to Caroline Hill, and my fault entirely for telling them what not to do instead of asking them to cooperate. My ideal line was not, "No Christmas trees," but "Would you focus on the story for me?" Grace, not law.

You'd think a man would learn, and sometimes I did. But not always. A year later, Year 10 are doing Christmas cards, and sitting in front of me is Caroline Hill. I hadn't forgotten entirely, of course. I got to the Christmas tree deal, and I moved so I could see Caroline and she could see me, and I said, very clearly and with careful enunciation, "No Christmas trees. No Christmas bushes. No Christmas shrubs, or hedges, or Bonsai plants. No Christmas cacti." They went to work.

Sometime later I did my tour, and I stopped at the elbow of Caroline Hill. She was working assiduously on a page covered by maybe seven Christmas trees, and as I began to say "What do you call this?' she anticipated the call and said "Not a Christmas tree, Mr Edgecombe!"

"No?" I asked. "Then what?"

"Christmas plantation!" she informed me. With a smile to light up the horizon. Game, set, match and entire tournament to Caroline Hill. Victory by an innings and 150 runs. My fault again. Double fault, I suppose.

It wasn't over. Three years later, at the end of Year 13, Caroline is entering her final chaplain's assembly and I am standing in the atrium waiting for the school to enter, as I always did. When her form class comes past me she breaks ranks, and detours, and hands me a rolled up A4 sheet with a ribbon tied around it. I made to open it and she said, "After the assembly."

"OK," I said, and we took our separate stations, she to her seat in the hall and I to the lectern on the stage.

I was preoccupied for the next 20 minutes, but when I got back to the staffroom I unrolled the sheet, to be confronted by a whole-page, full-colour, hand-drawn picture of a large and unapologetic Christmas tree, with a little note of appreciation from Caroline acknowledging the years. I still have that page.

I still have, also, the parable. Often in the years since, trying to tell a class the difference between law and grace, I have brought in the name and the story of Caroline Hill, and not a pupil in front of me requires any explanation at all. I wonder if Caroline is today a corporate lawyer.

There is another picture of the irrelevance of minutiae in a scene from *No Country for Old Men*, a 2005 novel by Cormac McCarthy. It later became a film. McCarthy's character, a sheriff close to retirement (the "old man"), is reflecting on the changes he has seen in his years of law enforcement and the damage he has witnessed to social structures, particularly by the drug trafficking of southern Texas. The sheriff says, "I think if you were Satan and you were settin around tryin to think up something that would just bring the human race to its knees what you would probably come up with is narcotics. Maybe he did. I told that to somebody at breakfast the other mornin and they asked me if I believed in Satan. I said Well that ain't the point. And they said I know but do you? I had to think about that. I guess as a boy I did. Come the middle years my belief I reckon had waned somewhat. Now I'm startin to lean back the other way. He explains a lot of things that otherwise don't have no explanation. Or not to me they don't."

"That ain't the point." I have talked of two categories of people who make an art form of missing the point when it comes to reacting to the Bible. Each would be horrified to be herded with the other. One group is made up of those religious champions who can't let understanding develop away from a literal seven-day creation period or a world-wide universal flood or a man being swallowed by a fish. They may even be right, but it ain't the point. The other group is made up of those cynics who want to stop at every creation day or flood account or man-swallow-ing fish and throw the whole thing out, baby, bathwater and bathroom. That ain't the point either. The point is to see past the trees and take good notice of the wood, and to apply good teaching to the challenges of life which have not only not changed at all since the days of Jesus, but may be even more visible than they were when more people assumed a religious veneer.

I was once asked something that was open to individual speculation, about which I had few views and had done little thinking. So I said, "Listen: I'm not the man with all the answers. What I do have is a fair acquaintance with the Bible. I'll just talk about what it says. OK?"

And my questioner said, "The Bible? Do you mean you believe it?"

I responded to the tone. It was personable enough, but there was the innate challenge. I said, "Certainly I do. Don't you?"

"Well, I haven't really read it." This was not too surprising — it is my experience that the people most sceptical about the Bible are usually those who have read it the least. She went on, "But it's kind of old-fashioned, isn't it? And isn't it full of contradictions? And anyway, how could you prove it's true even if it did look OK?"

I sighed, not too audibly. I said, "It's a tricky word, 'prove'. What can you 'prove' about ambition and pride and anger? Or sacrifices in a noble cause?"

"Oh," she said, "you just know about those things."

"How?" I asked her. "How do you know about all those things that aren't just physical facts? If it comes to that, how do you know about half the things that are physical facts? If you haven't seen it, you have to depend on the evidence of the people who did."

"But the people who say they saw it might be telling lies."

"Sure they might. But they might not be, too. If you really wanted to, you could keep on arguing ad nauseam about everything. Did they really land on the moon? Did Shakespeare write Shakespeare? Who won the election? You can go on about that if you want to, but you reach a point where most reasonable people say 'OK. On balance, it's convincing.' Can we do that with the Bible?"

"Fair enough. So, why do you think the Bible's convincing? Have you read it?"

"Certainly I have. I read some part of it most days."

"Why?"

"Because it goes a long way to give me light on questions about how I ought to live."'

"But isn't it all incredibly old?"

"Absolutely it's old. So is human nature. Wouldn't you be doubtful about a book written last month in Palmerston North and trying to tell you about principles of living that we should have known about since Adam and Eve?"

"Adam and Eve. Wait a minute. Garden of Eden, right?"

"Right. I thought you said you'd never read it."

"Everyone knows that story, Adam and Eve. That's half the problem. Science proves it's all a lot of rubbish."

"Science does not prove it's all a lot of rubbish. Science throws light on how the processes worked, not on who caused them nor on why he did."

"But who made God?"

"Think about it. God is the original maker. Only the original maker makes anything."

"So … God made God?"

"If you like. It's not quite what the Bible says. The Bible just says he was always there."

You can say what you like about the Bible, and many people have. My classes have asked me a lot of good questions about it — Is it true? Is it like a law for Christians or more of a guidebook (*should* we follow it or do we *have* to follow it)? Do you have to believe everything in the Bible to be a Christian? What truth was there behind the story of God's Bible? How do we know that what the Bible says is true? Some of those questions would keep you going for a while. But whatever you make of it, there is no escaping the fact that the Bible covers a wide expanse of very topical material, still, on social issues. Incidentally, among the questions listed here, the single word that intrigues me most is "was", in the query "What truth was there behind the story of God's Bible?" Was? It's not over yet, and its themes are very topical.

Which is a pretty good response to the "How do you know it's true?" idea. Injunctions to social justice or personal responsibility are, simply, true. They call you to what is, and to what is right, and to what should be. Bring back to mind Karl Barth's comment that it was what the snake said that mattered, not whether he spoke: we all recognise temptation. We know it offers our advantage at the expense of someone else's. Sometimes it suggests our advantage at a cost to universal goodness, or to absolute right. When Adam and Eve were tempted to enjoy the forbidden fruit and to avoid the cost, they moved for us all, with consequences that have impact on us all. Wherever we stand theologically, in our clearest moments, we know that.

It's about this time in a conversation when the bell often goes for the end of the lesson, but sometimes it doesn't. Then, the classroom teacher has to decide how long to keep talking to one interested party and maybe a clutch of others introducing a comment of their own from time to time, while not letting those who have dropped out of the conversation feel uninvolved. The worst conversations were those where someone began something that uncovered so many possible tangents that you hardly began on the first one when somebody else took off on the second and another party again wanted the third, or the fourth or the fifth. It was usually best to say, "Wait on a minute and we'll come back to it: let's chase this along first", and you were usually OK to do that. Unless the bell went first.

Chaplain's Assembly

As I have mentioned, I was responsible for the chaplain's function at Queen Margaret College for many years. It didn't start that way. When I began, it was solely as a classroom teacher of RE, and the chaplain's duties were carried out by another person. But I'd only been there a couple of years when the other person left, and the principal asked me if I would take over the chaplain's role; specifically, the weekly assembly on a Friday afternoon. So I did that from about 2002 until the end of the first term of 2019.

The school held a special assembly to mark the occasion when I finished as the chaplain, and I was invited to involve a few of the senior girls. I chose five or six I thought could handle it OK, and one of them, Siobhan, was to chair a section of the proceedings.

It turned out she could indeed handle it OK. She stood behind the lectern as one well accustomed to holding attention, looked at the school assembled before her and said, "I think Mr Edgecombe has held chaplain's assemblies here for 18 years. Once a week, give or take, say 32 weeks of a school year. Call it 570 assemblies. And in approximately half of those, he's given us the Good Samaritan."

Lies, of course, but the school loved it. So did I. I think she was later a tad nervous that I might have been offended, or hurt, but she needn't have worried. She was great. In fact, I tried not to become too repetitive or predictable in chaplain's assemblies, and I was often asked by either pupils or staff how I came to my theme each week. But if I did have to hammer anything to a point of predictability, I would be very happy to stand by the Good Samaritan, especially if I were allowed to look at the Prodigal Son for the other half of the time. Consider: they asked Jesus what was the greatest commandment in the law, and he said, "'Love God.' And a second, like it, is 'Love your neighbour.' Everything rests on these two."

The Good Samaritan is all about loving your neighbour. Jesus invented the story on the spot when some lawyer demanded to know who his neighbour was, and Jesus said, "There was this man …" The other parable, the Prodigal Son, is all about God waiting for a flicker of recognition from his two sons who are both bent on ripping him off, but he will be there for them when they want to notice it. That's all about loving God.

So thanks, Siobhan. I think your maths may be a mite general, but if my chaplain's assemblies had to cover any ground more than once, on the occasions when the school's Christian character was to be publicly acknowledged, I will take the Good Samaritan. And I would be very happy to put the Prodigal Son alongside it.

But of course, there was more to chaplain's assemblies than two recurring parables, no matter how central they might have been. It was my weekly challenge through the 18 years to come up with an assembly theme and to deliver it. We once had a new staff member, about 2013, who asked me, "What's your system? Do you have a lectionary you work through, or what?"

I had a number of principles I had arrived at early, but the truth was that there was never anything so organised as a lectionary. I worked on the assumption that chaplain's assembly was the place where the school's embracing of Christianity was up for public scrutiny by an audience who, by and large, had not embraced it individually. My principles were threefold, as I outlined them to Carol Craymer when she arrived as the new principal in 2004 and talked to me about what I was doing. One, I would read something from the Bible — however brief — in every assembly. Two, I would pray in the name of Jesus and three, my theme for the day would exemplify my absolute conviction that faith and life are inextricably entwined.

It was very easy for me to justify these things to Carol — not that she required me to. When I had told her what I was doing and why, I said to her, "They are my non-negotiables. If you don't think they are appropriate, you'll need to find another chaplain." Carol had no problem and nor, nearly 14 years later, did Jayne-Ann Young when she arrived as Carol's successor.

My logic was simple. It was that a school which advertised itself as "Christian" had better be seen to be so, as distinct from promoting a sort of generalised goodwill such as you could find in any decent state school, and calling it Christian. Certainly not all my hearers were Christian, but they had signed up to be there and for me to illustrate something other than genuine faith would be to sell them out.

Christian faith is learned from the Bible and from God, and in the Bible we are encouraged to come to God through Jesus: my points one and two. It meant that with all the courteous respect and goodwill in the world towards other faiths, none of them was going to take over the school's Christian platform by some process of our forgetting who we were. It meant a certain sensitivity was called for, but we ought to expect to model that anyway.

My third principle was the one that took away the comfort of a lectionary. I imagined that it might become all too easy for my audience to arrive at the end of morning school in a spirit of apathetic tolerance or something worse and to wait for the compulsory expression of the school's "special character" to be over before they headed off to the canteen. I'm sure a lot of them did that anyway, but I didn't want to make it any easier than it had to be. So instead of reading from the Bible in what they might have considered to be an arbitrary fashion and then trying to apply it to life, I started somewhere in the school or the world and went to what the Bible said about it. It kept you dancing, but it was worthwhile. And when the teacher who had asked about the lectionary left the school sometime later, she sent me an email that included a line I have treasured ever since: "The Bible was never an antiquated text in your hands."

Sometimes it was easy. Often a girl or a group would ask if they could advertise some worthy cause or other or perform an item at the chaplain's assembly: it was one of two occasions in the week (the other was principal's assembly, on a Monday), that offered the total school audience. I always tried to say yes. I wanted the assembly to be part of the school, and for the school to know they were part of it. I remember once hosting a dance group and the legendary Milada Pivac, deputy principal through a generation, asking me later if I thought that was quite chaplain's assembly material. I found myself saying what I had not previously synthesised, "If it can't be represented at a chaplain's assembly, perhaps we should ask if it has a place in a Christian school." That might be a bit cut and dried, but there's a germ in there somewhere. The only real dilemma I faced was the year the Senior Chorale, presenting their Big Sing repertoire before the public event, wanted to sing a Buddhist mantra called "Gate Gate". We went ahead with it, but only after I had pondered its implications fairly deeply and decided I could get my Christian teaching for the day from somewhere else in the chorale's repertoire. Billy Joel, if I recall.

The day's topic was made easy when someone put it before me that way. More often they didn't, and I had to reflect on what was important in the world and could be seen to relate, then prepare my material. And it was my experience that every week, somewhere, there would come a little feeling that this was it. It might come from anywhere — a conversation I was having, a book I was reading, a news item or a school event or a comment on the news or almost anything — but at some point I realised that this was it, and now I could do the hard yards. I came to regard it as a nudge from God, to be honest, and I believe it was. It didn't let me off the hook of preparation: indeed, it opened the door to a lot of thought and work. But I think that's how God's work is done anyway, as a partnership between him and a willing assistant. I liked it when the nudge came early in the week, and certainly it was good to have it by Wednesday night. If it was delayed until late on Thursday I was open to a certain anxiety, but once I was nudged I was away.

Our material, then, came from all over the place. The actual themes were probably limited enough — love God, love your neighbour kept recurring — but the pathway to get to them could come from anywhere. Including the Good Samaritan, as Siobhan acutely observed. I remember once discovering a *Dominion Post* article in which a police officer assisted someone who was walking over the Remutakas in driving snow and was headlined as a Good Samaritan for his efforts. Meat and drink.

Apart from Samaritans, though, we came from all over the compass. Australian cricket ball tampering, Christchurch earthquakes, Muslim mosque attack, outer space and the galaxies, entropy, the extreme grief of a disappointed women's rugby team, chorale items, charitable causes in the school, literary topics, a picture of Heinrich Himmler laughing, the Thai cave rescue, a summary of the school term just ending ... Piper, leaving school one December at the end of Year 13, emailed me as she went: "I just wanted to say that I always enjoy your discussions on Fridays and they usually provide interesting conversation amongst some of us Year 13's at Friday lunchtime. It's always nice to have something fresh to talk about other than social media!" Do you think I purred?

Claiming a reason to focus on my theme was always a minor part of it, and I would not infrequently begin by saying "I was talking to X or Y or Z the other day and she thought ..." Well, I was talking to a group of Year 12 girls sometime around 2010 and Ellen said to me, "I've always wanted to be the person that you quote in your assembly," and while I was framing a reply of appropriate modesty and pleasure, her friend Hannah said, "Everybody does." What really pleased me was the intimation of involvement: without it, no profound message of subtlety or power would find root anywhere. About a year later Olivia said to me, "You make me want to believe more in God." I hope, ten years later, that she still does, and countless hundreds more.

So what did I do with all these themes? Typically, as I say, I would try to root them in some recognisable context — "Person X was saying...", then illustrate with whatever event or story I had selected, and extrapolate some unarguable thesis such as that we are responsible for people around us. Then it was possible to say, "What the Bible says about this is ..." and then conclude with a prayer and head off to lunch.

It was always positive to include someone else in the assembly if I could. I remember once making some point about parenting and asking Rob Hawley, teacher of Physics, to respond to my questions.

"Mr Hawley," I said from the stage. "You've got a son. What are your hopes for him?" His response could not have been scripted. From the back of the hall and audible at the front of it came Rob's reply. "To get a job, "he said. "To get married, and have a family." There was a pause, timed as exquisitely as anything Rowan Atkinson might dream about in his finest hour, and then: "In that order!"

So it was good to engage a wingman if it were possible, but often it was not and we remained a monologue (though I was delighted when, late in my innings, a colleague on the staff described it as a sort of Christian version of *Prairie Home Companion*; I've always admired Garrison Keillor's narratives). But even if that accolade was rather too much, I did believe that a monologue was preferable to giving, say, the Bible reading to someone who might feel little sympathy for it. Much of your conviction comes down to a pause of the right length or a lift of the eyes at the right place, and not everyone could always do that for you.

More ambitiously, I once wanted to mount a role play that would involve a fairly eloquent partner purporting to be a student unpacking some literary themes and working without a script. I went to my best candidate from Year 12 and she fled from the idea in fear of the public. Same with a Year 11 girl I thought could handle it. In the end I went to Shweta, in Year 9. She took the whole thing on magnificently and with complete aplomb and someone asked me later, "Is Shweta really doing all those things that you were talking about?" No real surprise to me a few years later when Shweta turned out to be the Head Girl.

The question of school singing in chaplain's assembly was always a bit of a vexed issue. Sometimes — before Easter, say, or the school Christmas service — you would have a clear need to be able to sing something for a given reason, and you would practise it beforehand in a chaplain's assembly. And I have to say that Tim Jenkin and the music staff were always wonderfully helpful on those occasions. I particularly enjoyed watching Rosemary Russell, and after her Louise Logan, coaxing the best efforts from the school, and it was a good feeling of collegiality to work with them in that way.

But on a Friday-to-Friday basis, I never did establish an easy expectation of combined singing. It would have been good, and I felt the lack of it, but the challenge of finding material that was contemporary enough to be attractive, established enough to be known, solid enough to be worthwhile and general enough to not require massed hypocrisy in repeating personal lyrics was just too much. I rationalised it by telling myself that the school was not a church, but I never really felt that I was on top of the issue. One of the strands running through it all was that a lot of contemporary Christian music depended on statements of personal worship that most of my girls did not experience, and I did not want to compromise their integrity or insult God with mandatory lies.

There were exceptions. One year the annual chaplains' and RE teachers' conference delegates were visiting the school, and I asked a group of senior girls if they would prepare and present Stuart Townend's contemporary version of the 23rd Psalm during assembly. They did it superbly, and the school took it to its collective heart over the next few years. There were other examples of a particular song or a special event being well matched and the singing being a good thing, but in general, it never became regular.

Maybe I should have read the message given me a few weeks after accepting the chaplain's duties. I was in the music office that morning, trying to find something that might meet the day's needs, when in came

Francie, the school's music prefect. Perfect, I thought, here's the best source of advice I could have. So I asked her, "What do you think we might sing in assembly today, Francie?" She was matter-of-factly dismissive. "I don't know, Mr Edgecombe," she said, "but they don't hate coming to chaplain's assemblies, anyway, so I don't think it matters."

I was glad they didn't hate coming, and the evidence over the years was that that was true. It was, after all, a compulsory exercise, and it imposed its expectations. They were required to come in silence, for one thing: a school tradition. It was a good tradition, in that the chaplain on Fridays and the principal on Mondays had no settling-in time to reckon with; the girls came in, the staff came in, the principal or the chaplain got straight to the point in a receptive atmosphere. But, more subtly, it was also an expression of corporate commitment. I used to stand, often with the principal, in the atrium as the school filed past, with the sound paramount of feet on the carpet. There they were, the young and the senior, the large and the small, the pliant and the bolshy, with a shoelace trailing here and a loose tie there, and something about it was very moving. I once described it to Carol Craymer as we watched them together as "sort of ... beaut", and she knew exactly what I was trying to say. The school on display, a presentation of its dignity, alongside the historical stateliness of its nineteenth century central buildings.

So I was glad they didn't hate coming. Often, someone would suggest she enjoyed it. Not infrequently, a girl or a group of them, sometimes a class, would say, "Are you going to mention me in chaplain's today?" Mostly I wasn't, so I'd say something like, "Well, you never know your luck in a big city." But it was nice that they wanted me to. Vanity, it might have been, but it was also involvement, and I was grateful.

There was a delicious irony one year among all that. I had been asked about a shout-out by Ella, when she was somewhere in Year 10. She had given me no possible reason to score such a thing, and I laughed at her and dismissed the notion. She came back to it here and there in a sort of sporadically friendly nagging kind of way over the next few months. At the end of the year, I remember, she wrote me a story or drew me a picture called The Parable of the Mean Chaplain.

She progressed through to somewhere late in Year 12 and, for some long-forgotten reason that had nothing to do with her campaign, I did have a cause to mention her in chaplain's assembly. I did so with relish, and waited for my next encounter with her — and it turned out that she had been absent from school that day. Poetic justice then, and also a year later when, in Year 13, she led the group that sang the Townend Lord's Prayer, winning more than a shout-out on her merits. She never did revise her mean-chaplain parable. But a few years after she left school she visited me in my classroom for old times' sake, and had forgotten all about it.

Science and Faith:
No Cause for Conflict

Some of the things I met in the classroom over the years excited me. A lot of them entertained me. But there was one thing that simply depressed me. That was the view, much too common, that God had somehow come into conflict with science. "I believe in the Big Bang" was one remark delivered, more than once, as an article of faith held out as an alternative, and a preferable alternative, to anything that might include God.

I think a lot of that idea has developed from the unfortunate approach to the Bible that Year 8 confronted through the fog and the window panes. And that's hardly surprising, if both God-followers and God-doubters have insisted on believing that the Bible is saying things that seem demonstrably false. But it's depressing, just the same. I spent a bit of time devising ways to undermine the idea. Oblique undermining seemed to be a better tactic than outright confrontation, which usually sounds like either defensiveness or an assault. Either one puts you into a conflict you didn't want to encourage in the first place.

It's worth saying here that I am not talking about evidence for God. The Bible does not probe that issue: it assumes it, and moves forward accordingly. Nor do all of the sceptics stop to consider the question seriously: they also assume something, and move forward. If you expect God, you may see him, and if you don't, you may have to dismiss things you can't explain. But if God is, and is active in his world, he may well do things that are outside a measurable scientific norm. What I am addressing here is an unnecessary tension stemming from a kind of assumption that creates it independently.

You want to engage your students in thinking along these lines. Eliot, in Year 8, had been all about an approach to the Bible. For specifically creation thinking, we went into Year 9. Initially, we focused less on the Bible accounts – in fact, we rarely mentioned them at all until the end of the unit. With Year 9, I tried for a reduction to logical premises. I put ten identical coins into a box, numbered them from one to ten with a felt pen, and asked the students what the mathematical chances were of drawing out any pre-numbered coin. Correctly, they nominated one chance in ten.

It took a bit longer, but after a while you got them to understand that the chances of two in a row were one in a hundred, of three in a row, one in a thousand, and of the whole ten in a single consecutive sequence, the mathematical chances were one in ten billion. We tried it. The early stages, that is. The one in ten worked about every tenth time, as it should have, and sometimes we got the one in a hundred. Once, we hit one in a thousand. I never stood around long enough to seriously challenge the whole ten.

But then, I tipped the whole lot out and put them in my pocket. "Go on," I said, holding out the box. "What are the chances now?" They looked a bit dumbfounded, but they're courteous people and no one asked me, "Have you lost it?" Once they realised the question was for real, they said, "Well, none."

"No," I said. "Nothing in, nothing out." I could as well have quoted from *The Sound of Music*, but my voice is not up to a lot of public singing and "nothing comes from nothing" loses something when it's merely spoken. So I went on to say, "But there are a lot of people who want you to believe that the whole universe, not just ten coins, came from nowhere. On its own. Without an agency. Unprovoked. 'First there was nothing, and then it exploded.' I'll give you that we do have to reckon with an ultimate beginning somewhere, but with my theory — God — I only have to explain him. With the no-God theory, you have to explain every individual detail in every single part of a mind-bogglingly big universe, with no reason, of any kind, for any of it. And let me tell you, this is not a science question at all. It's an origins question. It's really a God question, and it's called faith. Science kicks in later, when we start observing and measuring that which has arrived."

"How do you know?"

"That it's not about science?"

"Yes."

"Because science measures things, and we are talking about how there came to be anything to measure. You start measuring when there is something there to get a look at. Before that, you can only wonder. I think it's God."

"Can you prove that?"

"Of course not. Same as the other option. Either way, it's before you get to proof."

We had another exercise, for which I divided them into groups of three and gave each group about 90 words taken from a written page and thoughtfully cut into individual pieces, one word per piece. Large print. Sometimes, to simplify things and reduce the chance of losing any, I put two words together. Then, with about 45 minutes available, their task was to make a coherent paragraph out of their words, leaving none unused.

They nearly all managed it, albeit with a variety of clues and confirming of details along the way. Then, when someone asked "What's this all about?" I could say, "It has taken you a long time to use three good intellects to make a sane paragraph, that already existed, out of 90 components you were kindly provided with. None of you found it easy. Yet some of you want to tell me, and are prepared to cite 'science' to support you, that the whole world as we know it came from nowhere, with no mind or agency, to assist it. Even if you are right — and no one can prove it — you need to know that what you are applying is faith, not science, which is measurable. My faith is in God. What's the other option?"

But I do think that my faith has more going for it than the no-God faith. I especially think that when I look at some of the other issues that are also beyond science, such as morality and love and culture. The real question, and I tried to suggest it to Year 9, is not about God versus science. It's best when it's not about anything "versus" anything. It is about "God? Or no-God?" There are eminent scientists on both sides of the God divide, just as there are people of every other specialist field on either side of it. Personally, I enjoyed the years when the Head of Science at Queen Margaret College was not only the most highly qualified teacher on the staff, but also a very level-headed and committed, and personable, Christian who was married to an Anglican vicar. It was very easy to point to her and ask if anyone wanted to challenge her credentials, especially on the day when someone asked me, "Mr Edgecombe, do you believe in God or science?"

It is of course pertinent in all the references to "science" to ask, "Which one do you mean?" Is God supposed to be nullified by the science of chemistry, or physics, or philology or hydrology or geology or etymology or something else? And *how* does the particular field of science, whichever one it is, arrive at that final step of faith that says after observation is complete, "And that leads us, beyond dispute, to here"?

One scientist who seems happy to adopt that position is Richard Dawkins. I understand Richard Dawkins to be an eminent biologist deserving of the highest regard, but I regard him as a lesser theologian. The literary critic Terry Eagleton once said of him, "Imagine someone holding forth on biology whose only knowledge of the subject is the *Book of British Birds*, and you have a rough idea of what it feels like to read Richard Dawkins on theology." Well, I don't know about that, and I certainly allow him to come to whatever personal position of faith that he finds compelling. But I do not allow him to state with absolute conviction that God is non-existent, in the face of the testimony of countless people through the ages that God is alive and active in their experience.

In passing, an editorial in *North and South* magazine in 2019 quoted Dawkins as wishing to see students taught robust thinking, because half of all Americans believe in angels and a third in ghosts. You may or you may not believe in either angels or ghosts, but if you are promoting rational thinking you should surely do better than simply dismiss the idea of them on the grounds that you don't agree with it. I know a man who summed up that approach in two sentences when he said, "I don't believe in Richard Dawkins. There is no evidence that he exists."

I took a friend along to the school once, a man who straddles both science and faith, and asked him to talk about it with a couple of senior groups. His name is Warwick Smith, senior government scientist at GNS Science through a 40-year career there and in the earlier DSIR. For a time he was Chief Seismologist and a senior adviser to the government concerning earthquakes and the detection of French nuclear testing in the Pacific. For 15 years, he was a member of a United Nations working group which addressed the detection of nuclear testing worldwide. His PhD is in geophysics from the University of California and he has served for 12 years as an elder at Titahi Bay Community Church. He addressed the groups as requested, and invited questions. One girl asked him if he believed the world was round. (His reply was brilliant. "Yes," he said dryly. "I've been around it.") But his major point was that science is about processes and theology is about reasons.

Science is science, theology is theology, and the world is richer for them both. Or, to be consistent, sciences are sciences and theology is theology, and the world is richer for them all. The British Jewish Orthodox Rabbi Jonathan Sacks sums the issue up by saying that science seeks to tell us how things work, and theology seeks to tell us why they should. He calls science the search for explanation and religion the search for meaning, and he has a book whose title is *The Great Partnership* — science and religion serving different, and complementary, aspects of the human quest for understanding. The girl who asked me if I believed in God or science brings me close to despair, because she crystallises so much misunderstanding on a scale so widespread that she cannot even see the implications, and nor can so many of those who have fed her the impression.

These are not academic themes. Sacks says that if the West loses its faith he fears for its future. It's a terrifying thing to be reminded of Nazi Germany and Stalinist Russia and remember that no secular morality could prevent their emergence. Nor, claims Sacks, does any secular morality have the power to oppose religious extremism. If they have to rely on forces within themselves, neither market forces nor liberal democracy will inspire sacrifice for the general wellbeing of the world.

Notice that he calls ruthless religious extremism a threat. He's a rabbi — he's not opposed to religion. What he calls for is considered religion with an informed and compassionate expression.

There is another mostly unstated assumption that came sometimes to the surface in my classroom, and it was summed up one day in the question, "Doesn't religion just cause a lot of wars?"

There's that word "just" again, but leave it for now. I suspect that all the religious wars we are challenged to recall are actually inclusive of a lot of other factors as well as religion, but let's leave that for now too. Let's say that "religion" has caused a lot of wars. It has certainly been involved in more than enough of them. But the term "religion" is a bit like "science": too broad to be really helpful, especially given that none of us can escape the label if we allow it to include humanism, godlessness and selfishness, all pursued religiously enough in their own right. What religion? Once we become specific we can begin to think critically.

To assume that religion causes wars and we should therefore give it up is neither possible nor honest. Nor is it logical. Economics causes wars too, so does politics, so does "science". We give up none of them. To suggest that we should, is parallel to saying that my brother once choked on his parsnips and I am therefore giving up food. We have to find a subtler approach. It will cost us some thought.

Actually, not only am I unconvinced that it's not really "religion" that causes conflict, I am also not convinced that it is genuinely "economics" that does it when an invasion occurs in order to secure a supply of oil. The real reason is human corruption and selfishness. But, when "religion" is involved in warfare, we might stop and take a look at the kind of religion it is. Not all religions are concerned with promoting the well-being of others, as some people suppose. It was Jesus who taught that, and they crucified him for it. On those occasions when wars have been pursued in the name of advancing Christianity — and there regrettably have been such occasions — those people doing so are acting outside the calling that Jesus gave them. That is, they have corrupted the cause they seek to promote. Other religions, with other ideals, would need to answer for themselves, but if they do not preach forgiveness then we should hardly be surprised by conflict.

Going back to Sacks. He argues that making science the basis of any belief that there is no meaning in the universe is to confuse explanation with interpretation. Any honest search for meaning in the world must go beyond science, even if that's where it starts, because science alone neither establishes nor negates a final meaning. What's more, the meaning of any system has to lie outside itself. Including the system we call the universe. What Abraham and the patriarchs gave the world was belief in a single God who was beyond the universe. That belief galvanised the human condition by giving it meaning, and in the meaning came hope. The denial of God reduces human beings to a desperate attempt to explain the world and everything in it from inside itself, and such a quest can never succeed.

Sacks's reasoning is that if God created the physical universe then he is free from its restraints, and if he made us in his image, then we are free as well. And if that is true, then people can change themselves, and they can also change the world. And that means that history is not limited to eternal repetition. In that sequence, he says, is the religious basis of hope.

Some cultures do not believe this. Inevitably, in the absence of a religious view, they give a shape of their own to some other form of recognised power. Nazi Germany and Stalinist Russia come readily to mind again. The ultimate force they created was the state, and history shows how indifferent to human value were the death camps of both regimes, and the demand for state-worship that spawned them. Such an indifference to human fate means that such cultures are tragic cultures. The same may be said for cultures based on other impersonal forces, be they natural forces or social, or economic. Their failure or refusal to esteem the value of the individual means that ultimately the culture will die. To establish human dignity, it is necessary to acknowledge a God who surpasses us but in whose image we have our being, and from whom we therefore take our dignity. And because that dignity comes from God and not from us, it is not reversible and it requires the community to treasure it and therefore, in the end, to also ensure its own collective identity.

He needs no commentary. But if we wanted any we might get it, again, from Cormac McCarthy's *No Country for Old Men,* where he gives us some remarkably similar thinking. The main story is about a cold-blooded killer tracking down a man who has stolen his money, and casually murdering people as he goes. The sheriff adds a perspective to the scenes he is witnessing.

In two paragraphs, the sheriff tells of one character's experiences in and after the Vietnam War. He says "They'd all done things over there that they'd just as soon left over there. We didn't have nothing like that in our war. Or very little of it. He smacked the tar out of one or two of them hippies. Spittin on him. Callin him a babykiller. A lot of them boys that come back, they're still havin problems. I thought it was because they didn't have the country behind them. But I think it might be worse than that even. The country they did have was in pieces. It still is. It wasn't the hippies' fault. It wasn't the fault of them boys that got sent over there neither. Eighteen, nineteen year old.

"He turned and looked at me. And then I thought he looked a lot older. His eyes looked old. He said: People will tell you it was Vietnam brought this country to its knees. But I never believed that. It was already in bad shape. Vietnam was just the icin on the cake. We didn't have nothing to give to em to take over there. If we'd sent em without rifles I don't know as they'd of been all that much worse off. You can't go to war like that. You can't go to war without God. I don't know what is goin to happen when the next one comes. I surely don't."

No one would seek to defend war as a preferred option. Including McCarthy. But if you have to consider one, you need a code of ethics to apply to it that will need to be bigger than science. Let the science provide the weapons to fight the war. Let God provide the ethics to tell you how to use them. Science and faith are not mutually exclusive, but parallel experiences of the universe. A train requires both tracks. If you ask God early enough, you might even get to avoid the war, but to do that you would need him to dictate the politicians' consciences as well, on both sides. That's a separate issue again, and it's still not the province of science.

What About God?

Not surprisingly, I kept getting asked through the years about the existence of God. It is a fair thing to wonder about the existence of God if you have never met compelling evidence for him, and many of my questioners had not. Not only that, but they are products of a society which reinforces an anti-God assumption without even necessarily thinking about it.

Let me illustrate that. Sometime in 2020 I found a headline in Stuff, admittedly in the "Paid content" section, that said, "A scientist released a painting of Jesus, and it changes what everyone believed." Yes, I know — paid content. But I clicked on the article, and when I got there, the "scientist" was re-described as an "historian" and the painting done by this historian was deemed revolutionary because she had given Jesus a sallow complexion and brown eyes. That's about what I have always imagined would be typical of anyone from the Middle East.

That is, Jesus' equipment did not include (and this was made explicit on the site) fair hair, blue eyes and a wardrobe made out of the white tablecloths that many American films like to give him. Now, all that's fair enough, but there are three subtle aspects to the headline we were given, and each one of them colours our outlook. One is the designation of this artist as a "scientist", which she may well be in her spare time but it gives her picture no special clout; the second is that "everyone" believes what this person is debunking; and the third is that the picture does in fact debunk it.

Quite simply, given that Jesus walked this earth long before the invention of the camera and that no one seems to have painted his portrait, no one knows what he looked like. Presumably, given his racial origins, he had the sort of appearance that I and this artist believe he might have had. I have never imagined Jesus as a sort of skinnier clone of Boris Johnson and unlike this artist, I have never drawn him, but when I do, the result will be the product of my imagination. Same as this person's. I have no problem with that, and I imagine that no reasonable person would have. It's a stance that leaves the door open, of course, for anyone else to give Jesus the blue eyes if they want to, but I guess that's a fair example of artistic licence. None of that is especially contentious.

What I do think is contentious is the implication that this artist's work is given extra authority by her description as a scientist. We don't even find out of which science she is a master: it seems not to matter. Chemistry? Soil enrichment? Genealogy? Nor do we know if her picture's any good. She's a "scientist": don't even think about it. I'm not too sure what significance, if any, attaches to the fact that the piece came from *Opera News,* Nigeria. The writer does say, "In our culture, we knew that Jesus looked like ... it was a piece of common knowledge for some people who believed in him ... however, a historian and a professor at the

King's College named Joan Taylor had proof that Jesus did not look like the images that we saw from different places." All that allows local interpretation, but it remains very sweeping, as well as implicitly dismissive. Nor do we know the nature of Joan Taylor's proof. It's a series of examples of a subtle perversion of critical faculty that has too often coloured the religious reaction of those within my classroom and beyond it.

The evidence about God is certainly open to interpretation. Given the significance and implications of the topic, it's fair to be very thoughtful about the evidence that is suggested. Being thoughtful is an active thing, often involving dialogue. So classroom dialogue about God was certainly appropriate, and as with any dialogue, a good first step was to establish whether it is real for both parties.

I have the good fortune to have never found the academic question of God's existence to have been a real challenge. I do not react well, though, to the suggestion that my belief in God is "just the result of your upbringing", or some other convenient dismissal. Such a dismissal is an insult to my adult thinking and to my life's experiences, and it is the sort of insult that I would try to avoid planting on anyone else with a different outlook. Or of a different upbringing, if it comes to that.

To be honest, I wonder if the academic question is as tricky as we make it. In the end, there can be only two possibilities, after all. We will make a number of extrapolations from either of them, but there can only be one answer. Either God exists, or he doesn't.

I was talking once, late in my time at the school, with a man who suddenly looked at me and asked, "You still employed?"

"Yeah," I said. "School chaplain."

He nodded. "So, what do you make of the whole God thing?"

Worldwide question, surely. Where to start? "Standard Christian believer," I said, although I think you could also debate whether there is such a thing. "The world just makes more sense to me with God."

He nodded again. "I've come to the opposite conclusion."

And so we talked, and listened, and agreed that faith was called for, for both of us. I enjoyed the conversation, and I hope he did too. Neither of us felt it necessary to use the word "just", and there was quite a lot of mutual goodwill. A lot of my classroom discussions, and all of them that were worthwhile, were conducted along similar lines.

In 1960, Yuri Gagarin made the first manned space flight from this earth. He left a Soviet launchpad and completed a single orbit before landing back in Russia, about an hour and a half later. Not too long afterwards the Soviet Premier, Nikita Khrushchev, made a speech which included the comment, on Gagarin's behalf, "I didn't see any God up there."

C S Lewis, Christian writer and Oxford don, picked up on Khrushchev's words in an article he wrote about this, called "The Seeing Eye". I earmarked it for my senior classes. Lewis commented that although the Russians had not found God in outer space, a lot of people through history and across the world claim to have found God here on earth. Or to have been found by him.

He wrote, "The conclusion some want us to draw from the Russian data is that God does not exist. A corollary is that those who think they have met him on earth were suffering from a delusion." This is exactly the ground, often unspoken, that was occupied by many of my classroom questioners. I saved the article because Lewis went on to consider other possible conclusions that might equally be drawn from the same facts. He identified them as:

"We have not yet gone far enough in space. There had been ships on the Atlantic for a good time before America was discovered.

"God does exist but is locally confined to this planet.

"The Russians did find God in space but didn't know it, because they lacked the requisite apparatus for detecting him.

"God does exist but is not an object either located in a particular part of space or diffused throughout space."

What I liked was Lewis's logical sifting of options. There is neither concern nor conflict in these remarks, but a consideration — what are the possibilities? He went on to consider them.

He simply dismissed the first two conclusions, as being primitive. Any religion that might relate to such inferences would also be primitive, tied to a view that God might be limited to something you might look at from outside of him. A lack of evidence in space for a God like that, Lewis remarked, ought to encourage us. The real threat would come from any evidence that a God so limited *did* exist.

He went on to draw the sort of analogy that marks so much of his work, and probably reveals him to be a teacher, when he said that expecting to find God as an observable character in his created world would be akin to reading a play by Shakespeare and being dismayed that Shakespeare was not in the cast. In a way, of course, Shakespeare is present in all his work, but he is not present as a listed character. He is not Hamlet. He relates to his world more as a playwright relates to his plays than as any of the characters in them do.

More than once over the years I was asked a question like, "If God is real, why doesn't he show himself?" In fact one day, a girl wrote that very question down, adding for good measure the words "just once." We talked about her question, asking what he would look like if that occurred and how we would know it was God. When I said to them, "That's exactly what Christians believe is the story of Jesus", the conversation, fairly, went in the direction of "How do we know that it's all true?"

In short, we will need more than a specific instance to convince us. To come back to Lewis, he develops the thesis that any mature view of God will come to understand that simply moving from one point to another, whether in space or on earth, will not change proximity to God. "A fish is no more, and no less, in the sea after it has swum a thousand miles than it was when it set out." What we will really need is to align our receptors.

So Lewis pursues that line of reason, asking how we might either reach God or, more tellingly, avoid him. There are people throughout history whose testimony is that God proved unavoidable. He classes himself among them.

But he offers some "advice" for avoiding God. Basically, he suggests distraction as the most reliable route: the distraction of money, status, sex and the things we feel indignant about. Other good God barriers are noise, crowds, social climbing, unhelpful reading. I imagine that if he were writing today he might include the internet, with or without conspiracy theories.

The British theologian Lesslie Newbigin has said, "Wandering about in a twilight where all cats are grey is not seeking the truth." That might be why so many religious traditions, and certainly not limited to Christians, find quiet meditation a helpful thing, and also why so many of my classes have appreciated the periods of quiet often built into their experiences.

Just maybe, God is nearer when he is not excluded, even when we stop short of noticing him.

Such were Lewis's thoughts on avoiding God. He went on to say that he was far less reliable about reaching God, because he had never looked for him. Instead, God had looked for him: the other way round. Lewis says that God stalked him, and that he is thankful for it. It safeguarded him against any later fears that his experience was only wish fulfilment, because he hadn't wished for it.

There is enough in there for a pretty meaty discussion with any serious-minded Year 12 or 13 group. It is lucid, it spells out options and it contains the personal factor. Any fair consideration of religious thinking can hardly do less. Lewis claims that God found him at a time when he was genuinely making an effort to obey his conscience; that is, a removal of the whole issue from the academic to the moral. I told you that the line between God and good was very thinly drawn.

Further to the question of God in space and the issue of where we are and where God is, we may remark that spiritual awareness may be equally well developed, or not, wherever we are. Some people seem to find God everywhere, while others do so nowhere. Lewis says that anyone who does not find God on earth is unlikely to do so in space. After all, he says, "We're in space already; every year we go a huge circular tour in space. But send a saint up in a spaceship and he'll find God in space as he found God on earth. Much depends on the seeing eye."

Which brings us back to "it's just your upbringing" or "just your opinion." Such a phrasing is dismissively simplistic, but the implications of the comment are fair. Is faith in God, or faith in no-God, really limited to upbringing or opinion?

Every person who shifted their stance away from where they started is evidence that faith is more than that, but it logically incorporates a range of things. One of those things will be upbringing (including a reaction against it) and opinions, as well as objective truth. If God were a rock, you might stumble across him. You might measure him and discuss him. But until you chose to use the rock in some way — for weighting down your tent flaps, perhaps — and therefore to involve yourself, you would never do more than make academic comment. And always, of course, you might choose to do less.

It's the same for everybody else. If you stumbled across me, you could measure me and discuss me as an object of greater or lesser interest. But once you begin the process of getting to know me, which would be an act of choice, I will become something you cannot simply measure. What, indeed, constitutes "me"? It is something mysteriously greater than 85 kilograms of ageing flesh and bone, and if I had a twin brother you would take a very short time to discover that there were two people there and not two copies of the same one, and a very long time to quantify how you could tell. And you would have to want to.

One of the questions that recurred from year to year and over all levels of seniority in the classes that I taught was, "Does God talk to people?" Sometimes we had its counter format, "Why doesn't God talk to people?" There are people throughout history who claim that indeed he does. The question then becomes "Why here, and not here?" and we've talked about it many times and in various forms. I devised a number of questions to help us focus.

The questions invited us to wonder about the sorts of person God might or might not speak to — Henri Charrière, for example, or Tony Campolo. We asked about the sorts of person we ourselves might or might not speak to. Almost every group agreed that how much anyone listened did a lot to shape how long you would spend trying to talk to them, and maybe God felt the same. And when we wondered about how

God might speak to us, the agreement was also very great: he would do so in a way that related to us rather than to any formula of "speaking", and no one else present would necessarily be impressed by our account of how it happened.

I remember once talking to a Year 9 class and telling them that Jesus is on record as healing at least three men who were blind, and doing it in different ways. He spoke to one, he touched one, and for the third, he spat into a handful of dirt, mixed the resulting mess into mud, rubbed it on the man's eyes and told him to go and wash it off at the local well.

Why, I asked them, did he go to all the process of spitting and mixing and asking the guy to go to the well, if he could have simply spoken and created the desired result — in fact, I said, why are there three different accounts to get to the same end? Year 9 didn't even pause to look at me with scorn. "Different people," they said. "Different experiences." And surely that's why it is possible for one person to claim a powerful experience from God and for his near neighbour to dismiss the whole thing as "just" his experience or upbringing or imagination or anything else that the neighbour, uninvolved, may find convenient as a means of dismissal. But when the neighbour begins to listen, the experience will be every bit as real, and is likely also to be unique. And equally dismissible to his near neighbour sitting on the other side. I never met a former astronaut among my students, but I met a lot of people who had not stopped to wonder if their concept of God was big enough.

There was a man called Noel Fellowes. English. We looked at his story, in print or on film in different years. He was a former policeman working as a taxi driver in the north of England when he was arrested in the 70s for a murder near a place he had recently been with his cab. Being innocent, he gave the police his full cooperation, and was shocked to be brutally interviewed and subsequently convicted of manslaughter and sentenced to a prison term, during which he was beaten by other inmates because he was a former cop.

His life after release was defined by these experiences, with nightmares and brooding, until his mother and brother, aided by his wife, coaxed him into a church where, he said, he had a mystical experience "and I knew it was God. I knew it was God. I knew it was God." He says it three times in the film, completely matter-of-factly and with no apparent attempt to convince anyone or to do anything other than convey his experience and his reaction to it. When the case against him and his conviction were finally quashed, after some fifteen years, he found himself able to quote Martin Luther King Junior: "Free at last. Thank God Almighty."

Certainly there are always those who are prepared to say, "But how do you *know* he was following God? Mightn't it all have been in his mind?" The best answer, probably, is "Sure. But he reckoned on God. And he was a lot closer to the action than I am." I will guarantee that those alongside the apostle Paul when he was dazzled and transformed on the Damascus road could have explained his experience away in half a dozen non-God rationalisations if they had felt like it. And for all I know, they might have done it. But the fact remains that his own conviction about it changed the face of the world forever.

Many stories left a lot of room for ambiguous interpretation. And that's OK. We had one called "Eddie and the Seagulls," about Captain Eddie Rickenbacker of the US forces who was marooned at sea for 24 days during World War 2 and who survived it, along with his raft mates. Completely out of food and water after eight days, they "had a simple devotional service and they prayed for a miracle." A little later a seagull alighted on Eddie's cap and he was able to snatch it: food and bait and later, fish. Added to the rainwater: survival.

Is that an answer to prayer? No one tells us. But there is gratitude. For the rest of his life Rickenbacker could be seen going down to the end of his local wharf and feeding shrimp to the local seagulls and, as they flocked in towards him, saying, "Thank you. Thank you." Gratitude is not a bad attitude. As Elvis Presley once famously asked, "Who do you thank when you have such luck?"

Even more ambiguous was the Mount Everest account of the British climber, Frank Smythe. In 1933 he was high on the mountain, alone by a combination of unplanned circumstances, and he later wrote about it. He spoke of a strong feeling, all the time he was alone, that there was someone with him. The impression was powerful and persistent, and it was positive — he felt that if he were to slip, he should be supported by a companion with a rope. Smythe was among the exclusive elite of pre-war mountaineers, seasoned and professional, and he was most unlikely to create a positive chimera or some other fiction from circumstances that he knew only too well were dangerous in the extreme, requiring all of his completely focused attention.

But the sense of a presence was so strong that when he reached a ledge he had been aiming for and stopped for a rest, he carefully divided in half his only piece of mint cake and turned to offer one to his companion, who in fact left him about that time.

Soon afterwards, on his way back down to camp, he had a visual experience. He happened to look up. There, floating in the blue sky, he saw two dark shapes that looked a bit like kite balloons. One had short wings. Although they were stationary, they appeared to pulse in and out as if they were breathing. He was completely arrested by the sight, utterly amazed, and he focused on them with intense interest. He thought his mind was OK, but he wanted to test it so he looked away from the vision to see if it followed his eyes. It did not, but when he looked back, it was still where he had seen it.

He looked away again, wanting to apply whatever testing he could to an occurrence utterly beyond his experience or imagination. He identified and named various details of the landscape, seeking to provide his mind with an objective test. When he looked back, the objects were still there, and they remained until a mist drifted across in front of them and obscured them from view. When the mist cleared, the vision had gone.

Smythe was sufficiently arrested by the whole event to give it space in the book he later wrote. He did not talk about God. His summary statement reads: "If it was an optical illusion, it was a very strange one. But it is possible that fatigue magnified out of all proportion something capable of a perfectly ordinary and rational explanation. That is all I can say about the matter and it rests there."

You might explain such occurrences in all kinds of ways, or none. But for every insistence that natural explanations will be most reliable, there will be another insistence on other factors best explained by faith. In a classroom, it is enough to allow for either or both, and not to become dogmatic about it. After all, Smythe was prepared to let it go, having first found it remarkable enough to comment on. And he was there. And we were not.

Going around telling stories was all very well but stories, of course, were not supposed to be an end in themselves. I remember Rob Harley, the television producer, once saying, "Never make a point without telling a story. Never tell a story without making a point." Your point could be as blatantly or subtly drawn as you liked, but it needed to be there. Sometimes the story *was* the point — and because I always remembered the sheer fatuousness of ever explaining a joke, I sometimes let the story go uncommentated upon rather than labour a point. But a story is a great vehicle for a moral or a theme, and it certainly beats the day-lights out of a lot of self-conscious preaching. If we allow the stories of Fellowes, Rickenbacker and Smythe to speak for themselves about God, we may still remark on their relevance to release, hope and gratitude, and intrigue.

On the other side of the acknowledging God equation, there was a point to ponder in a comment made by a talkback radio caller after the Christchurch earthquake. The caller said, "I am unable to continue to believe in God after this earthquake." Now you don't expect a lot of wisdom from the toxic swamp of talkback radio, and I hasten to say that I wasn't listening to it. The line was quoted to me by a friend who was. But his attention was gripped, and so is mine, by the response of the radio host, who asked, "Why this earthquake?"

It's a very good question. Is it OK somehow for a whole lot of other earthquakes, or floods or fires or drownings or deaths from Covid or cancer or truck accidents or haemorrhages or falling off high buildings or being gored by moose to occur and for God to be allowed to react how he chooses, but not so in this one which is close to home and where perhaps my friend was injured? It starts to sound selfish, actually — this one hurt me, and therefore God has fallen down on the job. Let all the Turks or Chileans or people I don't know suffer all they like, but if it hurts me, then God must have lost it.

You can table many reasons to believe in God. You might table a few for not believing in God. But to say that you might stop believing in him because you are suddenly involved in an event that has previously only affected other people, is more of a comment on you than it is on God. I remember, after a mass shooting at a school in Germany in the early 2000s, a news report in which a local youth was reported as saying something like, "Even if I believed in God, I would not believe in him anymore." I hope his logic satisfied him.

It's interesting to consider the kinds of things God gets blamed for. Without citing specific instances, you can bring to mind natural disasters, man-made disasters, illness, accidents, individual errors of judgement, political gaffes, acts of war, even individual criminal acts such as school massacres. Some of these things can be recognised by any impartial observer as the responsibility of very ordinary human beings. We're still left with the natural occurrences that remind us we live in a broken world, but if we are to blame God for everything we don't like, it seems only fair to attribute to him equal credit for any good thing we do like. Including days when there were no earthquakes, given that he must have stopped them. As for human villainy being God's fault: exit personal responsibility.

If it comes to acknowledging the presence of goodness in the world, it seems fair to ask anyone not believing in God why they should expect any. If the world is random, impersonal and brutal, then it is random, impersonal and brutal: no God to be attacked for the pain, no God to be thanked for the good. But even more subtly, no reason to expect any good in the first place.

There is a remarkable passivity about a lot of expectations in all this. If it's bad and I hate it, God should have stopped it. But if it's bad for my neighbour, shouldn't I expect to be an agent of stopping it? Or if it's good, might not God have allowed it? And if it's good for my neighbour, mightn't I expect to help in promoting it? It begins to look like a partnership between God and his people, not unlike the ones we read about featuring people like Abraham.

God, Truth and Practice

Through 20 years of Religious Education in the classroom, the themes of the day were dictated by the questions. That's true in any conversation, but it's very obvious when you're teaching a lesson. When you want to go in a particular direction, you ask a question to get you there. If the student asked the question, we took it until the interest waned. If she did not ask the question, then I asked mine, and probed around until there was some reaction that led to a conversation.

In the face of a good question from the floor, you don't want to be too long without something to say. On the other hand, you don't want to be talking just to fill the gap. Teacher's challenge. It's where the highs come from.

You remember the days you could look back to later and know you got it right. You remember too the days when you looked back later and knew you didn't. But I remember one day when there seemed to be nothing to say at all.

I have long since forgotten who she was, but there was a girl who asked me once in a thoughtful moment, "Mr Edgecombe, who is God?" I looked at her. I blinked. I wondered if my ears were working properly. I can't recall what my first words were, but they didn't happen straight away. They might have been, "I beg your pardon?" Such a response is not only a polite way of saying "What?", but it creates a second or two of thought time while she repeats it — or, better, says something slightly different — and you go into mental overdrive.

If I did say, "I beg your pardon?", it didn't help. I was still left devoid of inspiration. In the old days of blackboards, I'd have looked for the duster and earnestly cleaned the board and picked up a piece of meaningful chalk and walked deliberately to the other end of the board to write down some time-gaining thing while the brain continued to spin. But this was not the old days. No chalk. And anyway, I was too busy focusing on a single thought to be jazzing around with cleaning boards. I mean — *"Who is God?"* This is a question for the universe. Your hands flutter a bit and you raise an eyebrow. And you have to speak.

So I did. "Ah … God is …" my hands would have been gesturing here, "*God.*" She tried to look understanding. "I mean — you know —" She didn't know. But we were under way.

In the next few minutes, we talked about the creator of life, of the world, of the universe. We mentioned the source and the sustaining of everything. We talked about the inspiration to goodness and the rebuke to wrongdoing that all of us knows in a conscience. We talked about Jesus and the redeemer of the fallen and the lost. We covered all the theological ground and all the pop culture images that I and everyone else could think of.

Somewhere in it I had a thought. It probably came from God. Like so many thoughts, it began in a story.

"Do you remember Moses?" I asked them. Most of them did, by name if not in detail. "Basket," they said, "and plagues. And the sea."

"Yep, all good," I said. "And there's another incident."

"Wait on," someone said, "wasn't there a bush?"

"Oh yeah," said another voice." Take off your shoes."

"Holy ground."

"And the bush was on fire."

"No, it wasn't."

"He thought it was on fire."

I got back in: "You're onto it. What happened next?"

"God talked to him."

"Correct. And what did he say?"

"Ah ... didn't he tell him to go and see the King?"

"Let my people go!"

"You got it. And what did Moses say?"

We were onto a train by now, and the responses came and the story emerged. Moses, on being presented with a calling to inspire the ages all the way to the present day and offered the personal guarantee of God himself — "the God of your father, the God of Abraham, the God of Isaac and the God of Jacob", from whom he hid his face because he was afraid to look at him — Moses, at this high moment of historical drama, said: "Send someone else."

History of course records the fact that God declined to do that, so Moses' name is revered still, but before they got to this point Moses had paraded all the reasons he could think of to explain why he wouldn't be a good man to go, and unlikely to be well received if he got there. One of his stallings was, "They won't listen to me. Who shall I say sent me?" And God answered, "I am who I am. Tell them I am has sent you."

No playing for time now, but I had a whiteboard pen in my hand and I wrote in decent-sized letters, "I am who I am." We looked at it. I said, "What else could you say?"

I asked them, "Did you ever ask your mother 'How do you know when you're in love?' Who's asked their mother how you know when you're in love?" They all looked sheepish, but they all recognised it. "And she said, 'You'll just know.' And you thought, what a dumb answer. And it is. But in fact, there's no other thing to tell you."

They found this familiar, if not exactly conclusive. "Give it a few years," I said. But actually, what else can you say? Every single thing you might add needs adding to again. Every answer sounds complete but it never is. Every suggestion hints at a bigger truth. That's like defining God, even when he might have done it himself. So he goes to the biggest statement: "I am who I am. Tell them I am sent you."

"I am" is the shortest sentence the English language is grammatically capable of. Exclamations and one-word answers to questions are not sentences, so if you are preparing to argue like a standard Year 10 reprobate, don't start there. Every sentence needs a subject and a verb: someone who is doing something or being something. You can't have a shorter subject than the one-word "I": you can't have a shorter verb than the two-letter "am": you need no more for a sentence. The identity of God, the biggest idea we can be offered in the universe, summed up in the shortest sentence you can have in the only language I am capable of speaking. Not bad. And I was starting to feel a whole lot better about my "God is … God" comment of 20 minutes before.

So, "I am." God is. He is that which *is*. That is, the end of all questioning. That which, without qualification, *is*. Not, is … something, though that's also true, but when all the somethings are finished being added to, he still is. No wonder Moses wondered. Less wonder that I did too.

What is truth? Truth is, that which is. When my speech reflects reality, I have spoken truth. When you are holding to your ideals, you are true to them. When you don't let your lover down, we have true love. When the builder puts the plumb bob against the wall, he can see if the line is true. Bigger than facts, bigger than insights, bigger than any external measuring. Truth is that which causes us, when we see or read something that touches us at a level of awareness we have only subconsciously felt, to find ourselves nodding, "Of course."

It was not for nothing that Jesus said of himself, "I am the way, the truth and the life." Deeply ironic that Pilate asked him, the night before he was crucified, "What is truth?" He was the straight path to walk so as to know truth, to live in which is life itself. No wonder the crucifixion didn't last past three days. The real wonder is that it got started.

When the Queen Margaret College founders gave their school a motto (in Latin of course, back in 1919), it was about light and truth. Light: truth; truth: God. The founders wanted to give us more than small class sizes and well-drilled hockey teams. They wanted us to find truth: that which is. God.

That's why liars are such an assault on the delicate fabric of the moral world. Political spokesmen who are adamant that that which is true is not, who insist on lying for their own vainglorious ends, who seek to deceive people into supporting their agenda and building their own hubris: these people are not merely manipulative, even though they are that: they are mounting an attack on the essence of rightness. They assail God himself. They impoverish the world, even if their economy might run well for a decade or two. They reduce us all.

Other people enhance us all. There is a story told about a London minister who spent Sunday evening preaching up a storm about the virtues of honesty. At the end of the church service the woman who ran his Sunday School reminded him of a promise he had made to give five pounds towards some special effort for the children. He promised to bring the money during the week.

Monday was his day off, and on Tuesday he forgot it. However, as he got onto his usual bus and sat down after paying the driver, he realised he had been given an extra five-pound note among his change. He said later, "My first reaction as I realised the error was, 'How convenient. I can pay that Sunday School pledge.' And then I thought, 'No I can't.'"

So when he got off the bus, he went to the front door rather than the back, and stopped and said to the driver, "You gave me too much change by mistake. Here it is."

The driver grinned and said to him, "Not by mistake, Reverend. I was in your congregation on Sunday night, and I wondered how good your sermons were during the week. Well done. You just passed the test."

We all like to think we would pass the test. Sometimes we do. Sometimes we don't. Often, we have to work at it. A story like this is as good as any for focusing attention on the link between actions and words.

I once knew a man who owned a dog. On a miserable wet Wellington winter day, southerly howling, his dog interrupted a meeting being held in his house. His wife was part of the meeting: he was not. She looked at the dog and said, "Go. Go to John. Walkies!" John looked taken aback. "I wasn't going to take her for a walk," he protested. But fifteen minutes later, past the window, oilskins wrapped tightly around him, hat pulled down, went John, dog frisking happily on a leash.

I told my class about it. "This is an honest man. Is it a sin to lie to a dog?" I asked them. Basically, they thought it was. There were all sorts of reasons. Dog needs to know where she is, obedience training, etc etc. But fundamentally, the fact of lying to a dog is an attack on truth. Or, to say it differently, on God. These are high standards.

Then I remembered a man trying to get his printer to work in a way it wasn't calibrated to, so he set the setting to something bigger than he needed and said to me, "Got to trick the machine." And the question then became, "Is it a sin to lie to a machine?"

Well, I don't think it is either. Or more accurately, I don't think applying the setting you need to get the result you are looking for from an inanimate object counts as a lie. What you set on the machine is what "is"; what you tell the dog should align with what "is"; if the world is to run, we depend on following what "is".

And of course, liars know this, and they depend on it. That's why they tell lies — they rely on the rest of us following truth and therefore believing them, so they will gain a short-term benefit at the expense of everybody else. At the expense of God. I guess lying counts as idolatry — claiming for myself that which belongs to God. So the dictators and the tyrants who manipulate the public hold on truth by their lies and propaganda, and create the climate for a destruction of trust, are vile indeed, promoting the realm of darkness.

There is a contradiction in that paragraph. "At the expense of God," I said, and on the surface that seems to be true. Except that I wonder if it is. God is ... God, after all. Nothing I can do will reduce him in any way, just as nothing I can do will increase him in any way. The person who is reduced is the liar. It is not God.

I read somewhere, and I believe it, that the malcontent scribbling "Darkness" on the wall of his cell is not going to stop the sun from coming up tomorrow. There is in our time a popular columnist who has taken to referring to God with a lower case "g": his protest against religion. I enjoy his writing but I think less of him for this pettiness, and the irony is that he has affected my view of God in no way whatsoever.

So the liars and the dictators of history, with all their assaults on truth and on God, demean themselves. How can they not? If truth is truth, and I am detached from it, I am the loser. I guess that's why there are those who want to insist there is no such thing as absolute truth. It's a more consistent stance than to say that there is such truth but there is no God, but it's a statement that carries the seeds of its own falseness. How can I accept as true a statement that says there is no such thing?

In my floundering ineptness, I think I got it right that day, responding to "Who is God?" "God is ... God" is not so very far away from "I am who I am."

What You See Depends
on Where You Stand

I love the opening paragraph of John Steinbeck's *Cannery Row*. He begins with a striking view of the street and then he says, "Its inhabitants are, as the man once said, 'Whores, pimps, gamblers and sons of bitches', by which he meant Everybody. Had the man looked through another peephole he might have said 'Saints and angels and martyrs and holy men', and he would have meant the same thing." Truth, and every class I put it in front of could recognise it as such. If a few of our politicians and newspaper people and church people and social commentators in general could bear it in mind, we might all be enriched.

I don't want to use it here to open the thesis that no one is entirely a villain or entirely a hero, and that we all live in the struggle between nobility and moral squalor, even though that's true and we have discussed it in many classes at every level. Rather, I want to reflect on the angle of vision that brings about the views of saints and angels and holy men, or of pimps and gamblers and sons of bitches.

I have many times been part of those professional development courses that require you to do things you instantly forget. There are, however, some exceptions to the forgetting.

One of the exceptions for me occurred in Canberra, sometime in the 1990s. I was not teaching during those years, but was instead the National Director of Scripture Union in New Zealand, and I was attending a conference with my Australian peers. There was a morning when the course director put us all into pairs and sent us off into the neighbouring shopping centre to look at the world. She — or he, I can't remember — gave us a couple of minimal instructions.

One was that we were to walk together from the conference centre to the shopping mall, and we were to walk back. Another was that we were to stay in one place after we arrived at the mall. We were to stay together. We were to be there for a minimum of 20 minutes. And the final order was that, from the time we crossed the threshold of our conference room on the way out until the time we re-crossed it on the way back in, we were not to speak to each other. The walk, about 15 minutes each way plus the 20 minutes in the mall, was to be conducted in total silence. "Just look," she told us. "And listen. Then, talk about it when you get back."

My buddy for the exercise was Tom Slater, who was the State Director of Scripture Union in Victoria. We did as instructed: we walked out, sat, walked back, discussed it. There were three typical passages of conversation.

One was along the lines of: "Did you see that old guy getting off the bus?"

"Yes. I thought he was interesting. Did you notice he …?"

"Yes, I did. What about …?"

In other words, some things took the attention of us both, and we talked for a while about what we thought about it. I always enjoyed Tom's company and thinking, and it was rewarding to share these insights and speculations with him.

The second kind of conversation was something like, "What about the lady with the toddler?"

"You mean the wee guy in the red jacket?"

"Red jacket? Might have, I guess. The woman had a black bag."

"Yeah, I saw that. But the kid had a red coat."

"Did he? I never noticed."

Same reference point, different responses to it. The conversation there was along the lines of making sure we were talking about the same people.

And the third branch of it all went like: "What about the two high school kids in the magazine shop?"

"What magazine shop?" Complete went-right-past-you reaction, and nothing to share about it later.

Which was the point of the whole exercise. You and another, in the same place at the same time on the same mission, are likely to come out with two points of view. If that can happen in a physical location when you're conscious of it, how much more easily can a philosophical world view develop that is different from yours, leaving both of you with a picture that is less then complete?

We all see the world through individual lenses, and while that should create respect for the views of another, it neither invalidates nor justifies his viewpoint or mine. Not on its own, that is. Some things just are, no matter how I see them. I might allow your right to a view that there is nothing wrong with my sick mother, but with all respect to you, I'll listen more carefully to the doctor who calls around than I will to you. I will pay more care to my accountant's opinion than to yours at tax return time, too. You're still entitled to your view and to my respect, but if you dismiss the tax department as fake news or a hoax, I will retain the right to look past you. You avoid the taxes if you like. I will stay out of prison. And what's more important, I will make in the process a contribution to the common good, whose services I enjoy, and I will do so because it is right.

That last statement reflects my world view, which is that there is such a thing as right, because it is tied to God. My belief in God may not be complete, but it is not academic. It drives my social decisions and my actions. I pay my taxes.

You may argue, of course, that you pay your taxes too and you do not believe in God, but to quote Cormac McCarthy again, that ain't the point. The point is that my belief shapes my actions, unless I am deceiving myself. You and I might by chance parallel each other's moral choices for quite a while, but equally, we might not. If you argue that it doesn't matter, I will reply that it matters to me, because I believe God cares about what I do and I want to get it right, and if it doesn't matter to you, you have identified a gap between our life approaches that will, sooner or later, become marked and visibly important.

Early in my Queen Margaret career, I developed an assembly along these lines. After it, I was accosted by a couple of vocal sceptics from Year 10, demanding to know if I thought that atheists were devoid of morality. I was gratified by their engagement, but sorry about the confusion of my theme.

I was not saying then, nor have I intended to since, that people who exclude God from their reckoning are unable to make a positive moral decision. Nor, equally importantly, am I saying that people following God always get it right. History is littered with more than enough evidence to invalidate either idea — gamblers and holy men, after all. I am saying that at base level, I am required as a follower of God to look more broadly than to my immediate advantage. Others may choose to do that: I am required to. It simplifies a lot of the moral questions of life. It complicates some of the others.

I was asked about this one day by Bella, in Year 11. "Mr Edgecombe, what are you going to do if you get to the end of your life and find out you were wrong?" she asked me. I wanted to say about three things at once. I can't recall which of them I chose to start with.

But among the candidates for first answer there would have been the question, "If that happens, what will I have lost?" So far as I can tell the answer would be, "A certain amount of self-indulgence." Excesses not gratified, people not ripped off, time not spent in pursuing what I consider to be worthy causes. Since I don't regret any of those things now, I guess I'll be all right with it then, if that's how things turn out.

The second answer I might have used would be the very logical suggestion that if I am not to know whether my Christian beliefs are accurate until after I have died, and it turns out they are not, then I won't know about it then, either. No life, no knowledge: all I'll have is what I've had. And actually, that'll do. No worries.

But the third possibility would be the source of many worries. What if my beliefs turn out to be true but I haven't followed them? Too late then, and I've lost everything I didn't bother about. Such a possibility may not be an adequate basis for adopting faith, but it is a better question to ponder than the one I was given. The options must have stayed in Bella's mind, because she asked me the question again later in the year.

When I went to work for Scripture Union in the 1990s, they wanted to check out my principles and beliefs. Rightly: I would be representing the organisation in any number of public forums and, as in any enterprise, the CEO would be responsible for safeguarding its ethos. One of the questions they asked me at interview was whether I looked at the world theologically. I wasn't quite sure what they meant.

I am now. It means, did I see the everyday matters of the world in a way that reflected a belief in God? If I believe that God made the world, and me, and every other human being, then I am simply not free to treat people as a convenient vehicle for my personal gratification. My views on euthanasia, adultery, abortion, drug use, child care, quality education, political representation, slavery, economic dependency, the conservation of the planet, drunk driving — you name it: a belief in God, and the idea that the world is his, will shape an outlook.

Equally, a belief that the world is a chance collection of random particles perpetuated by no one knows what force and winding towards an unknown end without a possible purpose, will also shape an outlook. And two things need to be acknowledged. One is that the ideas of the God-follower and the God-denier will sometimes overlap. The second is that the views of two God-followers will not always overlap. I might refuse to go to war because I do not wish to kill another person created in God's own image and my fellow believer might go to war because he wishes to prevent people coming here to kill other people created in God's own image, but if we are true to our faith, we will have both considered the matter long and critically. Neither of us will go to war just to get a ride in a tank or enjoy the homecoming of a hero. I was appalled to see some American citizen, interviewed just before the 2020 US Presidential election, saying, "I'm happy with this presidency. It's been good for me." And I have to say that frankly, whether she was happy with the presidency or not, I believe she ought to have been thinking more widely than whether it was good for her.

Because it is not about me, and I am not the centre of the universe. That which is at the centre of the universe is, by Christian doctrine and a number of other doctrines, God. Once I remove him from there, I have created a vacuum that the recurring lessons of history demonstrate will be filled by something else, and that something else will be as a god to the person who put it there. The world thereafter will be shaped by reaction to the god installed.

I had the possible options for this spelt out for me with startling and dismaying clarity one day by a girl in Year 10, sometime around 2011. In the course of a lesson in which I had asked for some responsive writing she wrote: "My religion is witchcraft. I don't believe in God. I worship the moon goddess and the devil only." She asked me to tell her what I thought about that.

You always need to be respectful, and it is always good to be gentle. It is also necessary to be honest. Unusually, my response that day was to be written: more commonly, the question and answer sessions were verbal. But when you write, you can choose your words carefully, and nor are you going to be interrupted before you finish. Of course, a written response also looks very final and its phrasings lack personal colour, so there is also a need to be even more delicate. But this is what I wrote:

"You have your views and I guess you've come to them for reasons that seem good to you. I don't want to show you any disrespect. But if you want me to mostly tell you what I think, you will need to understand that I am trying still to be careful of your feelings.

"The moon goddess is tricky to get specific about because of course there have been so many of them in different cultures. But basically, multiple gods and goddesses all over the world come out of animism — the idea of different gods for various aspects of the world. The ancient Greeks, Romans and Egyptians are the most popular forms in our time.

Witchcraft is also pretty variable, but generally it's an approach to magic by supernatural powers that aren't God. Certainly it is consistent for you to separate witchcraft and God" — she had made the distinction as part of her writing — "because it would be impossible to try and make them fit each other, since they are mutually exclusive. So it is also consistent for you to link these things to devil worship.

"But you both puzzle me and you dismay me when you say in the same breath that you don't believe in God but you choose to worship the devil. If you really do not believe in God, for whatever reason, why do you believe in the devil? It seems perverse. But even if you do believe in the devil, why ever would you want to worship him? Let me remind you that the devil is, by definition, the emanation and essence of evil. Consider torture, murder, child molestation, rape and hatred, add in racism and slavery and exploitation of innocent people, remember genocide and grinding oppression and foul debauchery and destructive drug addiction, consider this recent dreadful massacre in Norway or stop if you want to at everyday selfishness and gossip and lies — all the works of the devil.

"Why, for any reason at all, would you want to tolerate any of these things, never mind worship them? Every decent person is called to oppose them. If, through the moon goddess and witchcraft you are seeking a kind of power, I have to say there are only two sources of power: God and the devil. You have correctly placed them on opposite sides. But you've backed the wrong side. When the final battle comes, God and the devil will meet in total conflict, and right will triumph. What we see in the world at present, all the suffering that worries so many of us, is the devil's attack on God's creation, and the time we live in is the period God has given us, before he acts, to choose our side.

"Effectively, we are part of the problem or part of the solution, and he is giving us time to choose. Then, sometime when the time is right, he will say 'Enough!' and march against the devil to finish him off forever. That's when we will see the end of the world as we know it, and that's when hell will come into its own — it's the place set aside for the devil and his angels. If what you say is true, you're playing with fire. Get out of it now."

My responses were rarely so personal or so direct, but then the triggers that elicited them were rarely so personal or direct either. World views are variable, but at base level they either affirm God or they don't.

This girl was clearer in her distinction than most people I met. She may not have fully understood the implications of the things she had said, or she may have been echoing an academic fashion or she might have been deliberately straight up. A lot of people wanted the comfort of such a line as "true for you", an attempt to avoid a basic issue by a negation of terms. Certainly we might see truth differently from different standpoints, but sometimes we just might be standing in the wrong place to see it at all. This girl put the light on a clear view of difference of chasm-like proportions, and there was no middle ground for me to stand on.

Points Not Too Strident

I have just finished citing perhaps the most unequivocal comments I ever made in all my years at the school. Usually, commentary was subtler, and a lot more two-way. It would have been that time, too, had the exchange been verbal rather than written. You didn't often want to swamp people, especially when topics were personal and delicate. Yet you needed to represent clear views from a firm foundation, if they were to be of any use at all. That tension was always close to the heart of the challenge.

If you have read this far and not discovered that I am a believer in the Bible, you haven't been paying attention. My belief comes from my conviction that anything to do with moral judgement requires a frame of reference greater than yourself, and of course the whole RE thing was to do with moral judgement. It also needs a greater frame of reference than, more desperately, whatever majority opinion might hold the popular vote just now. Hitler won a few popular votes.

That's why the Queen Margaret College founders did not bequeath the school the motto "By the light of Public Opinion and a Popular Vote." To that collection of Presbyterian elders, a phrase about light and truth was not a pious abstraction but a reminder of God, and they knew that and presented it to the school as a definition of special character.

When we consider God we may come to the Bible which, after all, has a fair amount to say about him. The other options are another religious faith entirely, or to deliver ourselves into the hands of any mystical zealot who happens to be passing by, like the ladies of the harem of the court of King Caractacus. Of course, some of them claim the Bible too, but that fact should cause us to consider it more carefully, not to discard it altogether.

But just because I held those beliefs, it did not mean that they were best expressed by taking a Bible into the classroom and reading it very loudly with eloquent gestures while standing on a desk. Even less did it mean that I might demand the acquiescence of anybody else while doing those things. In fact, when I look back after 21 years in the role, I wonder if we read it enough — and sometimes, one or other of my students was heard to voice the same concern. But it's too late now. It is, as the man once said, what it is.

Our age has a certain dread of imperialistic thinking. That's not a bad thing. But it did mean you often had to work hard to get an admission that the most appalling things should be called wrong. It also meant a common view that any thought I might hold is as good as any thought you might hold, simply because we both hold them. In the light of that, any appeal to moral authority had to be done with a carefulness bordering on commando stealth. The "my thoughts are as good as anyone else's" idea stems, of course, from the unimpeachable belief that individuals are of equal worth, but somehow this morphs into the idea that therefore their opinions are too. It's an idea that holds a degree of appeal until I need the advice of a plumber.

There's a lot of moral advice in the Bible about all sorts of things. There is good stuff about reliability, for example, in the books of Ecclesiastes and Ephesians. Respectively, they advise "Whatever your hand finds to do, do it with all your might," and "Serve wholeheartedly, as if you were serving the Lord." That's advice for the ages. But I don't think we ever read either Ecclesiastes or Ephesians. What we read was a line from Garrison Keillor, who said, ""Not many people were ever fired for not being brilliant, but the list of brilliant guys who wound up as shoe salesmen because they came late for the shift is as long as your leg." It was less authoritative, more rubbery. We could talk about that for a quarter of an hour, and we would extract all the inferences about smartness and duty and reliability that we might have got from Ecclesiastes or Ephesians and no one bridled. Garrison Keillor was a man from popular culture and we could listen to him on some sort of level terms.

We got another chord from Leo Tolstoy, the 19th-century Russian novelist. We didn't read him all, of course — if you're going to read all the way through a 19th-century Russian novel you are committing to a task about as light as reading the Old Testament in italicised small print just after twilight. But there's a gem or two to be found in both. So when Tolstoy remarks that it is "amazing how complete is the delusion that beauty is goodness", it should be no surprise to find the book of Proverbs went there too: "'My husband is not at home; he has gone on a long journey.' With persuasive words she led him astray; she seduced him with her smooth talk."

As a matter of fact, the Proverbs scene is graphic enough to just about make Tolstoy a safer classroom topic, but either way, the suggestion that attractiveness does not constitute virtue is very clear. It's a sort of antidote to half the messages of Hollywood, but they're more accessible than after-twilight small print. Not too surprising either to find a New Testament echo: Jesus himself said, "Watch out for false prophets. They come to you in sheep's clothing, but inwardly they are ferocious wolves." The sheep image is less electric than the lady with the absent husband, but you get the general point. So did Tolstoy.

Nor did any class fail to engage fiercely with a question asked by Digby Hannah, from La Trobe University in Melbourne: "Why should Nike be allowed to pay more to Michael Jordan to sponsor their shoes than the entire annual payroll of the Indonesian workers who make them?" It might as well have come straight from the Bible. Pretty well anywhere in the Bible — you can find the idea in a slew of places too numerous to record. But it didn't, and the more oblique approach served us well.

Avoiding stridency, though, still has to recall that morality is not the same as public opinion. A man called Ernest Lee Jahncke said, "Great moral issues cannot be resolved by counting noses but only by an appeal to what is right and what is wrong." Jahncke was expelled from the International Olympic Committee in 1936 because of his stand against the Berlin Games, the ones that became a propaganda platform for the Nazis.

Perhaps Jahncke, a Protestant, had his ethics informed by some acquaintance with the Book of Exodus where you can read, "Do not follow the crowd in doing wrong." Good advice, and even if it cost Jahncke his IOC seat, it just may have brought him a clear conscience. We often wondered whether a clear conscience might be a prerequisite for happiness.

An English vicar by the name of Becky Totterdell once wrote somewhere, "Happiness is a by-product of goodness." Jesus got there before she did: Saint Matthew in his Gospel quotes Jesus as saying, "Seek first God's kingdom and his righteousness, and all these things will be given to you as well." There was less tension in citing Jahncke or Totterdell than in quoting Jesus, but his teaching might still be called very current. With any luck, the United States Republicans might even get to understand it yet, after their 2020 election performance.

For commentary on that piece of history we might recall a comment of John Cleese, that monument of British television comedy, who said, "Most of the things we've got wrong can be explained by having an ego that's too big." It's a pretty good insight, and I wouldn't mind betting good New Zealand currency that it informs all his professional work. A Year 10 class and I once spent the best part of a lesson considering his comment, thinking up examples of it and being warned by it ourselves. As I write this, Cleese is still living — he's a contemporary voice.

The Book of Proverbs, in contrast, dates from about 1000 BC. In Chapter 6 of it there's a whole dilation on the themes of John Cleese, although he's not personally named there. Streamlined a bit, the relevant section reads, "A scoundrel and a villain goes about with a corrupt mouth, plots evil and deceit in his heart, stirs up dissension ... there are six things the Lord hates: haughty eyes, a lying tongue, a heart that devises wicked schemes, feet that are quick to rush into evil, a false witness who pours out lies and a man who stirs up dissension." This just might be the very earliest biography of Cleese's immortal character, Basil Fawlty. And not just Basil Fawlty.

We had an exercise we used to do in Year 8 to try and create some rigour in thinking about people's opinions. It was pretty obvious stuff really, but it was worth visiting because the implications are so significant.

We invented a woman. Not a real character in any sense of the word, just a cipher — "a woman" — and we gave her three friends, whom she respected greatly. One was a doctor, one was a plumber and the other was a financial adviser to the City Council. Our woman also knew a house painter, a lady who sold real estate and a receptionist at the local vet's. One day she hit her finger with a hammer, and two days later it was swollen and throbbing. From which of these people, we asked each other, will she seek advice? And why? And they all said the doctor, because he would know what to do about a sore finger.

Not too long after the finger finally came right, someone told her that house prices were soaring in her neighbourhood and she should see what her house was worth. Who should be asked now, we wondered? And everyone said the lady who sold real estate because she would know the subtleties of the house market.

What might happen to make her go and see the plumber? A leaky pipe. Why him? Because he knows about pipes. She wants to sell the house: who gets asked about that? The painter. Why the painter? Because he can get the house looking good to sell. All good. And why might she go to the vet's receptionist when her parrot develops glazed eyes and partial feather loss? To get an appointment with the vet, who may possibly have a better opinion on such a topic than, say, the financial adviser to the City Council (unless, as by now the girls were likely to be suggesting, the City Council lady was a part-time parrot specialist.)

There is a pattern beginning to develop here, and we are of course careful to say that we are not disrespecting any of the people we are by-passing in our quest for experts. We just recognise that not all opinions are equally informed.

It's worth driving the point home a bit. If the financial adviser has just swallowed turpentine for some reason not disclosed and we need to get the doctor there in a hurry, we won't waste a lot of time asking why it's the doctor. We'll just issue him directions to the house and despatch him at speed. Or her.

But is it all that simple? What if the painter said he was a rotten doctor? And the plumber said no one knew if he was any good or not but the vet's receptionist said he was a nice man? And your sister said all doctors were just out to make money and she never went near one? But your next-door neighbour said she would trust that man anywhere? There is a whole sifting of qualifications, opinions, prejudices, knowledge and points of view up for grabs here. So what about a claim such as that of Jesus when he said, "I am the way, the truth and the life. No one comes to the Father except through me."

It's an enormous claim, and we might want to ask some questions such as how can we tell if Jesus' words are reliable or not? Why would it be smart to ask someone? And when we do ask such questions, of whom might we choose to ask them? And it might be pertinent to ask these questions well before the turpentine has been swallowed.

There is a story told about three men marooned in a sea cave with the tide coming in and general drowning imminent as soon as the water level is high enough. They are quite different men: one is a philosopher, one is a physicist and the last one is the village simpleton, but they are all equally nervous. When the search party lowers a rope from the cliffs above and it falls within reach, their reactions reflect their backgrounds. "Ah," says the philosopher. "This looks like a rope. But it might represent the common wish fulfilment of all people in times of stress. This needs a little consideration."

The physicist is nearer the point. "A rope!" he exults. "Nylon, three-ply, breaking strain should be all right, where mass = force/acceleration of gravity —"

The simpleton didn't hear either of them. "Some python has lowered its tail into our cave," he said, "and I think I'll hold onto it until he slithers away." And he was long gone when the tide caught up with his two cave-dwelling fellows, and well placed then to find out his mistake about the snake.

Like all parables, it has its flaws. But if its central message is clear enough to make spelling it out an insult, specifying a secondary message might still be defensible. And a good secondary message here is that you need to get your questions asked before the pressure goes on because you cannot, as Thomas A Harris wrote in *I'm OK You're OK,* teach navigation in the middle of a storm. That's probably in the Bible somewhere too, but Thomas A Harris was an American psychiatrist, and you can present the comments of a psychiatrist with less resistance than you can offer the words of the Bible. But I'd be prepared to suggest the psychiatrist knew about more than a few of them.

Holding a Light Touch

It is hardly ever worthwhile arguing with people if you want to make a difference to their thinking. That's because, just when you are furiously concentrating on winning a point for your cause, they are furiously concentrating on winning a point for their cause. The only listening either of you will do is to find a space into which you can lob your weapon of mass destruction. Their weapon, you haven't noticed — and who cares about it anyway?

It's good for an RE teacher to remember this. If you can hear a point and ask a casually probing question, it is a far, far better thing than to shout the most obvious rejoinder. Every so often, I forgot.

Once was very late in my time at QMC, when I should have known better. But I was taken by surprise that day, and you never know how you will react when things get unexpected. We had been reading a story about a desperate woman in Auckland who, abandoned by her husband when her youngest child was a few months old, was providentially rescued from killing herself and all three of her children. Most of our conversation went well enough, but I was amazed to hear almost as much criticism of this miserable woman as there was understanding of her, and my amazement was compounded by some of the girls' wanting to defend the husband's departure because he was entitled to a chance at personal happiness with his glamorous secretary — who, of course, was not frazzled after spending hours at night tending his fretful infants. Anyway, we discussed the subtleties of all this for a few minutes, until I became aware that there was a girl in tears in the back of the room and someone else comforting her. I took a silent cue from her nearest neighbour and moved the conversation on.

At the end of the day I was visited in my empty classroom by Jacqui. She brought a friend. She was upset, but determined. "Mr Edgecombe," she said, "I just wanted to say how difficult that lesson was. That was a very delicate topic, and I don't think you were sensitive to it." She went on to give me, with tears, a lesson in subtleties and general appropriateness, and I apologised to her and asked her to convey my apology to the girl who had been upset. I thanked her for coming. I still admire her courage.

But here's the thing. I also still think I was absolutely right in my basic stance over the story. I had used the story before, without a problem. I was by then a very experienced classroom professional. Yet I got it wrong.

Mostly I got it wrong through circumstances I could not have known about, but they were circumstances that might apply on any given day in any given class, and I ought to have moved in such a way as to allow for them. Jacqui told me this. I could not have known what chords the story might touch — and that's the point. My handling of it needed to be light enough to allow for anything, and it hadn't been. If it had been an academic issue it would probably have been OK, but the power of a story goes past the academic. I knew that too. No excuses, really.

A year or two later, my error was a little different. It came when I was called suddenly away from the school to be with a close friend whose wife had collapsed, and who died that morning, and I left a story and some questions to be handled by a relief teacher. Some days after I returned, I was made aware of an email from a girl's parents who were critical of the nature of both the story and the questions. I was initially astonished, until I thought, "None of that would have been exceptionable if I had been there to field the reactions and to add the subtlety of approach." But I wasn't, and no relief teacher could be expected to. The parents had reacted to the work, but I think — still — it was in itself OK. It was in the absence of sensitive handling that the problem lay. My fault, again.

In complete contrast, I had had another experience of misjudging my audience years earlier, in my first term at the school, when I could be forgiven for misreading the vibe. When I arrived there, someone asked me, "What sport will you coach for your extra-curricular gig?" "Rugby," I said. It was the only sport I knew, and the school had no rugby team. "All right," they said, "you can help Mike Savage with the touch team."

Touch, I didn't know. But neither did Mike, who turned out to be an affable American with a knowledge of rugby about equal to mine of the American Electoral College system of politics. Sketchy. So I transferred my rugby skills to touch and he and I enjoyed each other's company in a long and generally unprofitable coaching partnership over the next few years. But right at the beginning of all that I was working one afternoon on passing skills, an aspect of the game I did understand, and trying to get the girls not to lob the ball to try and throw it further. "Stand closer together," I said, "and if you can't pass the ball that far, hang onto it. Whatever you do, *don't lob it!* Possession is everything in this game." I may even have staged a demonstration of a lobbed pass at this juncture, with a primed-up runner to intercept it to make the point; I can't remember. I should have. "If you lob the ball," I said slowly, "some big ugly girl from Wellington East or somewhere is going to come along and pluck it out of the sky and say 'Thank you very much' before she goes off and scores her try."

I completed this compelling scenario and became aware that my group had gone completely silent. There was a chill in the air. I looked around. Some looked away. Some glowered. "What's the matter?" I asked. No reply. I asked again, mystified. Someone muttered, "Not ugly."

"What?" I said. I was completely bewildered.

"Not ugly," the voice repeated. "You said some big ugly girl …" her voice tailed away.

I was still bewildered. "All right," I said. "I'm sorry. But this passing –"

I was telling the story the next day to a group in the staffroom, and I never got past the key phrase the first time before they spontaneously cracked up. In unison. Ann Mildenhall was especially entertained. "You'll learn," she said.

Mostly I did. I needed to. I had by then been coaching rugby teams for perhaps 15 years, good ones and others, and never in all that time had a squad missed a coaching point on the grounds of being offended by the phrasing. They had missed coaching points on maybe a million other grounds, but not that. I had, many times, rehearsed the drills following a penalty award, both attacking and defending, and in order to encourage quick responses had blown a whistle, waved my arms around, pointed randomly at some player and said, "Penalty. Against you. For being ugly." Their reaction had been to hurry to the spot and grab the ball. This new crowd stood around whingeing about the word ugly. And it wasn't even directed at them!

It didn't matter so much that day. But it mattered in the classroom. If the vibe was wrong, the lesson foundered. And arguments were not a pathway to changing thinking.

We had a session sometime around 2008 or 09 that I have often reflected on. We were in full flight on some long-forgotten but doubtless lofty theme, when someone challenged the concept of absolute right and wrong. "There's no such thing," she said. "It's only a common agreement that some things are unhelpful. There's no real right or wrong."

Well, fetch out your red rag and stand away from my horns. This is a popular belief in many quarters, and it feeds into many a social and political practice. It is also at a level of disagreement with all I stand for that is so deep that it may explain why I didn't just extend "right" to include "true", which is a short and not dishonest step, and then ask how anyone could be expected to believe such a statement if there were no truth to justify it. After all, if there is no truth, then the statement that says so cannot be true. And you don't even need morality for that, nor theology either, only logic.

But I didn't think fast enough to do that, and the discussion turned into an argument. The leading voice on the other side belonged to a girl who had that year had been largely responsible for the school's adoption of Amnesty International as a cause célèbre. About every second girl in the school, and more among the seniors, was wearing on her lapel a little plastic button, or two or three of them in varying colours, with the Amnesty International logo on them. She had been foremost in pursuing this worthy cause.

So I said to her, "Listen, with all due respect, you are a hypocrite." She blinked, as well she might. "You have been denying to us all that there is any such thing as right, but you have been making sacrifices for it all this term. That's hypocritical." I would not have made such a charge against anyone using inconsistency to their own advantage, but I thought the shock tactic might break through if used in reverse. I still don't know if it did or not, but I suspect that there might have been a better way to push back on the thinking.

I tried another way another day, on an occasion when another class was discussing absolute right and wrong. That day, when the suggestion came that nothing was inherently wrong, I said to the girl concerned, "Come out here for a minute while I spit in your hair." Their spontaneous disgust certainly reinforced my logic, but it didn't help my empathy.

A better tactic than getting personal about it was to move to a focus that everyone could agree on. It was fascinating to me through the years to observe, whenever we talked about wickedness, how soon the name of Hitler entered the conversation. It may be a triumph for the propaganda industry but, whatever, there he inevitably was. Stalin was a name that some of them had never heard of, more recent dictators likewise, but Hitler was a predictable shorthand for complete evil.

As such, he had his uses. I came across the question somewhere, "Is there anything wrong with Hitler these days?" and often presented it to a group trying to deny evil. Some of them valiantly tried to include Hitler in the argument, but no one could do it with any conviction. "He might have believed in what he was doing," "he thought he was right," "he was trying to help the German people" were, and were seen to be, a long way from saying, "It is actually OK to murder people by the million and lead a continent into chaos." Personally, it was the "these days" in the question that I always liked.

The idea of good and bad, right and wrong, ought and ought not, was never far from the surface. Neither should it be. It is, of course, close to God. If you want an idea of good, as most people do, but you do not want an idea of God, as many people do not, then you are in trouble because any idea of good needs an anchor and a reference point. Which is probably why some people wanted to destroy the idea of good, and also probably why the notion upset me so much.

Of course there are points on a continuum, and of course they shift. But only in the area round the centre. C S Lewis has been lucid in his writings on the nature of right and wrong, and I have often been grateful to him for sharpening my insights. He says that everyone agrees that there *is* a concept of right and wrong, and their differences occur only in contexts or by degree.

In fact, most of us agreed that some things are good, and some things are bad. Some of us had to sift it through for a while, and we often differed over details, but we knew what we meant. I never met a student who would not agree that murder, child molesting or racism are bad. At the other end of the spectrum, everyone I have taught has agreed that motherhood, loyalty, honesty and respect for others are good things, and even right. Certainly there were things between the extremes that change according to circumstance, but we were talking about the essence.

The girls have always understood conscience. Deep down, we know when we are doing right and we know when we have been guilty of wrong, even if no one else knows it and even when we're really trying to make excuses for ourselves. Sometimes girls have offered the theory that the idea of right or wrong is just a social construct that we have — though no one ever asked *why* we have it — but if you mention their breaches of school uniform and not their neighbour's, they feel offended.

Often, as we talked about good and bad, there would come the question, "All right, that's for our culture. What if someone's taught that what we think is wrong, is really right?"

It's a fair question. It calls for a broadening of examples — exceeding a speed of 90kph might be illegal in Lambton Quay, but will clearly not be a problem in a place where the limit is 140. But if you stay with principles without getting lost in the detail, it becomes clearer. Even cultures who shift the details of exactly *what* should be pursued or avoided, do not shift them very far.

The drug cartels of Mexico may insist I murder their selected victims, but they will not applaud me for turning my guns on them. My government might send me into battle and require me to attack the enemy with appalling ferocity, but I do not attack everyone at random for longer than it takes to put me away. Even where the details are shifted, or even perverted, there remains an idea of good.

I had an insight into some of this in my first year at Queen Margaret, with a Year 9 class. I asked them to write a list of five things they would call unarguably wrong. They dutifully thought their thoughts, and I began to list them on the board.

We got all the expected things — murder, rape, child abuse, various villainies and assorted illegalities — when Miriam looked a little apologetic and said, "My list's a bit different."

"That's fine," I said. "Let's have a look at it. What have you got?" She gave me her list. Five items, as asked: arrogance, selfishness, cruelty, complacency and deliberate ignorance. I put them in a single line on the board, between eating your pets and planting marijuana.

We talked our way through the various suggestions, agreeing that some things were always wrong but others varied with circumstance, and that if you were hungry enough it was better to eat the cat than to watch the children starve. (By some oversight, the reverse of that scenario was never considered.) I moved on to planting marijuana and some girl said, "Mr Edgecombe, you've left one out. It's Miriam's list."

"I know," I said. "I'm coming back to it in a minute."

We did. "What's different about it?" I asked them. It didn't take long. Someone said, "You can't see those things. They are inside. The others are things you do."

Someone else suggested, "Those are the things you are." And another girl offered, "It's like the difference between legality and —" she paused, groping for the word, and somebody said for her, "Morality." Brilliant. Not a sermon from me in sight, and all done without the shadow of an argument.

Year 9

(AND OTHER FAITHS)

The Theory of Edgecombe
and Other Conversations

In 20 years of RE teaching, there seems to be little ground we did not visit, although I suppose there must be an acre or so of it really. But some things we went back to again and again. And when a topic emerged yet one more time like a slug in a tide pool and I was about to groan, I needed to recall that I was the only one present who was also there all those other times. I remember once, many years ago, becoming irritable when I mentioned Abraham and someone said "Abraham Lincoln?" and I had to remind myself that she had not heard me explain a dozen times already that Abraham Lincoln owed his name to a more famous predecessor.

Sometimes, though, the angle was wonderfully novel. You never quite knew where an RE class might end up. Often it was a question that lit the fire, but sometimes it was a comment. And it might come from any-where, on any given day.

In 2020, there was a girl in Year 8 called Yovela. She was quite a small girl, with eyes that signalled engagement. She was the one who asked me at the start of her class's last lesson of the year if they might invent an on-the-spot Christmas drama, and then performed a most remark-able rendition of the star. But we were talking one day about the Day of Pentecost — itself an other-than-everyday topic — when Yovela offered a comment that I didn't think I'd heard correctly. "Would you say that again?" I asked.

So she did. "I said, it's just as well that Jesus isn't still here," she repeated. "It would be chaotic."

"Go on," I said.

"Well, think about it." She looked up, with the eyes dancing. "The whole world would be flocking there, and TV documentaries and every-thing, and everyone looking for Covid cures …" she tailed off, with an expressive gesture of open hands. "Probably better he was here when he was."

For a few seconds, I had a vision of the world as she had painted it. The idea flashed past my eyes of everyone trying to descend on Jerusalem at a time of maximum Covid lockdown and looking for financial return and probably political capital and a place in an international queue, and chaos seemed like a fair description. I decided she had probably hit it. God got the timing right, with Jesus coming when he did. No doubt he would be pleased to have Yovela's approval and, belatedly, mine.

Another day, the remark was decidedly more earthbound. Someone was asking why some people are so convinced that the way they interpret the Bible is right, and went on to elaborate: "Have you noticed the people who are most convinced they are right are the ones most likely to be wrong? Like Hitler or Westboro Baptist Church. Why is this?"

Wonderful. There, in a single observation, we had up for grabs dogmatism, paradox and public opinion as well as, for good measure, a link between Hitler and Westboro Baptist Church. You have to love it.

On the other hand, loving it doesn't mean you want to be cornered by it. Call me craven, but an early part of my response was to put a little distance between me and Westboro Baptist Church. To be scrupulously honest, I knew then and have found out since very little about the details of WBC, but any outfit that she linked to Hitler was one I was going to be most cautious about, and I had read one article that had described it as "arguably the most obnoxious and rabid hate group in America," that Baptist churches in general disowned. I did not want this moment to degenerate into a discussion, based on mutual ignorance, about how fair that statement was.

I started my response with the dogmatism angle. That, I have met. Why are the convinced-they-are-right people so often apparently wrong?

"Leaving out Hitler and the Westboro Baptist Church for the moment," I said, "it's fair to say that if anyone is convinced about something, they talk of it in pretty concrete terms, right?"

"Yes, I get that," she said. "But if you're convinced about the Bible, and I'm not, shouldn't you at least listen to me? I mean, doesn't it talk about tolerance?"

The correct answer is, "Not majorly." Certainly it talks about love, even for one's enemies, and a starting point of love is unlikely to give me a finishing point somewhere alongside Hitler. But some things simply shouldn't be tolerated, by anyone, and we talked about what some of them were. Then, if that's true, the focus comes onto how we might go about differing from people who embrace things we cannot tolerate.

We agreed that the level of listening is a good indicator of how positive the conversation might be. We thought that asking questions ahead of making judgements would tell us something too. We took quite a while to find our way through these issues, and we covered some very good ground, and the initiative for it came from her, not from me.

On another day, we had a subtler starting point when someone asked, "Is it wrong to criticise other religions if you don't believe in them, and believe in a completely different religion?" It didn't take long to identify the word "criticise" as central in that question, nor for someone to remark, "It depends on how you do it."

"Is criticism negative?" I asked them.

"Can be."

"Always?"

"Usually."

"But what if you've done, say, a work of art and you want it reviewed? Don't I have to criticise it then?"

"Review's not the same as criticising."

"Might be if I don't think it's much good."

"But you wouldn't just insult it. You'd say maybe we could look at this point here."

"Can we do that with religions we don't agree with?"

"Well, they probably haven't asked you to. With the art thing, they probably have – they're listening for your advice. Religion, you're probably just insulting them."

"Any way to stop that?"

They thought about it, and after a while someone said, "Well, it might be all right if you're talking to the person, and sharing questions and responses, and then your responses can be friendly and not just rude."

"Even if I disagree?"

"Sure. Not everyone believes everything."

It was better than a lot of the statements, or assumptions, I have heard. I told them how, years ago, I had been part of a Christian/Muslim dialogue group, for about two years. Once a month, half a dozen Christians and a similar number of Muslims met, alternately on Christian and Muslim premises, and discussed a paper brought by one team or the other on a pre-agreed topic. "How was it?" my girls wanted to know.

"Well, I kept going to it for two years. How do you reckon it might have been?"

"Pretty good?"

"Pretty good, yeah. We didn't argue, and I learned a lot. I don't know what they learned — you'd have to ask them. But they kept on coming too."

"You didn't argue. Did you agree on everything?"

"Of course not. I'm not a Muslim."

"What did you agree on?"

"God. One God, and we're accountable to him."

"What did you disagree on?"

"Jesus, for a start. They want Jesus to be a prophet. Christians believe he is God, in human form. One of the Muslims said to me one day, 'If you Christians would stop insisting that Jesus is God, there wouldn't be a lot of difference between us.' He had a point."

"Were you insulted?"

"No. We had a discussion group. People make different points. But I did get to say that Jesus being God was not a technicality, that it gave meaning to his death and resurrection. That's another major point of difference between us. I did say that agreeing on everything except Jesus is like saying there would be no difference between men and women if either of them just gave up being male or female. One point of difference, maybe, but pretty definitive. He said to me, and I said to him, a lot of things we couldn't have just got up and shouted about outside the mosque or somewhere."

The conversation was starting to broaden out about now. This was the point at which such discussions either did that, or petered out. If they petered, you went on with whatever had just been interrupted. If they broadened, you went with the tide. Ideally, the class would be engaged by now in some sort of activity that meant the girls who tired of the conversation could work on the bookwork, while those becoming absorbed could carry on discussing. Things weren't always ideal.

Anyway, this group came up with another question on the varied religions theme. "How can religions be so different, and each person who is part of one believe in theirs and not the others?"

The second part was easy. Clearly, if you're going to be part of a religion, you're going to believe in it. Equally clearly, that fact, by definition, means you are not believing in another one. Elementary logic and QED. The focus went on the first half — how can religions be so different?

About here, it is highly likely that I said something like, "I can't give a full answer to that. But I can give you a few ideas — some just-maybes. My ideas, OK? No authority, open to argument and I might even revise them in 10 minutes. Theory of Edgecombe."

I said something like that one day, and saw some girl writing furiously on the back page of her book. "What are you writing?" I asked her.

"Theory of Edgecombe," she said. "I've got about fifteen here."

I quailed a bit. I have no idea what they all said — I'd like to have read them, but it looked a bit self-indulgent — and I just hope they were all reasonable. I'd hate to think I'd be quoted on them, or that I was starting a new cult or something. Risks you take.

"Anyway," someone was asking, "what's the Theory of Edgecombe here?"

It needed a bit of a speech. I have said many times that "religion" is a tricky term, and that I like to define it along the lines of how the way we live is our answer to the big questions of life. Sometimes that's a de facto thing: we haven't adopted a known creed, just done over the years what we felt like doing, and on looking back we can see the patterns emerge. A lot of materialists are like that — it sort of happens by default.

But that was not the sense in which this questioner was using the word, so I had to put my practised definition behind the door while we talked on her terms, and to do that, I had to acknowledge I was doing it so I could pre-empt the inevitable "But you always say…" line that would otherwise surely come. We did that. We came to how can religions be so different.

"How did religion start?" someone asked.

"Well, I have to tell you that I wasn't there. But if you mean by 'religion' some awareness of big things we don't understand, maybe we can imagine some remote ancestor looking at the stars or a waterfall or a new baby and saying 'Man, where did that come from?' and the idea growing that someone bigger than us might have put it there. If that's the case, it all probably began on about Day 2 of human awareness. People reacting to the idea of a bigger force than themselves."

"Why would they do that?"

"I don't think that's too hard to understand. For one thing, if there is such a force – call it God, perhaps – and it has made people with a consciousness, you would expect them to have some sort of feeling for that which exists above them. Children, for example, don't need to be convinced about God. Child psychologists tell us that what they really need is to be de-convinced, by the forces that undermine their early acceptance. Left alone, children are far more likely to continue in belief than to adopt unbelief."

"But what if there isn't a God?"

"Well, people still seem to set about inventing one. Every primitive culture has worshipped something. Often, a lot of somethings. The Theory of Edgecombe here is that religion, or worship, stems from a knowledge that we are not as big as the world, and we need to react to it."

"So why different ones?"

"Think about it. Here's one group living by a big river that completely dominates their experience of the world. It has forces they can't understand. They worship the river. Two continents away, the people are over-awed by fire. Across the ocean, some person or other is possessed of great powers that no one can understand, and he – or she – talks about the world of awe and adds a few ideas that the locals adopt. Half a millennium later, these views have become a code of religious belief and practice, while the Big River people have evolved their faith with different variations."

"So it's all just local ideas?"

"I don't think it is. Some of it is. But it's more than 'just'. If God is real, and he's letting us know it, then the local ideas might give him a platform to build on. He might work from that base and rely on some enlightened locals to add more understanding."

"Why wouldn't he just show himself beyond doubt?"

"Personally, I think he has. What's more, I think he keeps on doing it. Look at the world. But if you mean a sort of phantasmagoria that nobody can deny, I think two things about that. One is that such a thing from a God of complete creative power might blow us entirely away. Literally. The Jews, for example, taught that no one could look on the face of God and live. Like walking on the sun, perhaps. So God has to use methods we can handle, and then there is always scope to deny them because they haven't convinced me yet. And the second thing I think about the phantasmagoria is that, even after it was finished, there would still be people who claimed it was all a nuclear explosion or something — anything — but not God."

"What's the option?"

"People who receive special understanding and bring it to others, who then either follow it or not. Abraham, Moses, Jesus, Mohammed, Siddhartha Gautama, Guru Nanak, Lao Tzu are all people who made such claims."

"Are they all equally reliable?"

"No. They're not all mutually exclusive, but they can't all be equally reliable. They say different things."

"So who do you choose?"

"The ones you find compelling. And I think that if you do that and keep an open mind for truth, you will find it. Maybe with a few changes of course along the way, but sometime. What you will *not* do is find it if you're not looking."

"So why have you selected Jesus?"

"Me? Personally?"

"Yes."

"Because he made the most outrageous claims, and if they are true, they don't leave any room for anything else. And I think they're true."

"What if they're wrong?"

"That's why they need to be carefully considered. That's where different religions come in too — Jews say Abraham but not Jesus, Christians say Abraham prepared the way for Jesus, Buddhists follow Gautama, Sikhs follow Guru Nanak."

"Can't you have them all?"

"No. You'll often find there's overlap, so you don't have to be rude about any of them. But going back to the Muslim guy's comment on Jesus: you can't say at the same time that Jesus is God and also a fake. So one answer takes you in one direction and the other takes you away from it. Different religions. That's where this conversation started."

Only One of You

One of New Zealand's more concerning features is our youth suicide rate. In 2013, to choose a year taken randomly from my time at Queen Margaret College, our female youth suicide rate was the highest in the world. The causes are complex and sensitive and I don't want to be simplistic about them, but whatever the details, a view of oneself as a valuable human being seemed to be a good thing to encourage.

We used to do a unit in Year 9 called "What Makes a Person?" I told them about my old friend on the train who had asked me, in my first week at the school in 2001, "What are they like up there at Queen Margaret College?"

I used to tell the girls that I had said to him something along the lines of, "Oh, you know. Girls, teenagers, stripey coats, about this high — pretty much all the same, really." I would be hoping for the first voice of protest, and if it were late in coming I would carry on with as extended a litany of factual but irrelevant details as I could sustain. Sooner or later there would be a: "Wait on."

So we would look at differences – who has blue eyes, who has brown. Who is shorter, taller, bigger (you had to become delicate about here), good at maths, swims well — you could go on and on, if you were careful enough. One year a Year 9 class made their very tall girl who was not embarrassed about it come out and stand back-to-back with me, for a tall-off. They were jubilant, and she was satisfied, when they adjudged her to be marginally taller than I was.

Then we went on to preferences. Who likes cats? Dogs? Hates either of them? Hates both? Why? Who prefers hokey-pokey ice cream over chocolate ice cream? Who doesn't like ice cream at all? (There have been a couple.)

Then we went to twins. Everyone had a story. One year I had no fewer than three girls in the same class who had twin sisters in other classes or in another school. I told them about a girl in my group at Teachers' College who was one of triplets: after knowing her for nearly a year before discovering a photograph of the three sisters, I was unable to decide which of them was the one standing in front of me. She was from Auckland: we were at College in Christchurch, and she had gone there to stop being "one of the triplets" and become an individual.

"But, would it matter?" I asked Year 9. "Surely triplets are only three versions of the same person?" They were contemptuous.

What does it take to make an individual? Twins have the same sort of chemistry, constructed in the exact same way and simultaneously, moulded by a similar environment: outcome, different people. At about this point, someone would offer the word, "personality". And you would ask, "Does personality make people unique? Or do unique people have different personalities?" Chicken and egg.

It seems that no one really knows. Nature or nurture has engaged enquirers throughout the ages, and doubtless will continue to do so as long as a thesis can still be wrung out of it. One thing my girls were united on was that the differences mattered. They were not impressed to hear that I once had twin players in a rugby team whose mother couldn't tell them apart when they were on the field, or that a former teaching colleague had once tried to kiss his fiancée's twin sister in a case of mistaken identity. Different, and important.

So we'd put a heading in our books, "What is a Person?" Under it, we would take a note beginning 1. DNA, with some detail, then add 2. Environment, with a bit more detail, then go to 3. "Personality", always in inverted commas to show it was a term of convenience, and we would add some more detail before I would ask them to write, "Some people" (I am one of them, as I would explain) "believe that personality represents the fingerprints of God."

Now, this is important. It's important scientifically: how can two people who are the same, be different? It's important theologically: *why* should two people who are the same, be different? This is more than an abstruse point of theological principle. It's important sociologically: how do I relate to two different people who look the same, and what does individuality mean in a world that differs from an anthill? It's important socially: if I am a complete individual, what does that say about my importance in human history? If God himself is interested in my life, perhaps it is more important than if he were not. Perhaps a high view of my neighbours might improve my treatment of them. Just perhaps, a high view of myself might enhance my understanding of self-worth. Perhaps a heightened view of self-worth might make a difference to those youth suicide rates.

We had a little poem in there, in some years. I lost it later, but it went along the lines of there being in the world both apples and bananas. Not everyone likes apples. Not everyone likes bananas. Some like both. Nothing the apple, or the banana, can do about it. So the apple might as well get on with being the best apple possible and forget about trying to be a banana in any attempt to win that lobby's vote. He'll never be a decent banana: he might as well be a first-rate apple. Same story for the banana. And of course, the world needs both apples and bananas anyway, whatever the individual points of view might be.

Then you would ask the class your questions — Why can't you be loved by all people? If you can't make people love you, what *can* you do? If you, personally, are to be the "ripest apple" you can be, what will it mean? That is, what qualities do you have to offer to the world and how can you make the most of them?

You would take your time on these questions, allowing reflection time to let things sink in. It was new-idea stuff for some of them, critical for others. Those who had heard it all before could roll their mental eyes if they had to, but the little kid losing the popularity game just might feel a bit better later than she did before you started. It's all about her, right now.

You could hardly elaborate on this stuff enough. I know a man called Ramsbottom. The day I met him, he was wearing a tee shirt emblazoned, in large letters, "BUM". When I asked him why, he told me that as a child he had always been embarrassed about his name and about the remarks of other kids until, when he was about ten, he decided to embrace it. Hence, the tee shirt. I told the girls about him.

We'd move on. Copying others may make you a "second-rate banana". What are some things you admire in others that you couldn't do yourself? Why couldn't you? So, what does that mean? How can you appreciate them? What can you do that no one else can do? Or, even better, what can you uniquely be?

What does the poem say about copying others in order to get people to like you? What is the most important message in the poem? How does that message apply to you, personally? What's the difference between knowing it's useless to copy someone else's abilities, and just generally giving up? John Steinbeck seems to be close to this when he wrote, in *East of Eden*, "You can't make a racehorse of a pig. But you can make a very fast pig." But even if you do, you have to wonder if a fast pig might be less appreciated than a fat one.

These sorts of themes are applicable at every level. Who am I if God made me, and who are you, and how do we treat each other? The abortion issue is coloured by it, and the euthanasia debate. Respect for political adversaries might become more obvious, and the debate less vitriolic. Resulting policies might show more respect for "the people" and less for self-interest or abstract principles. The world just might become a better place for more of its people to live in.

It's not as if such a view flies in the face of science. Science describes pretty well how we came to be, except for those details of difference that are still beyond a descriptive process. Why did we come to be? That's a question more theological, and those who wish to leave God out of the discussion debase us all by suggesting random aggregations of atoms that don't even have a reason to originally exist. The argument that God has to be explained, and because he can't be we should deny his existence, is not consistent with the equal argument that if he is denied there are a lot of other factors that can't be explained and, therefore, we should also deny their existence. Such as the difference between identical twins. And leaving God and all the subtleties linked to him out of that discussion takes you a lot closer to the experiments of the Nazi Doctor Joseph Mengele than I, anyway, ever want to contemplate being.

So I was always very happy to suggest that the individuals in front of me and around us all just might owe something to the mind of a creator who never repeated himself. No two snowflakes are quite the same? Well, I don't know, but fingerprints are well documented. Something about DNA. Dr Francis S Collins of the Human Genome Project said in 2007 that scientific and spiritual worldviews were not only compatible but "wondrously complementary". He described himself as a former atheist, and reported that once he began to investigate the evidence for faith, as he would have automatically treated every scientific proposition he dealt with, he began to reckon with the "why" questions — why is there not nothing? Why does mathematics describe nature so well? Why is the universe so well tuned to life? Why do we all have a sense of right and wrong? And it began to dawn on him that atheism was less rational than theistic faith.

Then, he had to ponder whether God could be interested in him, personally. His quest took him to Jesus, and he later wrote, "I can't identify a single conflict between what I know as a rigorous scientist and what I know as a believer." He spoke of the boggling figures involved in human DNA construction, and in the similarities and differences among human beings of every sort — so individually different, yet he says that the DNA is 99.9 percent identical. Without a trust in God, he suggested, the whole thing is unbelievable, even as the team of scientists stand watching it.

Well, I don't suppose he'd be impressed, but I think that too. I don't have his science; I just look at the world. I once asked a class to imagine something. "You're away from your family," I told them, "staying with an exchange family in Argentina. They have taken you to a national park, where there are high mountains and waterfalls. You are totally awed by the beauty of the place. There is a particularly high waterfall, with strength and power. The noise, the spray, the sun shining through the vapour, the delicate little flowers growing beside the pool at the water-fall's base, the rocks around the pool, a local bird singing in a nearby tree against the background noise of the falls, unfamiliar trees ranging off into the distance — reminds you of New Zealand a bit, and yet so totally different. Now, either write the letter home, describing the beauty and the majesty of the place, or write a poem, doing the same thing."

I wanted them to do two things. One was to "see" the details of a striking scene, and the other was to respond to them. Not one of us has ever looked at a starry sky without a sense of awe. Not one of us has failed, when we unexpectedly discover a striking scene of stunning beauty, to say to the nearest person, be they friend or stranger, "Look at that." Ursula responded to the waterfall exercise by writing: "The feeling that I get from this place is like the colour yellow. It's bright, warm, and feels safe. It's like being wrapped in a warm blanket, being able to close your eyes and know that everything will be alright. It's the type of place where you can be left alone with your thoughts mindlessly, letting them pass one after another. It's never busy or chaotic, but at your own pace. If you ever need somewhere to run away and/or escape, it's your spot. It's not some place in your mind that you have to drift off to, you can walk there and see, hear, smell and feel. It feels like a glass of water fresh from a spring." I love it. It's not "science", nor even academic. It's not even poetry. It's just a reaction, from the spirit, to a given scene. It's close to life.

I once stood on a bridge over the inlet near my home and looked at a baby seal wallowing in the water below me, and I looked down the road to find somebody else to show it to. No one there, so I looked the other way. No one there either. I felt robbed. I watched the seal for a while on my own, then checked the road again, both ways, and still found no one.

So I watched the seal on my own again, and then went on home and told my wife about it. She listened with a degree of sympathy, but it wasn't the same. To observe is to respond, and to respond is to tell the nearest bystander so you can both share it, and if you can't do that, the whole experience is somehow incomplete.

We all share that sense of wonder. I never told the anecdote about the seal to any class who failed to understand it. They all know the feeling, every individual girl I ever taught. That's the common human experience, that under God we know our place.

You knew, by the atmosphere in the classroom, when these thoughts were going home. But one day I was given documentary evidence of it. It was at the end of a year, when I often invited critical comment on the year's course, that one girl wrote — and it was over two years after the event — "One memorable lesson was when we were looking at a poem of a girl comparing herself and beauty. You took a moment to capture me. You spoke to each individual and told us that we don't require comparisons or judging beauty. We all are beautiful. You captured me there and the room fell silent. It was something so personal ... I'll always remember that."

That's human worth, in its context of awe. If we could lay our hands on that, affirming our person and our place, just maybe we could get that suicide rate down a little.

Islam, Narnia and Israel: Year 9

A lot of girls begin their Queen Margaret College experience at Year 9. While there are many who come up through the Junior School, there are many others who arrive for their secondary years following junior education at other places. For those from a state school, Year 9 is their first experience of Religious Education.

After we had begun the year with a look at what it means to be an individual, we would usually expand a bit into how and why an institution might differ from others that look similar to it. "What makes Queen Margaret College distinctive?" I would ask. And they would give me the gamut — girls, all ages from new entrants to Year 13, private, close to the railway station, Presbyterian, dual pathway (NCEA/IB), history — you name it. I would normally take the history as an excuse to look at Shakespeare's *Macbeth* for a couple of lessons, because Queen Margaret married Malcolm, the man who followed Macbeth on the Scottish throne, in 1057. And the play is made for RE, based as it is on spiritual beliefs and experiences connected to heaven, hell, and answers to prayer, as well as offering a deal of insight into motivation, ambition and power.

With that completed, we went on like everyone else in the school to contemplate Easter near the end of Term 1, and later we considered Creation. In Term 2, we placed a major focus on Islam as Year 9's part of the survey of world religions covered by the complete Queen Margaret course.

There were a couple of reasons for choosing Islam. By the end of Years 7 and 8 we'd had a fairly decent look at the Bible, and I always thought it was appropriate to consider the school's, and New Zealand's, major acknowledged religion before moving on to look at another one. Also Islam, like Christianity, is descended from Jewish roots, so it was a logical extension to go from the one to the other. And all that logic was reinforced by the fact that Islam, with something around 1.8 billion adherents, is the second most followed faith in the world, after Christianity.

Islam was also in the world news in my first year at the school. That was 2001, which was the year of the September 11 al-Qaeda attack on the World Trade Center in New York. Towards the end of my chaplain's tenure at QMC there was the mosque attack in Christchurch, in 2019. In between were various news-attracting events that confirmed that we should try to grow our understanding of an influential religious faith a little more broadly than social media comments might encourage.

There were a lot of girls — and parents — who were glad for us to be studying another religion. Some were curious, some were happy for novelty, and some felt freed from parochialism. It wasn't universal, however. I once had a girl who asked me, and so did her mother, if she might be exempted from the Islam unit because she was a practising member of another faith. I thought that was the very reason that she ought to be looking at this one, and as tactfully as possible, I declined the request, on those grounds. In the end she completed the unit happily enough, though she did ask if she might be allowed to not write out the Muslim creed, "There is one God, Allah, and Muhammed is his prophet." I had no problem granting that concession.

There is always a challenge in teaching about a faith not your own. By definition, there are elements of it that you personally disavow, and there are also subtleties of understanding that you hope you are getting right. Sometimes there was a Muslim girl in the class, and that was always helpful if she were prepared to add a voice. Not everyone wanted to do that, for obvious reasons, but for some years I enjoyed in the Middle School the presence of Adibah, who was very happy to take on the role of a sort of jovial voice of militia. I remember one day mentioning the prophet and adding to the mention of his name the standard Muslim phrase, "peace be upon him." Adibah looked up at me and said, more patronisingly than I can begin to represent here, "Good boy!"

You could work happily in that sort of context, and sometimes there was a springboard for more substantial comment as well. It was Adibah again who asked me one day, with concern, "Do you think Muslims were responsible for the Twin Towers attacks?"

Personally, I hadn't thought there was much doubt about it, but she was really angling to establish that not all Muslims would be well represented by such extremists as the Twin Towers zealots. It was a point well made, for her classmates and also for me. I had the distinction clear in my head at the time, but I'm not sure the emotional grip on it was established until years later when I watched in dismay as American evangelicals threw their support behind a President I deeply deplored on many grounds, including religious ones. Another reminder to be very cautious about generalisations.

We got to the political subtleties surrounding Islam later in the topic. Before all that, there was an attempt to consider history and dogma. As with everything, there was insufficient time to be more than superficial — you explained that, and hoped for the questions to probe at least some of it a little more subtly.

You began with the history, that Islam originated in Arabia in the early 7th century. A map or two helped with the geography. The term "early 7th century" then offered the opportunity for a detour through calendars and different ways of numbering the years: the Arab world was having 1442 when the world in New Zealand was having 2020. This took some absorbing for some of the girls, and we not infrequently added the Jewish variation (5780) or other related ideas. One year a Muslim girl in the class, Harriet, explained the lunar months on which the Arab calendar works. Sometimes you would be lured off into how Jesus could get to be born in some year "Before Christ".

Back on track, you introduced the Prophet, Muhammed (peace be upon him). About now, the variations of spelling became a feature, and it was possible to lose your way in pondering transliterations from languages with a different script.

Back to the Prophet. It was the Prophet Muhammed who gave the world the Koran, or Qur'an, the sacred Islamic scriptures, after his vision from the Angel Gabriel. Muslims believe that parts of the previously revealed scriptures, the Torah and the Gospels, had become distorted, and the new revelations were to put the people back onto the right path. Most of the revered figures of Jewish and Christian history are also regarded as prophets in Islam, with the significant difference that the most recent prophets take precedence over the earlier ones, and therefore Muhammed becomes the final authority. Jesus is also acknowledged as a prophet, but since Jews regard him as an impostor and Christians as God, this stance is anathema to both.

After the general background, we moved on to the basis of faith. We began with The Five Pillars of Islam, those duties that every Muslim must perform. The girls wrote them down: profession of faith (Shahada), regular prayers (Salah), giving to the needy (Zakat), fasting during daylight in the month of Ramadan (Sawm) and pilgrimage to Mecca (Hajj). Significant explanation at every point often gave opportunity for debate, especially around the legal requirements to practise the tenets of the faith — "What if you can't? What if you're on an aeroplane? What if you're sick? What happens if you don't do it?" And so on. The sorts of questions that were aired every single time that requirements of faith — any faith — were under consideration, and that highlighted the gap between a genuine wish to do something and a probably equal wish to be seen to be doing it.

The Five Pillars define orthodox Muslim religious belief and practice. We therefore spent a lot of time trying to be clear about what they did and didn't require, noting that a single honest, public recitation of the Shahada in Arabic is what is required for a person to become a Muslim, and the others followed as logical responsibilities consequent upon it. The formulaic nature of daily prayer was news to people mostly accustomed to a much looser format, and factors surrounding Ramadan were always fascinating. The giving of alms to the poor led us to consider how the amounts were calculated and then extracted from the faithful, noting how different Muslim nations demonstrated different requirements and levels of enforcement.

The Hajj took on a life of its own. The availability of numerous dramatic pictures of the Great Mosque in Mecca and the crowds approaching the Kaaba guaranteed interest and questions, and we were easily able to find anecdotes of a variety of pilgrimage experiences. Those from New Zealand allowed an immediacy of identity, and the story of a family from Hawkes Bay who some years ago wanted a pizza parlour to fund their hajj as a legal penalty for inadvertently including a bacon fragment in the family's pizza took us right into religious law and politics.

Then, with a coverage of the Five Pillars established, we looked for a few summary statements:

> that Abraham is the patriarch of the patriarchs, and Ishmael of the Arabs
> that the place of worship is the mosque
> that the faith is one of law, which Muslims must observe
> that Allah is holy and just
> that people are sinful and must strive for goodness to get into heaven
> that Allah is not obliged to forgive, and his followers must hope he will be merciful.

It took us some weeks of more subtle conversation than these points suggest for us to get this far, and then it was necessary to engage with current political factors and some of their distortions.

We were able to approach the religious background to various political events by establishing that Muslims allow no separation of faith and state, or church and politics, so politics is religious. This took some explaining in New Zealand, and so did the idea that Muslims abroad therefore see our politics as an expression of religion as well. Americans and the west are therefore seen as "Christian" and they appear to display an immoral lifestyle. The immoral lifestyle could be illustrated by a picture or two of a woman in a burka alongside another woman in a bikini.

"How," you asked, "does Woman A begin to understand the outlook of Woman B?"

The understanding that there are Muslims who see it as their holy duty to combat immoral lifestyles, and that it is their belief that a life sacrificed in a holy cause will allow entry into heaven went some way to explaining a number of world events. One of them was how anyone might recruit, from impoverished Muslim areas, a crew to attack the World Trade Center. The Crusades of the Middle Ages were also a necessary inclusion around here, illustrating that religious jihad has not always been limited to Islam and that the "Christian armies of the West" did very little credit to their faith either. And my private view that the Crusades had very little to do with genuine Christianity brought me back to Adibah's question about whether Muslims had attacked the World Trade Center.

The blasphemy laws of a number of modern Islamic states took us to religious political prisoners like Asia Bibi of Pakistan, or Meriam Yehya Ibrahim Ishag who fled Sudan in 2014. Amina Lawal of Nigeria was a high-profile example of Sharia morality law when her death sentence coincided with Nigeria's possible hosting of the Miss World contest of 2002. The world's focus on Miss World meant a high level of awareness of Amina Lawal, and these people could all be Googled. Their situations then needed to be both acknowledged and balanced with a nuanced view of their circumstances. Boko Haram and the missing schoolgirls in Nigeria, 2014; US President George Bush's war on terror; the presence of a Muslim Mayor of London, Sadiq Khan — there was more than enough religious/political material to last for the year, had we wanted it to. But we didn't, so the real challenge was to sketch an overall picture without forming a caricature.

We spent about a term on Islam, and by the end of that time we were in need of some contrast and light relief. I went to C S Lewis's Narnia series for children, and we read together *The Lion, the Witch and the Wardrobe*. To many of the classes I read it aloud, in its entirety. It took about three and a half lessons, but the hearing accorded it was always closely attentive, which said something for the currency of Lewis's prose.

While I read, the girls worked. On a clean page, they drew a large and compelling wardrobe door, in splendid and full colour, adding the title and author above and below it. They left the back of it clean, and on the next page, directly behind the door, they drew the forest of Narnia and a lamp post. When we had finished reading and drawing respectively, I cut around the door frames at top, bottom and centre with a craft knife, and they could then "go through" the wardrobe into the forest, past the lamp post. They could then cut out (and colour) some small coats and attach them to the back of the door, and then they glued the two pages together to keep them stable and a passage to Narnia consistent. The best efforts over this exercise were simply stunning.

With all that done we looked at some pictures from Lewis's life and of Magdalen College, Oxford, wrote down half a dozen central quotations from the book, discussed the Christian parallels of the story, and moved on to the next unit.

That's very simply stated. It does not begin on the implications of the story, never mind the detours or the associated links. A story in which a witch has captured a kingdom whose release depends on a saviour has theological implications for the ages. The characterisations of the children and the impact of their choices on their lives and those of others are rich in potential. The comments of the book's characters probed the outlook on life of us all, whatever religious views we might have. One of them is the professor, who talks to the children after Lucy's first visit into

Narnia, when they are completely unable to make sense of her reports. He asks them if she usually tells lies, and hears she does not. He reminds them that she is clearly not mad. If you eliminate lies and madness, you are left with truth: he points that out, and suggests that they believe her until something else turns up to force a review of that decision. He goes on to wonder to himself about logic, and why the children have not been taught it "in these schools."

Closer to Lewis's central theme, he has Susan asking if Aslan the lion — the Jesus figure — is safe to be near. The reply she receives, from the beaver, is scornful. "Safe? *Course* he isn't safe. But he's good." And when they meet Aslan they are inspired to noble thoughts and acts, "and something made Peter say" that the seducing of Edmund by the White Witch was partly his fault, because he had not been very nice to Edmund. And Aslan neither condemns nor exempts, and they are all called to a higher view. Then, fittingly, it is Aslan who provides the insight into the Christian understanding of redemption through sacrifice when he explains that the death of a willing and innocent victim in the place of a traitor would cause "death itself to start working backwards." Almost every class I took the book to had a majority who had read it before, but a lot of them had missed the parallels entirely.

We finished the year with a topic called "The Life and Times of Jesus." A map of Israel demonstrated that it was a real place, and a *Reader's Digest* film took us there. We noted ten Bible events featuring Jesus' life and teaching, and located the towns and areas mentioned in them on our map. It was more of a Social Studies approach than anything else, and the film was clear in its presentation of history and social customs of the time, many of which are very similar to social customs of the present day.

I made my first visit to Israel, for two weeks, at the start of 2019, and found it helpful to be able to add some colour drawn from personal observation. One example was the sycamore tree climbed by Zacchaeus when he wanted to see Jesus without being seen — and failed spectacularly in the second part of that wish — in Jericho. There is a tree there of the same sort, and it's leafier than the sycamore trees that I have known here. It made more sense of his thinking, while leaving intact the moral of his story.

The film was wide-ranging in its focus. Marriage customs, shepherds' practices, household tasks around baking and washing, Passover, traditions surrounding the Christmas story, local diet, politics — all there, and we could have extended it as long as we chose to. In fact, we took it through to a couple of weeks before Christmas and finished the year with the nativity. The film speculated on the nature of the Christmas star, and also covered the character and the gruesome history of King Herod, a nasty figure of a ruler both in the general view of history and in the account of him given in the Bible. The film explained divorce laws, and contracted marriages. About the only drawback was that the year was to end, with Christmas, where the film had logically begun, but we could get around that. By the time the unit was ended, the year was too, and we never suffered too much from a minor flashback to adjust the time sequence.

The Level of Discourse

It was Jessica who started it. We had been talking about *The Lion, the Witch and the Wardrobe* and the nature of temptation, when she had a thought. She put her hand up for permission to speak and said: "If Jesus was God, and he was tempted by the devil, does that mean that God can be tempted to do wrong?"

It was quarter to three on a Wednesday afternoon, with Year 9, and suddenly the children's world of *The Lion, the Witch and the Wardrobe* had given way to the sort of question that theologians have wrestled with through the centuries. I said, "Jessica, I need to be able to say about five things at once if I'm going to engage with that question. And I can't. So, can I say one thing and then another thing, and will you pretend I said them both at the same time? And then can I say another thing and we'll pretend I said that at the same time too?"

"Go on," said Jessica, with agreement from her friends. "See how we go."

I thought of two things to start with. One was the account in Matthew's Gospel of Jesus in the desert, being tempted by Satan. The actual line that begins that account reads, "Jesus was led by the Spirit into the wilderness to be tempted by the devil." The other thing was the teaching given to us by James, commonly accepted as Jesus' brother, who wrote: "When tempted, no one should say, 'God is tempting me.' For God cannot be tempted by evil, nor does he tempt anyone."

I thought of a few other things as well. Jesus: "Son of man, Son of God." Virgin birth. And Jesus as God. Trinity. Well, what else would you do on a Wednesday afternoon?

"Jesus as God," I said. "Yes and no. Or, better, yes but. We have to get our head around a few challenges here. Christians talk about "God" in three ways: Father, Son and Holy Spirit. So when they talk about "Father", they mean God but not Son or Spirit: when they talk about "Spirit", they mean God but not Father or Son: when they talk about "Son" — Jesus — they mean God, but not Father or Spirit. Then they complicate the whole thing by using the word "God" to mean sometimes Father and other times, all three."

"Wait a minute," someone asked. "Are you saying there are three Gods?"

"No, importantly I am not," I said. "I am saying God in three forms. If I have an egg, it's an egg. If I want to make a pavlova, I crack the shell and then separate the white from the yolk. I end up with three forms: shell (egg, but not *the* egg), white (egg, but not *the* egg), yolk (egg, but not *the* egg). One egg, three forms, different functions. Is this making sense?" General assent.

"So God (total) is represented on earth in human form (Jesus, Son). Son is tempted, Father and Spirit are not. Further, Spirit leads Son into the desert, to be tempted by the devil. If the idea of a devil is a problem for you, let's not talk about that right now: it'll become a distraction. Just think of evil as a force to be reckoned with and let that do. We can come back to the devil issue later if you want to, once we've cleared the other issues we have already."

They agreed to this as a fair enough approach, and we carried on. "How many things have you said so far?" they wanted to know. "Of your five?"

"I dunno. Let's add them up later. But we have Jesus, best thought of here as Son of God, led by Spirit of God, to be tempted."

Another girl put her voice in. "Hang on. If God's making Jesus be tempted, it doesn't sound fair. Why doesn't he come himself?"

"He is. Jesus: God. One with the Father. That's why he came. Distinct *representation* of the person of God, but same person."

"What's the Spirit?" someone asked.

"Um, personality. I can see your body: I can't see your personality. Your spirit. Who here plays sport, in a team?" Various. "We talk about team spirit. You can't see it, but you know how well it is when you see the team play. Especially you know how well it is when they lose. It's like the collective nature of the team. Grows among them, makes them do things."

"What was Jesus tempted with?" asked someone else.

"I'm just coming to it," I said.

"I know," said Caitlin. "Wasn't it about jumping off a building?"

"Yes, it got to that, later," I told her. "But before that it was a bit more immediate. He had been fasting for a long time and Satan said, 'If you are God, make the stones into bread.' Sounds OK, given that he's hungry. But the key words are 'If you are God'. To put it another way, Satan is saying, 'Do it my way.' What he didn't say, of course, was 'And then I'll be bossing God about.' And Jesus says 'Out. The whole reason I am here is to give everyone a chance to not do it your way.' In *The Lion, the Witch and the Wardrobe*, when the children don't do things the witch's way, the place can be put right. Until then, it's permanent winter."

"What about the building?" said Caitlin.

"Same thing. 'Do it my way. If you are God, you can jump off a building and not be hurt, and everyone will believe in you and you won't have to be crucified.' And Jesus says, 'Out. There is only one way to do what I have to do, and it is not your way.' He gives pretty much the same answer to the other temptation as well."

"So, did Jesus want to die?" from the same girl wondering about God making Jesus come to be tempted. "He seems like someone who likes life. Why did he want to die?"

"Put the question in the queue, if that's OK," I said. "Ahead of the one about the devil, but behind the one we're still on. People have often looked at this story and asked if Jesus really could have fallen to the temptation, or must he have been beyond it. Personally, I think we have to accept that he could have fallen. Otherwise, the whole thing's a charade. So I think he actually could have, but the key fact is that he did not. After all, the night he was arrested, he spent time in very earnest prayer asking God — Father — to find another way through it if it was at all possible. 'But if it's not,' he said, 'I'll do it anyway.'"

"So, why did he want to die?"

"He still didn't. But —"

There was a large sycamore tree growing outside the classroom window. "See that tree?" I asked.

Heads turned. "Yep."

"Let's say Caroline or Claudia or someone has climbed the tree. I don't know why she's climbed the tree — it probably looked like a good idea at the time. But she's up there. And she's in trouble. Branches too thin, and she can't get down. If you leave her alone long enough, she's going to fall, and she'll be hurt.

"And then I come along the path and I see her there. It so happens that I'm a very good climber of trees, and I know that I can help her down safely. I also know that if I do that, I can't get back safely myself. Those thin branches at the top won't carry both of us. She'll be OK, but I will certainly fall, and be badly hurt. I understand about trees, and I know that. So I have a choice. I don't want to go up, but I don't want her to fall. What's it going to depend on?"

"How much you want to help her?'

"Got it. So Jesus is not looking to die. He's looking to save the rest of us. Which is why he's got to be God — so he will (a) care enough and (b) have the qualities to be able to do it."

I don't know who asked the question, but it had been waiting to come. It was something like, "How can Jesus be God? I mean, Mary, Joseph —"

Fortunately, among all the brouhaha of a standard New Zealand Christmas, most of them had picked up something. "Not Joseph," someone said.

"Right," I answered. "Son of Mary, son of God. Mary is his mother, Joseph is not his father."

"How does that work?"

This is tricky. This is Year 9. Some of them are likely vague enough about a standard birth, never mind the virgin birth. I guess that's why I'm paid the big money. Anyway, it was always inevitable.

"Virgin birth," I said. "Mary becomes pregnant before she has any sexual contact."

"How?"

"Fair question. I know that doesn't happen, and you know it doesn't happen. We're asked to believe it happened.

"Step back a bit. Who invented this whole giving-birth system? God did. He made it so it works. If he can make a whole system that works, then he can also make an exception to the system for exceptional circumstances. Details? I don't know. But it all hinges on God, not on details.

"And here is where we need to have said a few things already, so we can get to this point. What you make of God will decide what you make of all the other issues, including the virgin birth. Basically, you look at the world with God in mind, or without God in mind. Everything else follows from there."

I had watched a television feature the night before about an unsolved New Zealand murder. It featured Greg King, the late defence lawyer who had defended the man who was accused and was challenging the police case. He said something along the lines of, "How you see the evidence depends on what you believe. If you believe this man is guilty, a number of facts begin to look sinister. But if you think he is innocent, or have an open mind, those facts take on quite different possibilities." Greg King may have got a mention in our conversation here, or not, but his thesis certainly did. And some girl went straight back to *The Lion, the Witch and the Wardrobe,* which was what this lesson had been planned to be all about, when she said, "That's like the Professor."

"What?" I said.

"The Professor. In *The Lion, the Witch and the Wardrobe.* You know, when Lucy comes back from Narnia and they all say 'That can't be true,' he says 'Keep an open mind until you know it's not true. Just because you never met it before doesn't mean it can't happen.'"

There was a very great neatness about it. We were ten minutes away from the end of the lesson now, and we had been brought back to the starting point. When we had read the book together, I had drawn their attention to various key scenes, and one of them was that one. Four children, one of them always truthful and one more doubtful: when their accounts of a magical world come into conflict, the other two side with the liar because his account lines up more easily with their assumed views. The Professor asks them which of the two is more reliable and counsels them to follow that line of reasoning when they weigh up the new information. "New to you", he reminds them, is different from "can't happen".

I knew my lesson was back on track when someone linked the white witch to the devil and Aslan to Jesus. No one did go back to ask about a devil, which was probably just as well: we didn't want to get as far as Hell's Pizzas at 25 past 3 and be hoping the owner's daughter's not sitting in front of us. But someone did ask, "Who is the Professor in the Bible?" and I was able to say "No one. It's not that sort of story."

Lewis always insisted that his book was not an allegory. In a letter he once wrote he reflected that there were people who believed he had begun with the lesson he wished to draw in mind and then worked back to a story to illustrate it, but he denied that process, calling it "pure moonshine." He said he couldn't begin to write to such a formula, and that what he had written began with the images and worked the other way around, with the Christian parallels weaselling themselves in whether he liked it or not. He explained Aslan by saying he was the logical answer to a question that wondered what Christ might become like if he were to enter a world like Narnia and set about redeeming it, and he drew a clear distinction between his own process and any genuine allegory.

We'd covered all this in an earlier lesson that had gone according to plan. It was one of the things that did not need to be said simultaneously with five other things. And that was just as well, because the bell was ringing by now and we can come back to the unmet questions when I meet the class again next week. Or, just as likely, we can start with the new question that Jessica, or someone, chooses to begin the day with for us. It's a wonderful world.

Year 10

(AND BIG ISSUES IN GENERAL)

"Other Religions"

Queen Margaret College is a Presbyterian school. I am a Christian teacher, appointed for that reason. It would therefore be a betrayal of the school's ethos and of my own conscience to teach a Religious Education course without a clear aim that all my students should know what the Christian faith is all about.

Given that a faith worth the name is not an academic affair, a corollary of teaching about it is that it includes an ethical outlook. Christianity and ethics therefore counted as two major strands of the RE syllabus.

But it was a Religious Education syllabus, not a Christian Education syllabus. So the Islam of Year 9 and attention to other major world faiths in other years made up the third major strand of the course. Every time there was a parent-teacher meeting I could guarantee that some of the parents I met would want to know if I taught about "other religions", and express satisfaction at hearing that I did.

The girls also wanted to know I was covering diverse ground. A few of them complained that it was not diverse enough, but when I look back I am unrepentant about that. I always saw a priority in my three strands and they ranked as I have listed them here: Christianity; ethics; other faiths, in that order. The reasoning was simple.

If the students did not hear about Christianity, the school had failed to meet its basic mandate. If they did not make an ethical link, I had failed to flesh out why any of it mattered. If they did not hear of other faiths, they understood less of the diverse world in which they live. But I always figured that while they could hear of various faiths equally well through other avenues if they needed to, the very goal of the Queen Margaret College founders was to provide a good education from a Christian starting point.

Having laid a broad if somewhat general foundation in Year 7 we then specialised a little in later years. The Christian faith predominated in Year 8 along with a side visit into Māori spirituality, Year 9 had its term on Islam, Year 10 looked at Buddhism and Year 11 at Judaism. Years 12 and 13 came into the picture late in my Queen Margaret service and were timetabled as "Ethics, Philosophy and Religion": we structured the course differently. There was also a little unit on Rastafarians in Year 10, not because their small numbers demanded inclusion alongside the bigger faiths, but because they were a logical and interesting follow-on from other work we had been doing on slavery and colonialism.

Teaching about a faith to which one does not subscribe is a call to being alert. It's not so much a challenge to demonstrate respect, since there is always an attempt to do that, as it is to speak with knowledge about things looked at from the outside. It's a different thing from speaking from the position of adherent. Although it's much freer to come in from outside, in that your own allegiance is not under scrutiny, there is often a subtle doubt that what you've read is quite what it looks like. So I used to say that to the class at the start of the topic, and the girls understood it. In the course of a remote lesson during the 2020 Covid-19 lockdown, on an abstruse aspect of Buddhism, one girl in Year 10 said, "I'm a Buddhist, Mr Edgecombe, and you've got that right." With her permission I made her my go-to person when I needed reassurance through the rest of the topic, and it was a very helpful thing.

The glaring omission from the list of religions covered was Hinduism. The reason was that its extremely complex nature meant that I was never confident I could get hold of a term's study in it without doing some branch of it a disservice while we were concentrating on a different branch. In short, I ran away from it. I talked about it one day to an Indian girl. She told me she was a Hindu and I said, "I have a confession about that," and told her my story, waiting for her appropriate expression of regret. She was very reassuring. "Oh no, Mr Edgecombe," she said, "you couldn't do that — it's far too complicated." She was very kind and I felt excused, but I wonder if I might have done better.

I did have an article I wrote for senior classes some time around 2005, in which I took Non-dualistic Hinduism as one part of a three-way comparison with Christianity and Islam in order to show that no one could "believe in" all of them at the same time. Not only were they different, but there were areas in which they positively conflicted, and I wanted to demonstrate that no logic in the world could reconcile the irreconcilable. We looked at what each of the three faiths said about the nature of God, or Ultimate Reality, about the Human Condition and about Spiritual Liberation. The article did no disservice to any of the faiths, and it certainly showed that you could not logically believe in them all at the same time, but I'm not sure either that it would count as a serious consideration of Hinduism.

On the subject of believing conflicting things, I recall two occasions — of the many — when I had to respond to direct questions about believing multiple things. Once was when someone asked me, "Mr Edgecombe, are there some things that you don't believe?" A question so phrased gives scope for a mercifully brief answer, and I gave it. It was, "Obviously." We'd have moved to the small print in the next sentence, but there was nothing more to add of any substance.

More direct, and less easily dealt with, was the question another day that asked, "Can Christians believe in any other religion as well as Christianity?" I knew where it came from. It was from the wish to not appear to disrespect anybody by disagreeing with them. I happen to believe that disagreeing with someone, if done kindly, shows a lot more respect than nodding blandly and turning the conversation to the weather, because it shows you have been listening. But it needs to be done kindly.

So I asked my questioner who wanted to believe different things at the same time, "Why would they want to?" She made the sort of answer I have just suggested, and waited for me to elaborate.

I did. I said something like, "Basically, there are three approaches to God that you can take, and they are represented in different religions. One is to say you're not interested, and since no Christian is saying this, you can count that out as part of a Christian/other religion combo. The second is to say that you're going to make God like you by doing certain things, but Christians know you can't do enough things, and their faith is in the sacrifice of Jesus and the gift of his grace. That's why they're Christians. So no religion based on following a law will sit well alongside Christian faith either. The third approach is to accept that you need God to forgive you, and to ask him to do it. That's where Christian faith necessarily begins. Then you go on doing good anyway but it's from gratitude, not from an attempt to make God pay you back as if it's a contract. Christians are onto receiving the gift of God. They can't buy into something else as well, because that would deny their central starting point, that God's free gift is all they have. No, you can't be a Christian and also believe in some other religion."

It was probably a bit more short-bits-and-pieces at the time than it is here, but that's pretty much the ground we covered. She thought about it a bit, and then pushed back on it by asking, "Isn't that exclusive?"

"Well," I said, "it's not exclusive, in that anyone is invited to join, but it is exclusive in that you can't get to first base and stand on the batting plate at the same time. This is not a sports tournament where you have to show equal favour to all the players. This is about commitment to faith that requires an approach to life. If you don't approach life, you've only got one other option. If your house is on fire, you don't show equal favour to the fire and the firemen. You make up your mind whose side you're on, and then you chuck on water or petrol. Not both."

It was not part of that conversation, but there was another day when a girl asked me, "Do you believe that Christianity is superior to all the other religions?" Frankly, you don't want to talk in these terms unless asked, and you'd rather not be asked; but if you are asked, you cannot dodge it. I looked at her, and paused long enough to make the point that this was not a case of firing randomly from the hip, and I raised my eyebrows enough to convey thoughtfulness and not spontaneous reflex, and I inclined my head and I spoke slowly, looking her in the eye so she could see I was taking her seriously. In short, I tried to engage with her, and to engage visibly.

And I said, "Yes, I do." It was all the more fraught because I had reason to think that she was herself a follower of another religion. But she looked back at me, seriously and thoughtfully, and she nodded and thanked me, and I thought then and I hope now that the conversation demonstrated mutual respect and not confrontation, and that it was true because it dealt honestly with a question that had been honestly asked and because she was not challenging me and I was not confronting her, except so far as two points of differing view cannot both be right. Incidentally, I remain prepared to dismiss out of hand the fatuous phrase "true for you", that you may read about all over the place where people aren't sure what to think. "True for you" is another way of saying that you don't think it's true or that you don't care if I do, but if you believe me when I put you on a bus to Napier and tell you it's going to Taupo, the consequent result will be true for neither of us, no matter what you believe.

There are of course many people who believe one thing but think they believe another. We often spent time trying to clarify the difference between mental assent and physical practice. Questions like "What religion was Hitler?" could be answered by "Nazi"; the resultant "Was that a religion?" led to a consideration of what beliefs drove Nazi practices and how such beliefs might be called religious. It was also a useful illustration — safe because no one ever wanted to follow Nazism or defend it, out loud anyway — of the fact that "religion" does not always have to mean "positive". You could also find ammunition to support that fact in the Crusades, and in modern day terrorist attacks conducted in the name of some sort of religious fervour, and in any number of current affairs articles reporting on regrettable events with a religious association. The attitude of Brian Tamaki of Destiny Church toward Covid vaccinations would have been illustration enough, but his worst excesses came a little late in my history to be useful. In fact, the files I built up through my regular practice of hoarding stuff I thought I could use are full of things that there was simply never time to use, and they covered every religious ground you could imagine and a fair amount you could not.

But it was never about covering the ground, or finishing the course. The point of an RE class, in my view, was to push the boundaries and open the mind to considerations not previously thought about. There was no exam to test their recall, and no performance to measure their understanding. I relied heavily on involuntary feedback to know how we were scoring, and I hoped that the real benefits were lodging in places from where they could be drawn on for years to come. I asked a Year 11 class at the end of 2013 to note some reflections on the course they had covered. Their responses, in light of the aims suggested here, were encouraging.

More than a couple of them picked up on the theme of forgiveness. One said, "QMC has taught me that the Christian faith highly values forgiveness. It is giving everyone a chance to say how they feel, ask questions (including controversial ones) and learn, in regard to faith. Having freedom of speech has played an important role in informing my spiritual understanding."

Another girl said, "Forgiveness and respect are very important to live a good life. The Bible readings in chaplain's assembly raise new questions and improve my understanding. Having them related to modern day topics helps me to understand better and enjoy Christianity more." I was especially pleased to note the links she made between the Bible and everyday life, as I was by the girl who wrote in a similar vein: "I have learned that Christianity and the ideas behind it come into everyday life regularly. It has taught me more about helping other people and learning right from wrong."

Also encouraging was the girl who said, "At QMC I have learned religion in a more real-life scenario, and I enjoy RE lessons because we are taught subtly (and sometimes not so subtly) about God. I really enjoyed over the years learning about other religions such as Muslims because what once seemed so foreign is now within my grasp of understanding. I now think of the world in a slightly different viewpoint other than a strictly materialistic world."

Similarly, someone else wrote, "I have learned that there is something out there beyond what we can see. It can't all be black and white; it can't all be hard science. There is emotion and coincidence and luck which involve something beyond science. Even if I don't personally believe that that special bit is God, QMC has shown me about spirituality."

The acknowledgement of a spiritual insight to a not entirely material world brought me joy. So did the expanded view of the "other religions" living in that world. That comment was reinforced by someone else who wrote: "Through looking at the way in which others lead their lives through culture and religion I've come to understand my own more and be more accepting and understanding of others." Her comment about better understanding her own culture and religion adds credence to my view that it is no help to wider understanding to dilute one's own sense of identity. Other comments from the same survey included:

"I have not so much learned new things as learned a lot of the reasoning behind my faith and ways to examine it and see how others view it. More understanding and wisdom than knowledge."

"I'm glad that QMC gives us the freedom to think and say whatever we think; that religion is not forced upon us."

"You have made me learn that I do not dislike the faith of Christianity, but what many have done under its protection. Not all Christians are like those I have read about: you have opened my narrow thinking of Christianity. There is no need to judge people because they are Christians as long as they do not force their religion on me. I find your way of teaching very good and you have made me kind of like religion. I would be a very narrow thinker in the field of faith. Thank you for teaching me and opening my eyes."

The last point had an echo, more bluntly put, in a comment made to me one day in a classroom by a girl who said, "I've learned that Christianity — excuse me — isn't as much bollocks as I thought."

There is a lot in there to give an RE teacher encouragement. Room for some reflection, too. Which is, really, what all of us need. Meanwhile, I recall a comment made by Lucy from many years earlier. She wrote: "A good RE class is like shopping. To get a really good buy you must take a brutally honest friend as opposed to a nice but unopinionated one. You get far more out of the experience and you choose the right dress." Truly a comparison made by someone in a girls' school, and how I love the rigour.

Beatitudes, Buddhism and Barbarism: Year 10

My friend who asked me in my first week what the girls at Queen Margaret College were like didn't leave the subject there. He also asked me what they would be studying.

It was a good question. I had looked at the syllabus I had inherited, and I must say I had done a bit of wondering about some of it. But Year 10 looked OK. Their first topic was headed "The Teachings of Jesus."

I told my friend this, and he grinned. Sardonically, I thought. "Where are you going to start?" he asked.

I had decided that the answer was in Jesus' Sermon on the Mount. Specifically, the Beatitudes. I figured we could take a long time or a short time over them, and it turned out I was right. Here they are,

from Matthew Chapter 5 which tells us that Jesus gave them first to his
disciples:

> "Blessed are the poor in spirit,
> for theirs is the kingdom of heaven.
> Blessed are those who mourn,
> for they will be comforted.
> Blessed are the meek,
> for they will inherit the earth.
> Blessed are those who hunger and thirst for
> righteousness,
> for they will be filled.
> Blessed are the merciful,
> for they will be shown mercy.
> Blessed are the pure in heart,
> for they will see God.
> Blessed are the peacemakers,
> for they will be called children of God.
> Blessed are those who are persecuted because of
> righteousness,
> for theirs is the kingdom of heaven."

Being the first topic of Term 1, the Beatitudes came up at the end of
the summer holidays, so I devised a lengthy introduction based on holiday
reminiscences. I asked them in the course of it what it might take to be
called happy. Then we poured scorn on the concept of "happiness" as a goal
in itself, and talked about it as a by-product of usefulness. Then we went
to such statements as "Happy are those who are sad," which did duty as a
paraphrase of the second Beatitude.

"Either Jesus didn't know much, or there's more in here than meets the eye," I would say. "I'm assuming the second."

To be fair, "happy" is a pretty weak word to replace "blessed". We went for "fortunate": fuller, subtler and a little less self-centred. It still left you faced by the idea that people who mourn might be thought of as fortunate, or that you could use the same word for someone who longed for things, such as "righteousness". We all knew as well that the role of a peacemaker is a difficult and delicate thing, allowing the possibility of attack from both sides. From Jesus' paradoxes came the conversation. And in his lines of explanation were the seeds of some very subtle dissection of theology and life.

Everyone is interested in being happy — after all, no one sets a goal of being unhappy. The Beatitudes suggested that happiness had less to do with lying on the beach, and more to do with fulfilling one's destiny. Jesus distilled this as the service of God and of one's neighbour. If we reject such an idea, then we are left to choose from a series of possibilities, all of which are likely to turn out to be some kind of self-service. Most of the evidence suggests that self-service rarely leads to true happiness, and most of Year 10 were able to work that out reasonably clearly.

We took our time over it. Girls throughout the school enjoyed elaborate and colourful book entries, and I asked them to enter each Beatitude on a poster-like half page. Pictures and colour. For my part, I found a story that might illustrate each Beatitude in some way, and we would discuss it. We rarely dealt with more than two in a classroom lesson, and we would cover a lot of ground.

My material came from everywhere. I told them about a man from Lebanon I had worked with in Australia when I was in my 20s. He was killed in a motor accident and his family were not able to come for the funeral. Mourning.

I showed them a ten-minute extract from the World War 1 film *Joyeux Noel,* when soldiers of both sides staged an impromptu Christmas truce (and were reprimanded for it). Peacemakers. We read a story about a little boy who kept ringing up the local telephone exchange — there was a whole detour necessary here on how phones used to work before we could start the story — and consuming the operator's time with trivial questions. Both of them benefited greatly from her being merciful. "Pure in heart" took us to the centre of the grace versus law issue.

And of course, "the kingdom of heaven". "What do you have to do to go to heaven? Do only good people go to heaven? Does God only bless those who rely on him? What if you're a really good person but you just don't believe in God?"

Excellent questions, demanding of sensitive and subtle responses, and many of those responses, or at least an approach to them, were to be found in front of us. It was worth pointing out that Jesus was not actually talking here about people "going to heaven" at all: more about heaven coming to earth in the shape of God's people representing it in an often ungrateful world. Meekness, a longing for good, peace-making, as distinct from peace-enjoying … gritty, demanding, and a long way from caricatures about harps and golden clouds.

I did, however, feel we should engage with the questions about how sporting or otherwise might be a God who "only blessed those who relied on him." For some years around 2005, I ran a little exercise.

I prepared for each girl a little packet of colourful postage stamps. Without telling them what was in the packets, I would promise to give one to any girl who wished to receive it. She would signify that wish by raising both hands above her head, with her eyes closed, before I counted to 10.

Most did it, though not all. Their responses were interesting. It was the closed-eyes that made the difference — individual, and vulnerable, and the whole thing became an exercise in trust. That was the aim.

Then, you could ask your questions — "What should the teacher do if some girl actually has only one hand? What if some girl failed to hear the instructions correctly? What if someone annoyed the teacher during the exercise and he refused to give that girl the gift? What if he gave two gifts to someone, at no cost to anybody else? What reasons might cause anyone to decline to play this game? What if someone did not play and later said that any fair teacher should include everybody in the handout?" You could go on or stop short, but it didn't take long to establish the link between goodwill and mistrust. And you didn't really need to suggest that God would be pretty mean to not reward goodwill, and pretty stupid to be manipulated by opportunists.

Once finished with the Beatitudes and Easter, we spent Term 2 considering Buddhism. A little history and geography to start the topic, and we needed a map. Throughout my years at QMC I found the general level of geographical knowledge in front of me to be pretty modest, and a map was often a good thing. I gave them an outline of Asia, extending from Pakistan to Japan and down to Indonesia, and they stuck it in their books and added a series of arrows to show the outward expansion of Buddhism from its northern Indian origins.

We noted that Buddhism is the dominant religion today of Burma, Thailand, Sri Lanka, Tibet, Cambodia, Viet Nam and Laos and has possibly 500 million adherents, though they can be difficult to define and therefore to count. Based on human rationality and relying very little on the supernatural, it looks to some people more like a philosophy than a religion. We didn't go into the difference.

We spent a bit of time putting the faith into its historical context, and teasing out the story of its founder, Siddhartha Gautama. Having established that he was born about 563 BC to an aristocratic Hindu chieftain near the India/Nepal border, and that he found spiritual fulfilment in neither the luxury of his youth nor the asceticism of holy orders in Hinduism, we were ready to contemplate his Middle Way of Buddhism.

It was possible to get all political when we talked about Burma rather than Myanmar, or when the status of Tibet came into question. Tibet especially, given that the Dalai Lama fled into India from the Chinese invasion of Tibet when he was a young man and remains the ranking Buddhist all these decades later. We didn't always chase the politics of it, but the time was never wasted when we did.

"So, what do Buddhists teach? Are they the ones in the orange robes? Do they worship Buddha?"

"Listen, we're coming to what they teach. Yes, they're the ones in the orange robes. Saffron, actually, and not all of them. No, they don't worship Buddha. The idea is that you become one." And we were away.

We started with The Four Noble Truths — that suffering is universal, that it stems from craving, that the best way to overcome it is to eliminate craving and the way to do that is to follow the Noble Eightfold Path. The Noble Eightfold Path is a complete way of life featuring Right: in vision, emotion, speech, action, livelihood, effort, awareness and meditation. "Right" is that which puts a person in sync with the universe.

The meditation angle became something of a feature. I was trying to explain it one day when I had the obvious thought: "Why not try some?" So I invited the class to sit for three minutes in complete silence and focus their thoughts on someone who had been good to them.

I had some doubts about this. I mean, have you ever asked 20 teenage girls to do anything similar? In the middle of a school day? Silence?

Anyway, they were up for it, and when we finished they wanted to do it again, longer. I doubt if any self-respecting Buddhist would have recognised our efforts, and hardly anyone's thoughts at the end were still on the person who had been good to them, but recognising that was half the point of it, and they had all enjoyed hearing the clock ticking.

We did do it again, though not until the next lesson. We did it longer, and in various classes, over many years. We did it in a Year 12 class one member of which had a younger sister in Year 10: fruit of their dinner-time conversation. We did it in one class who asked, "Can we see how long we can last?" and were still there, in total silence, 35 minutes later. We did it one day when an ERO officer arrived, sat for 10 minutes and left. I hope he found it relaxing.

But there was more traditional classroom work — notes on reincarnation and karma, and Nirvana, and a consideration of The Five Precepts. The Precepts were an excellent view of the application of the general principles — do not kill, steal, engage in sexual misconduct, make false speech or take intoxicants — and they allowed a world of conversation. The distinction between a precept and an arbitrary law was also worth making, along with the notion that no one was policing anything, but the penalties for lax behaviour came from the destruction that was inherent within it.

There was also a day late in my Queen Margaret tenure when I was asked about someone who claimed to be a Christian Buddhist, or it might have been a Buddhist Christian, and what did I think about that?

That was actually quite simple. In fact there is, in ethical terms, a lot of sympathetic overlay between the two faiths and a lot of recommended Buddhist behaviour looks a lot like recommended Christian behaviour, and I said that it was likely that the person claiming dualism was recognising that fact. "But," I said, "there is no overlay at all in their understanding of Jesus, and without a commitment to him no code of conduct can be truly called Christian. They are theologically far apart, in terms of the basis of their behaviours. So no, you can't be both. So far from a sort of mix bringing two faiths together, what is really happening is the creation of a third, that neither the true Christian nor the true Buddhist would be satisfied by. It is at least possible that the person claiming both has an in-depth understanding of neither."

We wrapped up our Buddhism topic by watching a TV3 documentary made around 2000 about a child from Kaukapakapa who had been recognised as a reincarnated Buddhist lama. The film covered his family's early thoughts about his special nature, then the steps to recognise him, and along the way a lot of comment about the nature of reincarnation. It took us to India, where he was to train for upwards of 20 years before being released into general life as a fully qualified monk.

It also took us on his farewell trip around New Zealand, during which he was presented to the New Zealand public in a variety of gatherings and settings. And it was not until I had taught my last lessons on Buddhism with Year 10 that I was rummaging one day through an old folder of memorabilia and discovered an invitation to his Wellington meeting: "New Zealand Karma Kagyu Trust announces the recognition of a seven-year-old New Zealand boy as the incarnation of a high Tibetan Lama. Venerable Pong Re Sung Rap Tulku Rinpoche has been officially recognised by the Head of the Karma Kagyu School of Tibetan Buddhism, His Eminence Tai Situ. To honour this very happy occasion, the Trust invites Mr Ken Edgecombe, Chairman of the Council of Wellington Churches, to a celebratory afternoon tea to meet Rinpoche at 3:00pm, Saturday 6 November 1999 in the Wellington City Council Building, Meeting Room 2." I don't remember attending the event, but the girls would have been interested in the immediacy of it all. Then again, it might have looked like name-dropping. C'est la vie.

Having "finished" Buddhism around the end of Term 2, we considered a topic called Symbolism. All the world depends on symbols and a lot of them are religious. We drew flags to recognise some international examples: India, Israel, Cambodia, Pakistan, South Korea, Japan, Ethiopia, United Kingdom: carefully chosen to give us Hinduism, Judaism, Islam (twice), Taoism, Shintoism and Christianity (twice). Symbolism was an elastic topic. You could extend it as long as symbols could be found, or truncate it when you wanted to move on. When we did move on, it was to William Wilberforce and the abolition of slavery. Christian faith in action opposing barbaric practices.

We began this topic by seeing the film *Amazing Grace*, the story of the marathon campaign to end slavery in the British Empire. Its main character is William Wilberforce, who was both a dissolute young man and a Member of Parliament (I know, I know!) before meeting God and consequently redirecting his life. Following an inner struggle between becoming a religious recluse or continuing as an MP with a dedicated cause, he chose the cause. *Amazing Grace* allows a glimpse also of John Newton, who was not only something of a mentor to Wilberforce but who also wrote the classic hymn of that title, after a career in slave ships and a liberating and epochal encounter with God.

A story like Wilberforce's carries a double sting. For anyone inclined to Christian complacency, the clear message is that purity of doctrine ought to lead to social involvement and it might be costly. For those inclined to mock the idea of faith at all, it provides evidence beyond the academic of the power of the gospel. William Wilberforce's life tells of commitment and courage.

It was a topic of major significance in its own right, and when we finished it we followed on with a short view of colonialism in Africa and some of its social and political legacy.

The implications of slavery and colonialism are clearly both huge and sensitive, and a little dabble was always in order. Black Lives Matter in 2020 justified on its own some view of the background that shaped so much of current American attitudes. And out of it all came also some religious aftermath in the shape of Rastafarians.

There are not that many Rastafarians in the world, and their orthodoxy of practice is so loose as to make them very difficult to recognise, never mind to count. Furthermore, their religious dogma is almost all derivative, drawing heavily on Jewish and Christian scriptures and applying teachings found there to African and American history. Had it not been for Bob Marley and the Wailers, it is likely that they would have remained largely unknown to history.

But there was Bob Marley, with his dreadlocks, and there were the Wailers, and a quick look at their lyrics reveals a lot of focus on African Americans and their history as subjects of exploitation. "Buffalo Soldier" summarises it well: the song talks about the African people being stolen from their homes and carried as so much cargo to America, and in a fight for survival ever since. True when the first slave ships arrived in the American colonies in 1619. According to Michelle Obama in her book *Becoming*, published in 2018, true still. Four hundred years.

Marcus Garvey began the Rastafarian emergence, unwittingly, when he preached economic and political independence for blacks in the years before World War 1. Picking up on his theme, Leonard Howell drafted the first six tenets of Rastafarians in 1933: largely anti-white racism and since revised. But he preached the idea of an African destiny, based on the fact that Ethiopia under Emperor Haile Selassie had resisted European colonialism better than most. The red, green and yellow of the Ethiopian flag became the colours of Rastafarians in America, and Haile Selassie was elevated into a Christ-like figure of salvation and hope. As Tafari Makonnen before becoming Emperor, with the title of Ras, or duke, he also gave his name to the religious group.

Rastafarians are without specified buildings or a priesthood, and their sacred texts are mostly Biblical. Their adherents are therefore loosely delineated. Following Old Testament dietary restrictions, some do not eat shellfish or certain types of meat. But others do, and neither side wishes to police anything. The dreadlocks come from an Old Testament injunction to not cut the body: the same injunction caused Marley to resist a cancer operation and contributed to his death at the age of 36. Although the religious strands can be easily described, recognising their authority in followers' lives is more tricky. But they represent a significant piece of world history, and considering them and their implications gave Year 10 a worthwhile finish to their year's RE course.

For Love or Money

It can be a tricky thing to ask a group of girls wedged between Science and English at 11:15 on a wet Tuesday morning to give their thinking to the big questions of life. While some of them do arrive eager to explore the intangible, others are very keen to do quite other things. You need to catch their attention. It often helps if you can focus complex issues into succinct statements.

Sometimes you can do it by telling them a story. Sometimes you might try asking them a question. Sometimes you ask them to ask you a question. This last approach is best done if they write their questions down, but you need to be ready then to try and respond to them.

You get a whole cross-section of current thinking reflected in the questions. One day, in lieu of a question, one girl wrote a statement which seemed to me to capture the spirit of the age in a lot of the western world. It was about halfway through my Queen Margaret tenure and I've forgotten who she was, but she said, "I do not have any questions: I do not want to live my life with questions bothering me. I want to live free and in peace and let my imagination do the work for me. Sometimes I wonder what life means but to be honest I do not really care. My life is limited and I do not want to waste time by thinking about such things." So there you go. I wonder what ten years' living has done to her outlook since? Eat, drink and be merry is a soothing philosophy while you're doing it, but the shine wanes a bit when the merriment does, or when the eating and drinking are taking their toll.

One of the start-the-thinking gimmicks I came up with was to put in front of them the words: "In the end, it all comes down to love or money, and the greatest of these is money," and to ask, "Do you agree?" Very few of them did. There were always those who tried to have both love and money, or who wanted to not differentiate between them, but you needed to stick to "in the end." When all else has gone, what's it to be – love or money that conquers? Do we keep slaves for profit or release them, for their freedom and ours? There were not many who were prepared to stick with money.

Both Jesus and the Beatles were onto this, of course. "All you need is love" has become a byword since 1967 and Jesus was a fair bit before that with, "You cannot serve God and money." Having temporarily removed materialism from the frame, you could then move on to consider the nature of love.

Which is where you wanted to be. "What is love?" was a question that Year 11 engaged with often, and they were always interested in it. Their suggestions covered a lot of wonderful ground – giving, supporting, "being there", encouraging, offering and receiving forgiveness and, most sweepingly of all, sacrifice.

We had a story about sacrifice. It was about an American mother just after World War 2. She had lost her husband, she had three teenaged daughters and money was scarce, but somehow she found enough for herself and her daughters, and also she generally found something for anyone passing through who might need a bit of this or that.

The story is told by one of the daughters, who recalls how the local church launched a special Easter effort for a poor family and how she and her sisters sacrificed, joyously, for weeks and saved $70 for the special offering. "We could hardly wait to get to church!" Once there, they gave their $70 with great pleasure.

Their happiness collapsed that afternoon when the pastor arrived at their house and gave their mother an envelope containing $70 in the recognisably new banknotes they had swapped for their variegated savings at the bank, and seventeen $1 bills. "We didn't talk, just sat and stared at the floor. We had gone from feeling like millionaires to feeling like poor relics of the parish."

The following Sunday, having reluctantly acceded to their mother's insistence that they return to church, they heard a visiting missionary appeal for churches in Africa who needed money to buy roofs. He said $100 would put a roof on a church. "We looked at each other and Mum reached into her purse and pulled out the envelope. Margaret put it in the offering."

When the offering was counted, it yielded a little over $100. The missionary was excited. He hadn't expected nearly so much from a fairly small group of people. He said, "You must have some rich people in this church."

"Suddenly it struck us! We had given $87 of that 'little over $100.' We were the rich family in the church! Hadn't the missionary said so? From that day on I've never been poor again."

She can't have had much money, though. A footnote to the story says that in 2011 she was 79 and, with her husband, living on Social Security.

But it had never occurred to her in childhood that the family didn't have enough to help a child who needed clothing or a place to stay. Her mother always came up with something. "That might explain," the editor added, "why she and her husband have 13 children — 12 of them adopted — and have fostered 77 others."

In my very early years at QMC we talked one day in a Year 10 class about giving to needy people, and one girl remarked, "I would really like to make a lot of money when I grow up, so I can help people in need." It was a noble sentiment and I appreciated and affirmed it, but like any teacher of, say, Mathematics, I saw my primary task as being greater than to make people feel good, and I felt the need to push back on its basic assumption. "How much are you giving now?" I asked. "Because if you don't give a little when you have a little, you're not likely to give a lot when you have a lot." The spirit of giving comes from the heart, not from the bank account, and our American woman gathered that from her mother and applied it throughout a life in which the bank account was probably always very low.

I don't know who coined the line, "Some people are so poor that all they have is money," but I wish I did know. I have quoted it many times. Without putting guilt on anyone, it is proper for us to acknowledge responsibility for everyone.

Because on any international scale, the girls I worked with, and I, were all very rich. One index of wealth claims that if you have food in the refrigerator, clothes on your back, a roof overhead and a place to sleep, you are richer than 75% of people in the world, and every one of us fits into that top 25%. Another index says if you have money in the bank and also in your wallet and spare change in a dish someplace, you are among the top 8% of the world's wealthy. We're all in there, too. And when we turn away from simple cash measures, we might ponder another claim that people who have never experienced the danger of battle, the loneliness of imprisonment, the agony of torture or the pangs of starvation are ahead of 500 million other people in the world. If we are to wait for wealth to inspire our charity, we may wait no longer.

When you talked of sacrifice, when you talked of forgiveness, when you talked of love, you were close to the life of Jesus, and you were close to God. I rarely made those links specific, believing as I did that there was a line to be protected between describing the Christian faith and seeking to promote it. Sometimes I wondered if I drew my lines too far away from the boundaries, although I know there were girls who would dispute that, but I always felt that if I sought to hold conversations about love and forgiveness, I could rely on the girls to join the dots for themselves. Late in my time at the school I had some unexpected encouragement in this.

The weekend before New Zealand went into national lockdown for Covid-19, in March of 2020, Prime Minister Jacinda Ardern suggested that citizens in the older age bracket might isolate themselves early. Before I had even heard her announcement all my four sons were on the phone to encourage me to do this and one of them, James, offered to go to the school and take my classes for me. It was no empty offer: he is a very fine teacher who had resigned from his last teaching post the year before and had not yet begun at another. So he went.

I asked him that evening, of course, (and on the phone, of course!) how he had got on.

"Great," he said, "I enjoyed it."

"Anything stand out?" I asked.

"Year 11, at the end of the day," he said. "They really got into their stuff." They had been left a page entitled "You be the Judge." It held the summaries of 15 moral issues with three options offered after each one for them to react to. One option sought to benefit them, one benefited the opposite point of view and the third was a fence-sitting option. My biggest regret was not being able to talk the issues through with them myself.

There were all sorts of issues on the page — people lying in public life, people in shady business deals, matters of ethics and morality not defined by law. One of them was about a man's opportunity to betray his wife, taken from a 1995 film called *Mr Holland's Opus*. Should he leave his wife and go away with one of his students, or go home and work at his domestic problems?

"One girl at the back was really fired up about it," said James. "She stayed on after the bell went and all the rest of the class had shot off to the bus, and what's more the school was closing down for Covid as well, from that minute, but she came up to the front of the room and insisted on carrying on the conversation. I'd already told her where I stood on the issue, which was where she stood too, but she wanted to make sure I got the point. She said to me, 'I've been taught by your father for five years, and I know what he would think about this. And I agree with him!' She was thoroughly onto it."

I was intrigued to hear this, to say the least. I don't think I had ever talked specifically to this girl's class about marital fidelity. "Did she tell you what I'd think about it?" I asked James.

"Yep," he said.

"Was she right?

"Yep," he said. "Totally."

The lesson is almost too obvious to draw, so of course I'll draw it. It is that I don't need to spell out all the implications of every issue. I need to be consistent and transparent, and give them room to spell things out for themselves. They might even get a little help from God. Chill out, Mr RE teacher.

There was another illustration of the same truth the following year. It was the Year 12/13 EPR class this time, and we had heard the story of a young man escaping the drug cartels of Central America and in flight — illegally — into the USA. His cause is picked up by a retired English teacher, who goes to extreme lengths to represent his interests to the American authorities, at great cost to himself, all the way to the President, and finally wins him acceptance into American society. And in the middle of it all a voice from the floor said, for all of us, "This is applied Christianity, isn't it?"

There were only two, very lightly drawn, references in the story to anything identifiable as specifically Christian, but — it was.

Sometimes the sting in a story is spelt out and made obvious. These times, not so much. Either way, it was often useful to try for a light touch. Perhaps the best stings worked their way under the surface and stayed unnoticed until they festered into attention later. A girl once told me that her mother thought her RE lessons had taught her to think, listen and respond with thought and compassion, and she thought herself that learning to listen and to respond with a critical depth had been a major part of what she had gained. And I have to say that, as an outcome, that'll do me.

But a story often took you where you could never go alone. What can an elderly man say to a group of young women about sexual mores? If he's smart, not too much. But he just might quote from a famous writer, say someone like Steinbeck, as follows:

"You ain't got nothing," Suzy said. "Bugs and snakes and a dirty house. I bet some dame threw you over. That's what you're substituting for. Got a wife? No. Got a girl? No."

Doc found himself shouting, "I don't want a wife. I have all the women I want!"

"Woman and women is two different things," said Suzy. "Guy knows all about women, he don't know nothing about a woman."

Not much left to add for a discerning reader, and the classes were always full of discerning readers. But if you did want to add anything, it just might be a poem, such as Mike Starkey's "Mary He Said". Starkey gives us five short verses of the sailor speaking, things like: "When the child grows tell him he has a father who loves him dearly Mary he said" and "If they say a sailor has a girl in every port say you don't believe their lies Mary, he said", before he is shredded by the girl in the last verse which reads: "The name's Alison, she said." Sting like a scorpion, bigger than a bee.

On the money versus love issue, their thinking was nearly always very encouraging. Money, they collectively decided, was stuff, and stuff should come after people. It was very useful stuff, and very desirable stuff, but it came after people. And that was great, because it gave you a platform to start exploring, "What does 'love' mean, in a world of diversity and multiple values?" I recall a couple of questions I was asked by Year 10 some time around 2010 or 2011, and what I said in response to them. I recall them very clearly because I wrote them down at the time along with my responses and I gave the girls a copy to have in front of them as we talked about it. Verbatim, here are the questions and my written answers. I included the first one in a longish story I wrote to respond to a dozen or so questions at the same time, so it has the style of a piece of fiction with characters in dialogue, but the question is as it came:

"If 'God' tells you to love everyone equally, what *value* does that place on love?"

And my character, Uncle Bob, asked, "How do you mean?"

"Well, if I love you, you're special. And if I love Sophie, she's special. But if I love everyone, no one's special. So haven't I really cancelled it all out, and lost the whole point?"

Uncle Bob considered it for a moment, and then he said, "No, you haven't. You will keep on loving people in different ways — your friend, your mother, some lucky young man. But that doesn't stop you from loving the neighbour over the fence, or the checkout girl at the supermarket, or the person who teaches you English or even the person who steals your cell phone. You'll love them in different ways. The point is, you will want the best thing for all those people so you will show them kindness in your dealings with them, whether the dealings are large or small. You might smile at the checkout girl and speak to her courteously, you might try to give the bus driver the right change to make his job a little bit easier, you might try to understand the cell phone thief before you fly into a rage, and even then make sure you treat him justly and not viciously. All these things count as love, and we owe them to everyone, and that doesn't neutralise anything." I still think I could live with that answer, and I still think it's a pretty good question. The second one was probing too:

"If someone believes in a religion and makes actions accordingly, which people in other religions see as wrong, does it make it wrong if that's what the first person believes is right? Like with terrorists' bombings for example: they believe that the bombing is the right thing to do but we see it as wrong because we don't believe in that religion. How do you judge it?"

This is a deep question, and the somewhat laboured style is an indicator that its author is wrestling with its implications. Year 10, after all! I was still writing responses to this group of questions, and what I wrote for her read:

"I think this question is really asking, 'Does belief in a religion justify everything I do in the name of that religion?' And the answer is 'No, it doesn't.' There is good and bad religion, just as there are good and bad economics, and good and bad politics, or music, or tastes in fashion. The fact that we are — rightly — tolerant of the rights of other people to follow a range of religions does not mean that all the religions they choose to follow, or maybe their expressions of those religions, are equally admirable. Indeed, by definition, they can't be. If I seek to pursue a course of action that is clearly abhorrent, such as child sacrifice or oppressing women or bombing random citizens, then any attempt to justify it by claiming a religious mandate should open the religion to scrutiny, not justify the behaviour."

In a conversation, you would cover a bit more ground and respond as you went to the secondary questions that would inevitably emerge, but as a written piece, this will do. Love wants to respect: love cannot pretend. Here is the tension, in philosophy as in life.

And as long as you believe in truth, it's important. It is no good trotting out the old line that "It doesn't matter what you believe as long as you're sincere", because if you believe it you will try to follow it and if you try to follow it and it's wrong, you or someone else is going to get hurt. Probably you and someone else. As a baseline I much prefer "It doesn't matter what you believe as long as you're insincere." Once you genuinely become sincere, it starts to matter. I think it was C S Lewis who said that rubbish does not cease to be rubbish just because you are talking it about God. If you are right, I should affirm you. If you are wrong, I should challenge you, even if I do choose to do so gently and with sensitive respect. You should do the same for me. And if we are not sure, we should talk about it. Such talk, decently conducted, might be included under the general banner of love.

Year 11

(AND CURRENT AFFAIRS)

History, Choices, and the
Unseen Outlooks: Year 11

By the time they got to the start of Year 11, most of the girls I met were developing the ability and the will to engage in a quite subtle probing of issues. The first RE topic of Term 1 sought to build on that fact. I called it "Values, Choices, Decisions", and everyone began by identifying five core values that she held dear. The years threw up a great variety of issues, but typically we would be offered things like family, friends, truth, education, happiness: mostly personal values but sometimes more universal items such as justice or equality. I'm not sure I was ever offered qualities like selfishness, meanness or vanity, even from people who exhibited them. It was an encouraging view of aspiration, at the very least, and it's fair to say that it was a generally honest one.

We defined our terms, of course. "Choices" were the options life gave us every day: to go to school or to avoid it, and so forth. "Decisions" were the discernible outcomes — what we could be seen to have done in response to the choices. "Values", then, were what drove our decisions. If I am at school while my cousin is surfing and my friend is disfiguring the Queen Victoria statue on Kent Terrace, we are demonstrating quite different values no matter what we might think we hold dear.

We played around with these concepts quite a lot, looking at lines like J K Rowling's "Our future does not depend on our abilities, but on our choices," and Joseph Stowell's "Our lives are not shaped by the dreams we dream, but by the choices we make." I also liked to add a comment made to me many years ago by a friend who said, "Show me your cheque book and show me your diary, and I'll tell you what your values are." Even when I had to explain what a cheque book was, the principle was pretty clear.

So we looked at a pile of situations, likely and otherwise, asking "What would I do?" and "What does that tell me?" Every year, as part of the exercise, we considered a situation in which "Your best friend has appeared in the gown that she has bought to wear to the school ball and asked you, 'Do you like it?' You don't. Do you: (a) say it looks great; (b) say it doesn't look great but the right accessories might help; (c) avoid the question?" It created heated debate, year after year. There were girls who wanted to idealise truth and still choose (a) in the name of "friendship", and discussion was often willing. One year I was asked, "Mr Edgecombe, do you have a wife?" and when I said I did, received the response, "Not for long!"

We had a story to help us probe the topic too. I drip-fed it to them in nine instalments. It featured a Year 12 girl in a school a lot like Queen Margaret College. She is a respected and trusted senior student but, after eight grey-area situations requiring her decisions, gets it wrong each time and is finally on the verge of expulsion. The question then is not,

"What should she do now?" but, "What should the principal do now?" Some years I brought the principal along to give a view from a genuine decision-maker and always we would ask, "What are this girl's demonstrated core values?" Basically, they came down to vanity.

Term 2 took us into the "other religion" for the year, and in Year 11 it was Judaism. There were girls who couldn't differentiate it from Christianity, and therein lay half the benefit of the topic. I had to choose whether to start it with Abraham and work up to the present or go the other way around, flashback style. I always began in Hitler's death camps and went back, as an illustration that Jews have consistently been involved in political situations, not always by choice.

So our first identified Jew was Simon Wiesenthal, who was once dragged out of his concentration camp to be asked for forgiveness from a dying Nazi who had committed vicious anti-Semitic crimes. Wiesenthal declined to absolve him, and indeed spent the rest of his long life — he survived the camp and died in 2005 at the age of 96 — bringing Nazi war criminals to trial.

Apart from anything else, Jewish and Christian attitudes to forgiveness help the onlooker to discern between the two faiths. While Christians point to the words of Jesus, "Father forgive them, they don't know what they are doing," Jews are as likely to look to the words of Samson, the judge whose story is recorded in the Hebrew Bible, which Christians call the Old Testament. Having been captured and blinded by his enemies, Samson in his dying moments called on God for a restoration of his supernatural strength, one more time, "in vengeance for my two eyes."

We considered Abraham, the "first Jew", who followed God in faith. One God, that is, the Jews' great contribution to world religion. Then the Patriarchs, including Joseph. Moses, who led the people out of slavery through the plagues and the Red Sea, and gave the Jews the Passover, celebrated to this day as a memorial of God's care in adversity and a beacon of hope for the future. "Next year in Jerusalem", through the trials of the years, including the Holocaust.

Moses gave me a curved ball in a tricky context one day when we were seeing the film *Prince of Egypt*. Showing a film these days is a pretty straightforward thing: you have it on MP4 and you shut the curtains and play it through the data projector. But it wasn't always like that. Even when the old battles with the Bell and Howell movie projector and the loopy film and the school film room bookings had become ancient history, there was a time when you had to organise the television monitor and the video and a suitable room, and once you got there you wanted to make the most of the time you had available. So it was a logistical challenge as much as a theological issue when, as Moses confronted the burning bush and the film travelled on, a girl about four in from the end of the row asked me in a sort of a loud whisper, "Mr Edgecombe, have you ever been on holy ground?"

It's an intriguing theme. It was the more so because I knew this girl was Jewish. She may have been something of a lapsed variety of Jewish, but nevertheless there she was, and this was Moses, prophet of God, shoes off on holy ground, and a short form of "Yes" or "No" or "Sort of" didn't remotely look useful and you couldn't have a conversation of any subtlety in the middle of a film room where everyone else was shutting up because I had told them to and Moses of course had his challenges but here I was having mine. "Talk to you later," I mouthed. But of course "later" she had moved on and the period was finishing and she had to go to Maths or somewhere and I had to take the video monitor back. But I was able to suggest a view of holy ground that was less "other" than the film had suggested, and to sow the seed of thought that God might speak to us in various ways and that that might create holy ground. Sowing seeds that you hoped might feed later understanding seems to have been central to the years.

The other significant memory I have of that girl was at the prizegiving of her final year. Queen Margaret College has a custom of presenting a Bible to the Year 13 girls before they leave, at their final prizegiving. The chaplain stands by the pile of Bibles, identifies the next girl in the line, checks the name against that in the Bible and passes the book on to the principal, who does the actual presenting (while the chaplain is identifying the next girl and matching her to the next Bible). It's all done at high speed in a leisurely style, at the end of a lengthy and tiring hot night with all the school and their whanau present and anticipating supper, and you don't want to mess it up or slow things down. Easy, if you're the principal.

Trickier for the chaplain, especially if the cover of the Bible lifts the name slip away when you open the thing up and you're already looking down the line to see if the next girl is really the next girl or is one or more away. About every third slip does that and you always wonder why, if the Bibles are all the same, there needs to be a slip in there anyway but no one ever wanted to listen to that question.

Anyway, there we are at prizegiving the night the holy ground girl left. It is, actually, some weeks since we have physically sighted these girls, because they all go on exam leave a month and a bit before. And I'm standing there, madly identifying Bibles and matching girls and looking nonchalant, when there appears in the queue a girl I have never seen before in my life. The name in the Bible says holy ground girl. The girl coming bore no resemblance to her, whatsoever. I checked the next Bible. No dice. The line moved onward. The Bible before matched the girl before. The principal began to turn towards me. Thinking at the speed of sound and moving with studied grace I thought "Not my problem.

She can have this one as she goes past, and she can sort it out later", and passed holy ground girl's Bible to the principal to give to this stranger who, as she walked past me, caught my eye and flickered the merest shadow of a grin. It was Holy Ground herself, with a haircut that suggested a couple of dozen starlings had been working on it for a fortnight and that looked like something no member of the male sex had ever seen before in his innocent life. It was only a large, Bible-covered table that saved her from being hurled vigorously off the stage into a non-comprehending audience. The principal shook her hand and looked to me for the next Bible. The line moved on.

Going back to Year 11, after Moses we did a quick continuing summary of Jewish history, Biblical and subsequent. The dispersal of the Jews through the centuries, including over 350 years' banishment from England, to 1657. The attacks on the Jews during the Crusades. Their preservation as a people by their religion and by great moral strength, developed by undeserved suffering which enabled them to resist persecution. Also by the envy, distrust, and greed of those who opposed them. The Jews' outlasting the empires of the Egyptians, Assyrians, Babylonians, Persians, Greeks and Romans, the medieval empires set up by Christianity and Islam, and the regimes of Nazi Germany and the Soviet Union, all of which oppressed Jews, Judaism or both, and all of which seemed impregnable in their day. They disappeared: the Jewish people live. The formation of Israel in 1948. The disproportionate influence of Jews on current world events, not least by their presence in the United States, New York being the second biggest Jewish city in the world.

It's a topic worthy of a course of its own. We gave it a term. It's a start.

We read the words of a couple of Jewish spokesmen, one being Jonathan Sacks. He argued that the civilisation of the West rests on particular religious foundations, and that in times when we have ignored those foundations we have lost "much that makes life gracious, free and humane." His people's experience under Nazi Germany certainly seems to bear that out. He talked also about how religion can go wrong.

As well as that, he spoke about how participating in positive religious acts helps define those acts. He argues that taking part in a seder service on Passover, which involves telling the story of the book of Exodus, is different from watching a film or reading a book about it. When you enact it, he says, it becomes part of you, and you become part of the community. So the faith rituals and the prayers of community contribute to the nature of the participant. He suggests that this is why there were so many Jews in the fight against apartheid, and why Rabbi Abraham Joshua Heschel marched with Martin Luther King.

Sacks called prayer a way of seeing. To illustrate it he quoted Iris Murdoch, the novelist, as saying that she might be looking out of a window, interrupted and aimless, when she sees a kestrel and is absorbed by it until she returns to herself, and finds the challenge she has been neglecting has become altered. She called it "unselfing." Sacks says this is one factor of prayer.

For another Jewish spokesman, we read a comment or two from Diana Wichtel. Wichtel has been a *New Zealand Listener* contributor and is the daughter of a holocaust victim. In 2017 she wrote a book called *Driving to Treblinka*, and she talked about her daughter's experiences as a Jew in New Zealand. She wrote: "When my daughter went to do a communications degree, she was asked to write an essay about experiences of racism. She wanted to write about anti-Semitism. She was told she could write only about something she'd experienced, and she said she had experienced it. No, she was told, she hadn't. There wasn't any anti-Semitism in New Zealand."

In response, Wichtel mentioned a person who once reacted to an article of hers by asking, "When have the Jews ever told the truth about anything?" and went on to claim that America's dropping of the atomic bomb on two Japanese cities was "a Jewish-initiated holocaust." She said that every once in a while, when the holocaust was discussed during her own school or university courses, she would say "My father's family were murdered by the Nazis." But, she said, "It never went well. I learned to shut up."

Anti-Semitism in New Zealand? Most of us have not seen very much of it. But most of us are not Jewish. And it's pretty easy to not see things that might directly affect maybe 0.13 percent of the population, max. But we were very conscious of the Black Lives Matter events of 2020: not many African-Americans in New Zealand either. Media. So what *are* we called to see, and to notice, and to do something about? A girl asked one day, "Do we owe anything to anyone else?"

We talked about it, and there emerged the thought that if we did not, then couldn't murder be justified? And we said that if we owed nothing then yes, it could, and so could many other injustices. We decided that being human meant that we do owe to others. We owe courtesy, honesty, reliability, respect, faithfulness and a range of related decencies — call it love. And suddenly an attitude to Judaism became relevant for us all, again. Even for a population percentage of 0.13.

We talked about all these things for a long time, and emerged from the study of Judaism about the start of Term 3. It morphed quite naturally into forgiveness. It did that on at least three grounds.

One was the Jewish and Christian views on forgiveness, the implications of which had been introduced to us by Simon Wiesenthal. Another insight on that also came directly from the holocaust, though not from the Jewish perspective.

We watched on YouTube a BBC *Hardtalk* interview, posted in 2017, featuring Niklas Frank. Niklas Frank is an elderly man who was then living in northern Germany. But in World War 2 he had lived in Poland with his parents. His father, Hans Frank, was Hitler's personally-appointed Governor-General of Poland, and responsible for the deaths of millions of people. Niklas Frank's BBC interviewer, Stephen Sackur, drew from him a picture of a man defined all his life by his father's actions, and when Sackur asked him, "Can you not move on? These are not your actions, they're your father's. Can you not forgive him?" Frank replied, "Too many victims."

It's powerful stuff. It's a few years old now, of course, but the up-to-date examples in news items and elsewhere created a difficulty, not of where to find material about forgiveness that mattered, but of how to select from the wealth of it. How about a man who donated a kidney to his wife and wanted it back a few years later when they divorced? What about a young man very publicly charged with domestic assault and included in the All Black team soon afterwards, with a degree of widely-expressed opposition to his selection? Or a child molester of years ago who repented of his actions, later became a minister of religion and confessed all to the police who later came looking for him, and then served a prison term? Or a Muslim man who was shot and blinded by a white supremacist after the 9/11 attacks and who sued the governor of Texas to prevent his assailant from being executed? Or a South Auckland family whose child was killed by a drunken teenaged driver and who wanted to protect the young man responsible from lasting damage in the aftermath?

There was more material in all this than we could possibly use. Especially was that so when it was linked to justice — can you morally forgive someone and punish them at the same time? Should you? Does forgiving an offender disrespect the victim? What difference does the offender's attitude make? When are we in the position of the forgiver, and why? And when would we like to be forgiven ourselves? "Forgive us our sins," says Jesus in the Lord's Prayer, "*as we forgive* those who sin against us ..." What is all that, or any of it, going to mean to me this week, or this afternoon? Over the years we had some powerful, and very personal, conversations along those lines.

Years 12/13
(AND CURRENT AFFAIRS)

To Forgive or to Fester

A classical bullseye target has four rings. The one surrounding the bullseye is called the "inner". It's a pretty good place to land a shot.

It's a tricky thing to teach "religious education" without teaching "religion". That is, you need to be careful not to take advantage of a captive audience. You teach "about" religion. You might preach at people in a church, and you'd spend your time there aiming at the bullseye. But a school is not a church, and a delicate hit on the inner might be a better score than a dogmatic bullseye.

Working on this theory and remembering that Christian faith is all about forgiveness, I often sought lesson material on forgiveness rather than on Christian dogma. Everyone was interested in it, and you could allow the individual to make her own links. People generally prefer to do that anyway.

Forgiveness material is available everywhere. The range is from the historical and the profound to the trivial and the banal, and everything in between. For many years, I turned to a Garrison Keillor monologue from *Prairie Home Companion* for Year 11. It was called "Ronnie and the Winnebago".

You had to prep it a bit — explain who Garrison Keillor is (one sentence would do it), talk about ice fishing (a few more sentences with a picture or two; a comment on frozen lakes and fish), and explain about the Winnebago. A Winnebago is a motor home, or in New Zealand terms, a campervan. It's a luxurious sort of a campervan. It's called a Winnebago after the company that makes it, which is in Winnebago County, Iowa, and which in turn is named after the Native American tribe whose ancestral land it is. Thus does a people become a consumer product. They'll get to it one day.

But the Keillor story, even when presented on a voice-only CD with no visuals, never failed to catch the girls' attention and their sympathy. Its hero is Ronnie, three years out of high school when the story is told and just rejoining general society after three years in self-imposed isolation. A voice near the beginning of the story says, "Ronnie. We haven't seen you since — since the Winnebago."

They are ice-fishing. The narrator takes us back three years to the night when Ronnie, just leaving school, takes his father's Winnebago to go ice-fishing himself. He has a group of friends and too much booze and it's late at night, so he didn't ask his parents about the Winnebago ("he didn't want to disturb them") and they went out to the lake. He did pause momentarily when he saw that the season's icehouses had all been packed away … but there he was, with his friends, so they fished all night and went to sleep about sunrise, still on the frozen lake.

They are awakened about noon by the voice of Ronnie's uncle shouting at them from the shore, and Ronnie realises, to his horror and too late, that the ice is in melt mode and there is open water between him and the shore. In the best effort that he can make to gain dry land, he nonetheless writes the vehicle off as he beaches it. He sends his friends home with his uncle and waits in the wreckage of the Winnebago for his father to arrive, some half hour later.

The dialogue that follows the arrival of Ronnie's father is as good a lead-in to about six worthwhile themes as I know of anywhere. Basically, it goes like this, in the most matter-of-fact of rural tones:

> Ronnie's father (whose name is Don!); "Are you all right?"
> Ronnie: "Yes, I'm all right."
> *Pause.*
> Father: "I'd rather you hadn't done it. But you have, and I'm glad you're all right."
> *Pause.*
> Father: "I suppose you were thinking this is insured?"
> Ronnie: "It's not insured?"
> Father: "No. I only insure it for the summer, when I would be using it."
> *Pause.*
> Ronnie: "I'll pay you for it. I will pay you for it."
> Narrator: "And so he has." Three years, two jobs (both no-account affairs), no university, no meals out or movies, living at home, drives "the ugliest car in the state of Minnesota," for which he paid fifty dollars, and pays off the debt.

Year 11 and I then consider whether he is forgiven. It takes them about 15 seconds to say that he is, citing the evidence that his father shows more initial concern for him than for the vehicle, that he continues to live at home during the three-year stringencies, and all the evidence is that the relationship between him and his Dad is a civilised one. There is always a voice that wonders if he can be genuinely called forgiven in that he does in fact pay the debt, but it is always quickly balanced by another voice pointing out that the debt-paying is his own idea. Forgiveness, we decide, really comes down to restored relationship, and I am able to point out with an absolute minimum of sententiousness that the same applies to our dealings with God.

So the story serves us well. But it's not over at that point. Running parallel to all the narrative about the Winnebago there is a sub-plot. It concerns, not surprisingly, a girl, whom Ronnie has met while he is working as a waiter in some scungy dive much loved by drunken students, and with whom he thinks he might be in love. But he is not sure. When she announces unexpectedly that she is leaving Minnesota he is sad, and his eyes cloud with tears, and he is tempted to take her hand and say something that "he wasn't sure he meant," but he didn't do that. He didn't do that because he had "just finished paying off one obligation and he wasn't sure that he wanted to take on another," and he realised that making a promise to a woman that you are not sure you can keep, "means driving your Winnebago into very deep water indeed."

So now, after a consideration of forgiveness, we are launched into thoughts about love. Does he love this girl? Does she love him? How can you tell? And again, the wisdom takes a very short time to unearth. The answers are "No" and "No", and you can tell this because if the love were real, there would be no sudden announcement of a plan to which he had not been previously admitted during its gestation.

It's been a pretty full lesson by now, but if we haven't run out of time we can always think about the overall assessment. These events cost Ronnie a lot. What does he lose? What does he gain? Does he end up winning, or losing? I always want us to decide that the answers are money, wisdom, winning, but we often have to take a little longer than the time we have left if we're going to get that far. But that's OK, because this is one of those journeys where the travelling is as important as the destination anyway.

Ronnie's is a light and domestic story and it has a wide appeal long before you get to any sort of theme. Rather more gritty is the story of Debbie Morris.

Sometime in the mid-90s there was a book and a film called *Dead Man Walking*. The film starred Sean Penn and Susan Sarandon, and it was the story of the dealings of Sister Helen Prejean, a Catholic nun, with men on death row in the American south. It became a focus for the anti-death-penalty lobby.

One of the condemned men represented in *Dead Man Walking* was Robert Lee Willie, who was executed for murder, kidnap and rape. Sister Prejean was his spiritual adviser in the months before his death. One of Robert Willie's victims was Debbie Morris, and in 2000 she published her account of her ordeal and its aftermath, using the title *Forgiving the Dead Man Walking*. In it she told of how she had been kidnapped by Willie and his accomplice when she was 16 and raped repeatedly over some 30 hours before the men reluctantly released her — Willie, she believed, would rather have murdered her. She heard him planning it with the other two, and saying that releasing her would prove to be a big mistake.

She tried to move on with her life after the crimes and Willie's execution, and she eventually married and had children, but she always lived with hurt and resentment, and fear.

"The fear comes in parking lots," she said, "and anywhere I stop while driving alone at night." She had been kidnapped while sitting in a parked car at night. Taking her two young children to an empty park near her home was out of the question, even during daylight hours and never mind that it was over 1300 kilometres from where the kidnapping had occurred and a long time later. She became anxious if she and her husband sat too long in a parked car. She told her story when she was 37 years old: the crimes against her had been committed 21 years earlier.

But the nightmares lessened and the fear weakened its grip as her Christian faith became stronger. She quoted from Matthew's Gospel: "If you do not forgive men their sins, your Father will not forgive your sins." She learned to assert herself and to correct people who referred to her as a victim: "I am a crime survivor," she said. Years after the event, with Robert Lee Willie long since dead, she was planning to visit his accomplice in jail as soon as the authorities gave her permission to. She ran a website for a long time, and lectured widely on faith-based healing, forgiveness, and crime victim rehabilitation. It was her comments on forgiveness that attracted the attention of senior classes at Queen Margaret College for some years.

Morris believes that crime victims and their families need to understand that their healing does not depend on the fate of the criminal. They are able to heal and to find joy in life no matter what happens to him and ultimately, his life is irrelevant to them.

She talked about her experiences in the months surrounding the death of Robert Lee Willie. She said that she was initially terrified that he might escape from prison and attack her, then she hoped that his conviction would release her emotionally, then that his execution would do it. But those externalities did not release her personal ghosts. In the end, she began the process that led towards healing only after she told God that she was prepared to begin to forgive. "I learned that unforgiveness leaves behind a prisoner," she said. "And that prisoner was me."

Perhaps that final statement was Debbie Morris's most powerful teaching point, along with the understanding that forgiveness is a process and not a point, that it takes time. And the first step in the process is being prepared to try. It is the step of willingness.

A story like Debbie Morris's requires a deal of sensitivity in a classroom full of teenaged girls. It's a powerful story. Perhaps one of its useful aspects was the opportunity it gave us to address the phrase that has become a predictable cliché, "Forgive and forget." It was a line nearly always offered at some early point in the discussion, but we came to see that forgiving has a healing function perhaps especially when it is impossible to forget.

We agreed that no one wants, naturally, to forgive anyone. There is a sense of moral superiority in refusing to forgive someone, and we do not want to let anyone off lightly when they have done us wrong. Nor should we. But we heard about another woman who drove often past a prison where a man was being held for a crime against her family, and whenever she drove past she screamed her rage and hatred at the prison. "Without in any way criticising a person suffering things the rest of us can only wonder at," I asked the girls, "who suffers again every time she shouts?"

And they said, correctly, "She does. He doesn't know she's shouting. He probably wouldn't care. If he's callous enough, he might even gain some sort of pleasure from it." Logically, you assume she knows all that. Yet she does it, no doubt for a form of emotional release. Perhaps the release of that kind of torment is part of what Jesus was talking about when he invited his people to bring their burdens to him. Certainly it was the experience of Debbie Morris that when she told God she was prepared to forgive her assailant, "as much as I was able to", that the process began.

It is worth noting that this is not the same thing as "forgiving yourself." "Forgiving yourself" is another phrase I heard a lot in these contexts. I can understand it too, because there are people who nurse their own private guilt, real or imagined, long after everyone else, including God, has absolved them and moved on. Guilt is a very healthy thing when it prompts us to go and heal the ruptured relationship, but it is a lethal thing when it shapes us long after the healing has already been offered by the other person concerned. Forgiving yourself is not a substitute for confession and repentance, and for the gift of forgiveness offered by the person you have wronged. It comes after those things. There is an order of events, and it is good to move through the order correctly, both when we forgive and when we need to be forgiven. The same is true of our dealings with God. You can't preach all that in a classroom, but to land a few shots in that area of the target is to score pretty close to the inner.

Where Did We Get To? Years 12 and 13

During my years at Queen Margaret, RE had a chequered time in the senior classes. In the beginning of my tenure there, Year 12 had a period a week in their timetable just like everyone else, but there was nothing in Year 13. Later we experimented with a voluntary model in Year 13, but just for one year and we never got to iron out the creases or invent some subtleties. A few years after that, RE disappeared entirely and without trace from Year 12, for reasons no one ever explained to me or them (and six months later Erana, in Year 12, accosted me in the corridor with "What happened to RE in Year 12? I'm not OK with it.") Finally, in 2019, it was converted into Ethics, Philosophy and Religion and reintroduced to both Years 12 and 13, NCEA classes only.

Predictably, the new designation of EPR had its pros and cons. But it allowed a wonderful freedom to look at virtually anything with a moral or philosophical tinge or a religious feature, and the tenor of classroom discussion looked very similar to the best of the previous years. Partly for that reason, I never introduced a deliberate study of any particular world faith into the senior course. What we did was to look at a number of modular topics and allow ourselves to go where the material took us. That turned out to be virtually everywhere. It had a lot going for it, but it was less focused than we'd been in earlier years, and I came to wonder if that was one of the cons.

We did one unit on six pieces of literature which offered some sort of ethical or religious overtone. *To Kill a Mockingbird* was one, *The Power and the Glory* was another. We had another unit on six films, including *Citizen Kane* and *Sully*. I say "six", and I prepared these units in groups of six, but I'm not sure we ever completed six pieces in any of them. We tended to work on one or two or three and move on to something else, sort of by osmosis. We had six Bible stories, and six Current Events, but I don't think any mathematician would be impressed if they took take the total course covered and divided it by six, and then measured it against the lessons actually taught. We kept finding one-off pieces that interrupted the tidy system. But I didn't care, and the girls didn't either. Ethics? Philosophy? Religion? For sure. In there somewhere.

There was one story that I used, though not as much as it deserved, that spanned 60 years and three continents and allowed a view of ethics, religion and philosophy all at the same time.

There are a lot of people who think that the name Timbuktu is a make-up representation of Nowhere. There are doubtless good reasons for them to think that, but they are wrong. Timbuktu is a real place, situated in modern day Mali. Sahara Desert.

In 2012, Timbuktu was attacked by al-Qaeda. A flow of refugees left the city for Bamako, the Malian capital about 860 kilometres to the south, a 24-hour drive. Among their leaders was a man called Nouh Ag Infa Yattara. He is a Christian, thought to be perhaps the first Christian in Timbuktu, and he is a Christian as a result of his dealings with an American missionary he met in his boyhood. Timbuktu is the fourth holiest city of Islam, and some of the Tuareg tribesmen in the area do not take kindly either to westerners or to Christians. Consequently, the young Nouh's faith was often tested, but he was strengthened by many stories of Christians in situations he considered more challenging than his own.

He stayed committed into his adulthood, and he established a Christian church. He and his wife, Fati, built it into a strong group of "Muslim Background Believers", and they would become an early target for radical extremists if the city fell to al-Qaeda. So in 2012, Nouh left for Bamako.

About 25 years earlier, around 1986, Nouh had had an experience that had meant a lot to him, though it would likely have been overlooked by any casual onlooker. He had been talking one afternoon to a missionary in Timbuktu — not the one he'd known as a boy — when a group of children brought a young westerner into their building. His name was Steve Saint, and he was an aid agency worker from Bamako. He was visiting Timbuktu because he had been able to get a ride there and he couldn't stay away from a place so fascinating.

He was worried though, because the plane he had arrived on wasn't able to take him back, and he had not been able to find anyone driving a truck. He had known it was chancy when he left Bamako, but he'd reckoned the risk was worth it. When he'd left the Timbuktu airstrip, the pilot had said to him, "Good luck — and don't go anywhere without water." A lot of westerners have just disappeared in the desert. (The Lonely Planet guide advises travellers in Mali to "avoid the regions bordering Mauritania and Niger as well as north of Timbuktu, as they are the domain of desert bandits," and mentions that the border of Cote d'Ivoire has been closed by on-going unrest. It also advises travellers to be vigilant in the south, and remarks that trying to get around Mali in the hot season is "strictly for masochists.") Apart from that, it seems to be OK.

Steve Saint had done his exploring, was having no luck with a truck and was beginning to attract the notice of the locals. He was also wondering just where all this would lead him. Then he met the missionary, and Nouh.

Steve was interested in Nouh. How had this man become a Christian in a place like Timbuktu, and what had inspired him to persist in Christian faith when all around him were opposed to it? So Nouh, interpreted by the missionary, told him.

He mentioned the stories that had inspired and encouraged him. One of them was about an incident that had occurred in South America 30 years previously, and some years before he'd met the first missionary.

In January of 1956, the world was shocked by the killing of five young American missionaries by the Auca Indians of the headwaters of the Amazon River, in the utterly remote Ecuadorian jungle. One of them was Nate Saint, the pilot of the plane the men had used to make their contact with the tribe.

Nouh had been told about these men by the original missionary. He explained to Steve how much it had impressed him. "They willingly risked their lives to take the gospel to some savage Indians in South America," he said. "They were all killed." His eyes widened. "I've lived all my life in the desert. How terrifying the jungle must have been! The book said these men let themselves be speared to death, even though they had guns with them and they could have fought off their attackers. If they could do that, surely I could live for my faith at home."

The missionary had been looking at Steve during Nouh's comments. Now he said, "I remember that incident well. One of the men killed had the same name as you."

"Yes," said Steve. "Nate Saint was my father. I was four years old."

"Your father!" said Nouh. "So, the story is true?"

"Yes," said Steve. "It's true."

Not only was Steve able to assure Nouh that the story was true, but he was able to share a glimpse of how it had affected him. As he grew up without his father, whom he had revered as a child, he had felt a real sense of loss, often when he would have liked advice or support. Most recently he had been thinking of his father that very afternoon, as he was anxious about a ride out of Timbuktu in a truck. More than once he had wondered if his father's death was necessary, or had done any good for anybody else. Now he was hearing, from a man in a place he had scarcely believed in, that there was good indeed.

Nouh and Steve and the missionary talked through the afternoon, and they took him back into town just before dusk. When they got there, they found Steve's friends at the airstrip, with the good news that plans had changed and there would be a spare seat back in the plane after all. Steve had his ride organised.

He reflected on it all as they flew back over the desert. It seemed incredible to him, that God loved him — and Nouh — so much that he had given them both exactly what they needed, at the ends of the earth. From the Amazon jungle to Timbuktu? Steve gave Nouh the assurance that the story that had given him courage was in fact true: Nouh gave Steve the assurance that his father's death had indeed been used for good. Nate Saint, by dying, had given Nouh a faith worth dying for, and Nouh, in return, had given Nate's faith back to his son, Steve.

Nouh and his wife Fati returned from Bamako to Timbuktu after the French and Malian armies re-secured it against al-Qaeda in 2013, although the area remained volatile. Together, and with their son, they initiated a number of practical ministries of compassion to the many poor people in the area, especially women and children. In the years after his return, Nouh was active in aid programmes, Christian evangelism and in representing the Christian community to the Malian government and to the United Nations.

Nate Saint, Steve Saint, Nouh Ag Infa Yattara — all people who expected to make sacrifices for other people because of their faith. Not all of the stories in my classes were quite so pointed. But I often used them to try and illustrate faith in action: real people's experiences of God being allowed to change their lives for the good of others and, as well, stories guaranteed to create interest for their own sake. At the end of 2020, Sharon in Year 12 wrote for me, among other reactions to the course, "I love your stories."

I'm glad she did. They came from everywhere. Since it is my conviction that the Bible has a lot to say to the modern world, they sometimes came from there. And I was pleased with a comment made by Amy, at the end of her Year 13 course, when she said, "Thank you for the years. I know a lot more about the Bible than I would have otherwise. I like the way you've focused on the moral side of it."

To be honest, I'm not sure what my options were about the moral side of it. But I think she meant that the treatment was not academic, removed, or religiously legalistic. Nor, I would contend, should it be. A friend of mine on the History staff of Massey University once said that you can't apply the Bible without getting personal, and I think he's right. But you don't have to always spell out the obvious.

The best material had a sting, but the sting did not always come at the end of the story. Sometimes it was the thing that caught the eye in the first place, and a consideration of it led us to a narrative. I was reading something by the English writer G K Chesterton one school holidays and came across his comment that there could be no art without morality. One thing led to another and 65 Power Point slides and three lessons later my senior class were engaged in producing their own artwork to illustrate a moral or philosophical point. Katie asked me in the process whether something she was drawing was insensitive; Charlotte later wrote, "It's nice to talk about art and culture for a change — we talk a lot about morals and beliefs, however having new things to think about keeps it interesting." There had been a variety of topics in the 65 Power Point slides — and their selection had been rendered difficult only by deciding what to leave out.

Among the things kept in were a couple of poems, a pop song, a selection of satiric photographs, a tattoo, a political meme and a couple of cartoons one of which focused on "Alternative Facts" — it nearly derailed us — some pieces of graffiti from the West Bank of Jerusalem and a Korean sculpture that was upsetting the Japanese government by its depiction of wartime "comfort women", more accurately described as sex slaves.

There were questions about the nature of art, and of morality, and of objective standards. Our unit happened to coincide with the announcement of the 2020 Parkin Drawing prizewinner, who collected $25,000 for a page full of forward slashes produced on a typewriter and who was later challenged for plagiarism: the judge denied any. We wondered about what constituted art: Eleanor suggested that the typewriter gave the work more status than a computer would have done. We went to Robert L Short's book, *The Parables of Peanuts*, and considered what made some work "art" and other work "entertainment."

We thought about films, and a novel, and political photographs. We left out advertising, in the interests of keeping the topic brief enough to not either pall or morph into a cancerous invasion of the rest of the course. We covered a lot of ground, not arriving from a story to a sting in the tail but by starting with a ready-made sting and going back to a cluster of stories.

For the record, Short's thoughts about art suggested that while art might seek to entertain us, as any other medium might, it also goes further than entertainment. Its effect is to take us into a reality we might not have otherwise seen, or that we may now see differently. Art may allow us a view of our own lives, perhaps with implications for how we may live them better. If entertainment allows us temporary escape from life, art equips us for the return, and will always have "something to say."

So not all our material was Biblical, nor Christian, nor even visibly religious — Ethics, Philosophy, Religion, after all. 2020 was the year of Black Lives Matter, and while I don't think every American social thread is necessarily paralleled in New Zealand, some of it has echoes and this one was on a scale to provoke comment. I went into the EPR class with my comments provoked.

"What do you think?" I asked. "Should we have a look at it?" They thought we should. I thought they would. I had already begun preparing.

Where to start? Well, their knowledge of history was likely pretty sketchy. What about a sort of timeline of key events? We should start in slavery, and we could end up in emancipation.

I went back to the arrival in America of the first slave ship. 1619. And I stopped right there. *1619!* They finished the Civil War in 1865. I talked about it that afternoon to Jacqui Brown, Head of the Senior School. "Did you know …?" I said, in that tone of voice peculiar to people who, when they ask that question, are always secure in the belief that you do not know. And Jacqui said, "Wow! *Wow!*" I talked to one of my sons that evening and he said the very same thing, in precisely the same tone of voice — "Wow! *Wow!*" And I knew I was onto something.

I have raved on to many a class over the years about how very fortunate New Zealand is — we don't know how lucky we are, if you like. The European settlers arrived here about the time that slavery was abolished in the British Empire. Consequently, we have never had a history of slavery to fuel our social attitudes. And I have said to my classes that American racial attitudes have had to overcome such a history, and it's different. But until I wrote the numbers down and looked at them, it had not occurred to me that the Americans had 246 years of slavery to define their views, compared with 150 and some years since. They've still got over 90 years to break even. No wonder they still have ground to make up. No wonder Barack Obama, the former President and famously their first black one, said in 2013, "I think it's important to recognise that the African American community is looking at this issue through a set of experiences and a history that doesn't go away." Masterpiece of understatement.

Well, I did my timeline. It came to 19 pages of items chosen to represent racial events between 1619 and the present day. I started pruning.

I got it down to nine pages. Then a Power Point to go with it. 54 slides this time. I reckoned I was ready.

In the olden days of teaching there used to be a thing called Chalk & Talk. Teacher talked to class and wrote things on the board. It has become most unfashionable. We all deride it. For this document, we didn't do Chalk &Talk. We did everyone-has-the-article-electronically, and Power Point. And I talked. And when I got a bit worried that everyone might be asleep or mentally absent or something else, I said to them, "Are you OK with this?" They all were. The stuff spoke for itself.

We had three lessons on Black Lives Matter. It was systematic in so far as the items were in order of time, but the selection process was whatever took my eye. It included the Civil War, the founding of the Ku Klux Klan and some of their sorry history, a summary of lynching stats — approximately 6,500 black people between 1865 and 1950, and some since — and various high-profile incidents through to the 1960s.

Civil Rights movement. Martin Luther King. Recent random acts of compensation such as the naming of streets after black victims or the awarding of posthumous awards or pardons to people long since gone. Another lynching, in Texas, in 1998, and the execution of the murderers in 2011 and 2019. Taking the knee; Black Lives Matter.

And then, the day I was to begin presenting the lessons, there was a news article telling of a "far-right militia" group that clashed with Black Lives Matter protesters in Louisville, Kentucky, in anti-racism protests. "The heavily armed group was pictured shoving guns in the faces of BLM activists amid tense scenes … hundreds of far-right activists in combat gear and armed with semiautomatic weapons faced off with protesters. In less than an hour, police wearing riot gear came to the stand-off and cleared the park entirely."

We talked about the significance of these and other events. We never opened nor quoted the Bible, but its teaching was inherent in our comments. And one voice not in the classroom later added a perspective which would have thrown light on it for us all.

The month after we finished the lessons, I was in central Wellington, talking to a New Zealand-domiciled American who had lived and studied in New York. He said to me, "When I graduated, in the 80s, I went to the South to visit some of my university friends. My first visit there. Before I went down there, I thought we'd fought the Civil War a hundred years ago. In the South, they're still fighting it."

There is a window on difference, right there. The Civil War, a beacon of liberation to some, is a landmark of frustration for others. No wonder there are people who feel the need to say out loud that black lives matter. No wonder either that there are others who wish to stop them from saying it. As I said, we did not use the Bible in the three lessons on Black Lives Matter. But we have on other occasions heard the exhortation of Jesus to treat all people with respect and love. We have many a time rehearsed the fact that the "Good Samaritan" is not a story that was told because Samaritans were good. It is a fictional story that chooses a Samaritan to be the good example precisely because those hearing the story regarded them as bad. Most of my girls didn't know what a Samaritan was. It was a person who came from Samaria.

Samaria was an area in the Palestine of Jesus that all self-respecting Jews avoided. They avoided it because they regarded the Samaritans in the same way that Republicans regard Mexicans, or the way that the KKK regarded blacks: as shifty, dirty, reprehensible agents of social unrest and general concern to all decent people and intrinsically unamerican. It is likely that, if Jesus had been setting his story in 2020 Phoenix or downtown Chicago and had been asked to illustrate the idea of neighbourliness, he might have said, "There was this Mexican," or "This African American". Given that the girls knew this background, we didn't have to preach a Bible message over the ground of Black Lives Matter. Racism to Jesus looked a lot like racism still does. The aim in Years 12 and 13 was to find a broad sweep of religious or philosophical origin and to sort out its ethical application.

So our classroom material was intended to engage attention and allow a chance to shift the perspective, and people might engage at various levels. They all enjoyed a story — everyone does. After all, it's what the television industry exists on. And when the implications emerged, they sometimes went where you predicted, and they sometimes went quite elsewhere. It hardly ever mattered, as long as they went somewhere. I was delighted at the end of 2020, when Bethany said to me as she finished Year 13, "The questions you face us with and the discussions you bring us into give me just about enough thought processes for a lifetime!"

Another girl, in the same class, took her thoughts a little further back. "You've taught me since Year 7," she said, "from sliding camels to what constitutes art." The reference to art went back about six weeks; the perennial sliding camels went back to Year 7 when we took Abraham to the Promised Land by a route he never followed. It was six or seven years in her experience and about 4000 years in world history. Good spread. You always did hope for a bigger picture.

Faith and Life

I have already said that throughout my time at Queen Margaret, my deeply held conviction was that faith and life could not be separated without major disservice to both. It gave rise to some subtle classroom commentary, which I sometimes manoeuvred for. Sometimes I was manoeuvred into it.

I was asked one day, "Are people that drink and do drugs and consider themselves Christian, truly religious?" The question drew a link, as it should, from belief to behaviour, but it left out all factors of motive, intent or grace, of weakness matched against deliberate folly, of earnest failure in contrast to hypocrisy, and likely a few other implications as well.

I backed up a little to create a wider angle, like an All Black goal-kicker. I often did that. I said that it came down to the relationship between what you believe and what you do, and of how much you are trying to succeed even if you fail, as against not even trying in the first place.

Certainly Christianity does not advocate the abuse of drink and drugs. In fact, it teaches against such abuses, and against a bunch of other behaviours as well. So, does someone who does the things that the faith teaches against count as a true follower of that faith? The same question, of course, can be asked about any faith.

At the time I was asked the question there was a man who had recently started coming to my church. He was alcohol dependent, and I think he had some drug problems as well. But he was beginning to understand some of the teachings of Jesus and of the church, and he was genuinely keen to follow them. Could we call him "truly religious", I asked the girls? He'd started, he wanted to move forward, he still had a way to go.

We considered the proposition, "If you have to be perfect, if you have to get it all right, to be called 'truly religious', then none of us qualifies, however hard we try." Then we wondered about, "But if you don't try at all, then surely you can't qualify either?" Then we got to, "So the question becomes, what are the factors in the middle ground, where an effort is being made even though mistakes or failures continue to occur?"

Not only does the Bible not talk about people getting it all right, but it doesn't even talk about what percentage of it we have to aim at. It talks about how we all got too much of it wrong, and how we need to ask God to forgive us. Then, but only then, we need to try to get as much right as we can — and we will still make mistakes, errors and failures.

The issue is one of being forgiven, and then because we are forgiven, we will try to do well. When I look at someone else, I cannot know if they are forgiven or not, so it is hard for me to know if they are "truly religious" and making mistakes in spite of their best efforts, or irreligious and calling themselves by some name — such as Christian — for reasons of their own choice. The best answer to the original question might be "maybe" — maybe Christian and weak, or not Christian but deluded.

I knew another man. Richard. He was the pastor of a church in Auckland. He told me once about a Chinese student called Wing Lee, who turned up at his church one day with some of his flatmates. Richard and Wing Lee were later to get many an airing at Queen Margaret College.

Wing Lee was new to New Zealand, from Shanghai. He was short of friends and glad to be accepted by the church community. He stayed among them throughout his university course, maybe three or four years. He made a number of friends, and he also became interested in the church's teaching. A lot of it was about Jesus.

"What does Jesus want us to do?" he asked Richard. Richard answered, "He wants us to love God and to love other people."

Wing Lee thought about it. "How can I love God?" he asked.

Richard said, "Mostly by loving other people. But tell God you want to, and ask him to help."

Wing Lee asked, "How will he help?"

"Various ways," Richard answered. "Watch, and see what he does."

And Wing Lee said, "How should I love other people?"

"By doing the right thing," Richard said. "You'll know. And by adding a bit — do more good than you have to."

Wing Lee finished university. He went back to China and got a high-powered job in a finance company, with a lot of international contacts. One day, he talked to a man from Poland, whose name was Szymon. Szymon had to send Wing Lee $2000, to make an investment and cover some incidental costs.

But he made a mistake, and he sent Wing Lee $500 too much. Wing Lee thought, "Great! Here's $500 for myself. And Szymon thinks that's the right sum so he will never ask, and no one else knows about it — all covered. How very nice."

But as he started to tap on his keyboard, he suddenly had a thought. And he seemed to see his old friend Richard, back in Auckland, and to hear his voice saying, "Jesus wants you to love God, and to love other people. Ask God to help."

He didn't really have to ask God — but he did, anyway. "God, what should I do?" he asked. He knew what he had to do. He picked up the phone and he rang up Szymon. He said, "Szymon. Your money. You've given me $500 too much."

Szymon was blown away. "Wing Lee, I didn't know that," he said. "No one else did either. And they never would. Why are you telling me? I've never had a phone call like this before in my life." Wing Lee said, "God told me to." And Szymon said, "Well, because you're so honest, you keep the $500."

But Wing Lee said, "No, that's your $500. I shouldn't be paid just to do what I ought to. That's nothing special. It's what anyone should do." So he paid the money back.

But the next week, three more businessmen in Poland all rang Wing Lee up, and each one said, "Will you work for us? We want you, because Szymon says you're an honest man, and we can trust you." And Wing Lee was paid — honestly — more than a thousand dollars more than he thought he would be paid that week, and with promises of more business ahead.

Jesus said, "Whoever can be trusted with little things, can also be trusted with big things, and whoever is dishonest with little things will also be dishonest with big things. So learn to follow God, and do not be turned away by money."

I don't know how much Wing Lee understood about the subtleties of Christian faith. But he knew what he could see ahead of him to do, and he did it. I don't know how much the substance-dependent man at my church knew about Christian faith either. But he was different and so were his problems, and perhaps he found them harder to master.

The whole question of wishing to follow God and therefore doing good to everyone else was neatly flipped on its head one day by Georgie, in Year 11. She had been involved in such a discussion and then she asked, "If the point of following God is to love our neighbour, why don't we leave God out of it all and just get on with loving our neighbour?"

It's not true to say the question left me speechless, but it did leave me grappling for where to start, and it wasn't until much later that it dawned on me that I had just been offered perhaps the greatest travesty of Christian thinking I had ever heard. The nub of it, of course, is the conditional – "If the point of following God is to love our neighbour ..." Loving the neighbour is not the point of following God. It's just the inescapable outcome of it.

This was a day when I didn't get it right. I talked about how we needed to rely on God to enable us if we were going to consistently love our neighbour, and that we did not have in ourselves the resources to do it unless God provided them. Georgie listened respectfully and added to the conversation, but I don't think she was convinced. It sounded, even to me, a bit like a convenient argument that didn't get to the heart of it. And of course, it didn't get to the heart of it. The heart of it is that Jesus said the greatest command is to love God, and the second command is like it: love your neighbour. In that order. To go straight to the outcome without the basis and to look for the fruit without the root is to lose everything at once.

C S Lewis wrote: "Aim at heaven and you will get earth thrown in. Aim at earth and you get neither." I once heard Judge Andrew Becroft, then serving as New Zealand's Children's Commissioner, say that seeking justice does not make you a Christian, but if you're not seeking justice, there's something wrong with your Christianity. What I believe and what I do, all tied up together. Building built on sound foundations.

I asked a senior class in 2020 what characteristics they thought might pertain to "the kingdom of heaven" – that is, the qualities that seemed to belong with such an expression. Gloriously, there was not a harp nor a cloud nor a golden street in sight, nor any other ethereal thing. What they gave me was a list that included respect, love, truth, loyalty, hope, fulfilment, purity and peace. If your life is anything remotely like mine, you will recognise the need for a very great help from someone like God if you are to get consistently anywhere near any one of them.

When I became a part-time teacher in my later years at Queen Margaret College, some of my travel on the train occurred in off-peak hours. Those trips have a different flavour from the commuter rush. I sat next to a man one day and, uncharacteristically, we talked (and discovered, in that quintessentially New Zealand way, a mutual acquaintance), and he asked me what I did. When I told him I taught Religious Education in a girls' school, he asked a question I have often been asked: "Do they listen?"

It's a fair question. But, generally speaking, the answer is, "They do." On any given day, of course, someone won't, and there is also the odd individual who arrives with a supercilious look and defends the right to maintain it, but on the whole and by a vast majority, if I listened to them, they listened to me. The result was an interchange of ideas and outlooks that enriched me and I hope was useful to them.

There were little pieces of evidence that suggested it was. I had an email once from a young woman in her second year out of school. She wanted to tell me that while she was in my class I had talked about taking a few minutes every now and then to sit in silence and reflect on life. "You told us that when I was in Year 8," she wrote, "and I've done it every so often through the years since. It's a wonderful, calming thing, and you get a new perspective." She said she had been having a trying year, and she wanted me to know my advice had helped.

I mentioned it to my class that day, and one of them nodded. "I remember you saying that," she said. "It was in a chaplain's assembly. I do it sometimes too." Somebody else agreed. I was delighted — by the fact that anyone remembered it, for a start, as well as by the fact of someone's doing it. We live in a noisy world, and to quieten it down a bit is to give an opportunity to subtler things. Maybe even to God.

An approach to listening might even sometimes be an overt teaching point. There was a brief time in my career when I taught at Mana College, a state school in Porirua which has a lot in common with Queen Margaret College along with a few points of difference, and I took my Year 12 English class out onto the rugby field, spaced them out at 30-metre intervals on their own and left them there for 20 minutes with the instruction to listen to the world around them. Nothing else. Just listen.

When they came back inside, they were alight. "Did you hear the seagulls? The dog? That kid shouting, the mother calling it, the car door slamming ..." No sound heard was dramatic or extraordinary in itself, just everyday sounds that *had been heard*. We miss most of the world around us, simply by not hearing it or seeing it. Look at the commuters on a train: they all gaze into phones. It used to be newspapers. I read a book. No one sees the world. Time alone, without distraction or time constraint or phones, just space to be and to see what it does for you, usually has to be deliberately created. And if all that's true, how much more might we miss of the subtler manifestations of God, which we might not recognise when we're alert, never mind when we're not.

Remembering Mana College, I sent a senior class outside one day at Queen Margaret College too. I laminated a couple of dozen quotations on little, brightly coloured slips. Different quote for each girl. I waited for a lovely sunny day and gave them a slip each.

"Go outside," I told them. "Go alone." Recalling my long-ago exercise in Canberra and the power of solitude. "Find a comfortable place, stay on your own, read your quote and reflect on it. When you come back, tell me about it."

This was an opportunity for considered thought, rather than just listening or looking, and I asked them to write me their responses when they got back. I was a bit disappointed, to be honest: some of them engaged with it well, but some were quite superficial and a few gave evidence of not having joined with the spirit of it at all. That didn't nullify the exercise, just suggested that some training might be in order. The tricky part about that in Wellington is guaranteeing a pleasant day when you want one, especially when you have your class only once a week and the lead-in time is complex.

But on any given day in the classroom, there might come a moment when the listening became intense. I did not habitually spend my time, as some of my friends seemed to think, dealing constantly with incipient rebellion or widespread lassitude. For some consecutive years leading up to about 2010 we considered in Year 12 a film called *Ghosts of Mississippi*, an American civil rights film culminating in a courtroom scene. One year I had to show the last section of it in a science laboratory with a single row of about six seats at the back, and when the jury came to announce its verdict, the entire back row of my class was leaning forward and holding hands, completely and emotionally intent on the outcome. When the foreman delivered "Guilty" they spontaneously raised their hands in the air in triumph, and I swallowed vigorously before I was found reduced to tears in my own classroom. They were moved by the film. I was moved by understanding that these people I worked with were so wrought upon by compassion and justice, and by simple right.

There were other days, with different starting points. When we talked of love, marriage and personal commitment, there was not unusually a total, pin-drop silence. Sometimes I would wonder if I might be moving too far into personal space, and I might say "Look, I'm sorry. Let me move along," and invariably the immediate and spontaneous reaction would be "Carry on!" I had a couple of stories that would sometimes create a similar effect: "Information Please", the one about a little boy to whom a telephone operator was kind; "Something for Stevie", about a young Down Syndrome man looked after by a group of truckers. The point in common was that they all presented something of the sacred. The encouraging, energising, thing about the girls I taught was that the sacred did not typically pass them by.

Other evidence of listening, apart from the classroom atmosphere, came intermittently from girls who sometimes chose to write some reflections when they were leaving. More than one girl used phrasing like "Makes me re-think my life and values" or "A greater understanding and curiosity about religion", "Question our decisive answers to life's 'big questions'", "Left us all a little more open-minded in a quietly non-judgemental fashion."

Such comments are more than personally energising. They are an encouragement to believe that in a world influenced too greatly by transient social commentators, there was a place for more considered deliberation. It may not be quite the reaction the strongest revivalist preachers look for, but there must surely be a value in such comments as "RE classes have been this wonderful opportunity to breathe, recollect my thoughts, listen and really reflect on what life is all about, and for giving me a sort of moral compass that I can carry with me — to be thoughtful in the way I treat the world and the people in it, and in times of distress, to appreciate the beauty within our world." I would not have dared to lay out such a list of goals as a working manifesto; to see it voluntarily delivered by one of the participants was to believe again that there is hope.

Current Affairs

In 2019, I read Laura Hillebrand's book *Unbroken*. It's the story of Louis Zamperini, pre-war Olympic athlete captured by the Japanese while on wartime service in the Pacific and brutally mistreated before coming home and marrying too soon, then almost destroying his marriage and himself with alcohol. His wife drags him off to an evangelistic meeting run in California by Billy Graham, the evangelist of international status in the years after World War 2. Zamperini responds there to the claims of God and is subsequently able to put his life together, without booze. I thought I might use it in the classroom, but I never did.

I have on my files the story of Sir Kim Workman, knighted in 2019 in recognition of his campaigns for social rights in New Zealand. I never used that either. Nor did I use Suzanne Aubert, aka Sister Mary Joseph, who started a home for orphans and the under-privileged on the Whanganui River and two hospitals in Wellington.

What these unused files in my possession illustrate is that there was always a welter of material available for classroom use, so much so that you simply could not find room in your course for everything you'd hoarded. Current affairs, of course, have a way of quickly losing currency, so I came to use the term to mean anything I had currently discovered, not necessarily anything that had just happened. It didn't matter too much how old the events were. What mattered was how well the themes had worn.

Having said that, 2020 was a year that allowed plenty of scope to morally explore the modern world. I undertook a deliberate policy during the year of not mentioning Donald Trump, the US President, in my classroom, because he had a way of derailing everything there as surely as he did it everywhere else. A sort of orange herring, and I could mostly do without him.

But he was not entirely avoidable. One day, on a discussion of honesty and its impact on public morality, I said something like, "That's what I deplore most about the present American President: his habitual lying is an undermining of civilisation. This is not a political comment. It's not my job to make political comments. This is a morality comment — where are we if we can't trust people in public life?"

I thought it was a rhetorical question and was poised to move on, but a hand went up and I asked for the response. It came in an American accent. "Could you give us an example of the President's lies?" she asked.

This was one more time to be dumbfounded. I sometimes am dumbfounded, though usually not. Having nothing to say is not a strength in a classroom full of students. They are apt to think less of you. But here, this day, I may have gaped like a goldfish.

It was not like the day they asked me who God is and I simply wondered if there was any response to make at all. This was the unlike pole —

so many options, you splash about landing one. Finally I said, "If we start at one of his first, and least significant, lies, we could say his claim to have had the biggest inauguration crowd in history. The photos proved him to be wrong, so he said it again, louder. And then if we come up to date" (it was about July of 2020) "and get a bit more significant, we might say his claim that he inherited nothing to fight the Covid pandemic with. He's the guy who disbanded the pandemic unit. And please note — I'll say it again — this is not a political statement. It's a comment about morality, and fitness to govern."

I remembered the American accent though, and also the general rule of thumb in any class. "And you have the right of reply," I said. "We don't have to move on until you've said anything you need to come back at me with." She waived that right, and we moved on.

There was a news item that caught my eye around 2015, give or take. It said that university campuses throughout the USA and Europe had voted to cancel contracts with Coca-Cola. I wondered if someone had become conscious of their diet, but that was not the thrust of the protests. It was all about water.

Coca-Cola had established a bottling plant in the village of Kaladera, in India, at the end of 1999. Kaladera is a desert state, and farmers rely on access to groundwater to cultivate their crops. Coca-Cola uses vast amounts of water, using almost three litres of water to make one litre of soft drink.

Consequently, the article said, there had been a serious decline in water levels since Coca-Cola arrived, and farmers could not irrigate their lands and sustain their crops. Whole families were at risk of losing their livelihood, and locals feared that Kaladera could become a "dark zone," an area that has been abandoned for lack of water.

Coca-Cola was also said to be having a devastating impact on water supplies elsewhere. El Salvador accused them of exhausting water resources over a 25-year period. Similar stories came out of Mexico. It would be very surprising if there were not a raft of other incidents as well. After all, the company made a deliberate drive after World War 2 to be available all over the world, and by 1995 was represented in more countries than the United Nations.

We spent a bit of time kicking around the responsibilities of big corporates and of business in general, and then in early 2016 we found a news item from New Delhi that read, "Coca-Cola Co. has closed a bottling plant in north India that activists had campaigned against, signalling challenges the US beverage giant faces as it seeks to expand in the world's second-most populous nation." No detail, no elaboration, just a little reminder that no one lives to himself … if someone can be found to call him to account.

Another article, an editorial in *The Guardian* from late 2019, talked about a possible need for a moral code for scientists and mathematicians. All very well, the writer said, for a person to pursue pure science or mathematics because they could, but when an unscrupulous user took possession and a nuclear bomb emerged, could the scientist claim to be uninvolved and innocent?

Less dramatically, the writer went on to argue that people have lost control of their personal data, that it is too easy for misinformation to spread on the web and that online political advertising needs transparency and understanding.

And then, just on a year later, the events of the United States election and its aftermath threw those exact points into bold relief. Certainly the liar is responsible for the lies. But is there a responsibility also for those who help spread them?

We took the general principles from these articles and asked a few questions that might apply close to home. What should you do when your boss and you do not see eye to eye? Should an individual member of a national sports team be allowed to wear wristbands supporting — or opposing — political or moral stances? Or be allowed to not advertise selected commercial products? If so, who should decide which ones? Should a teacher resign from a school with official policies to which he or she cannot subscribe? You're a landlord: should you allow your tenant to advertise cigarettes? Or stop him from displaying hateful billboards?

And then, of course, whose "should" do we follow? On what can we agree as a basis of behaviour? When you want to stand for truth and I want to stand for pragmatism, who referees it and by what rulebook? How do my big beliefs shape my specific actions and attitudes? And how do we react when someone else imposes repercussions on our moral standards?

The last question could be illustrated by a woman called Corrie ten Boom, whose family lived near Amsterdam before World War 2. Devout Christians, they had a life history of helping people in need, and when that category began to include persecuted Jews, they kept on doing what they had always done.

It got them arrested, and Corrie's sister, her elderly father and two other family members were all murdered in concentration camps. She survived. After the war, she became something of a Christian celebrity, providing an inspiration to hundreds of thousands of people as a speaker-in-demand in more than 60 countries. She testified to God's love and encouraged everyone she met with the message that "Jesus is Victor."

She was knighted by the Queen of Holland. Yad Vashem, the Holocaust Museum in Jerusalem, asked her in 1968 to plant a tree in the Garden of Righteousness, in honour of the many Jews whose lives her family saved. Her tree stands there today. In the early 1970s her book, *The Hiding Place*, became a best-seller and World Wide Pictures released the major motion picture in 1975. She wrote many other books. She died on her 91st birthday, in 1983.

You cannot tell the story of Corrie ten Boom without being overtly Christian about it, and it's close to obligatory to become Biblical as well. It gives classic illustration that deeply held faith shapes personal behaviour. In Berlin in 1947, she met a man who asked her for help. She recognised him. He had been among the more brutal of her wartime guards, and her body automatically tensed at sight of him. He told her he had become a Christian; he had asked God for an opportunity to ask one of his victims for forgiveness, and he said, "That's why I'm here. Will you forgive me?"

She prayed silently for wisdom, wrestling with her emotions, and felt a warmth flow through her arm until she took his hand and said, "I forgive you everything," and read with him some Bible verses from 1 John 1, about the forgiveness of God.

When the man told her that he was unable to forget his own sins, she stayed in the Bible. She read that God will put the sins of a penitent person as far away from him as the east is from the west. "If you repent," she said to the man, "he casts them into the depths of the sea, forgiven and forgotten, and puts up a sign, 'No Fishing Allowed.'"

Corrie ten Boom wrote that in her post-war experience with other victims of Nazi brutality, it was those who were able to forgive who were best able to rebuild their lives. Those who found it impossible to do so, or who chose not to, often moved into deepening cycles of hatred and despair.

We read the ten Boom story in a Year 12 class in 2007 and Rachel said, "Find forgiveness there? You'd have to be supernaturally nice." It would be hard to cap that as an assessment of the character of God, but later in the same conversation Nicole came pretty close. We had extended our thinking from Corrie ten Boom to God and she said, "When it comes to forgiveness, God hasn't left himself any choice."

Dead right. And wonderfully phrased. Since God has promised forgiveness to all who want it, he would betray not only his promise but his very character if he failed to honour his promise. It must have been 10 years later that Amy made her comment about the Bible being used with a focus on its moral side. What encouraged me was that all three of these girls found the moral, spiritual and theological aspects of the Bible to be entwined. If we read it well, they become indistinguishable. If we read it really well, they become personal as well.

Parables in Lockdown

The Bible material of the EPR classes might be divided into two sorts. One was the narrative selections that featured notable people — Abraham, Moses, Daniel et al — and the discussion of character and implication was always probing and rich. The other sort was marked by the more teaching passages.

During the remote learning sessions of the Covid pandemic lockdown in 2021, we looked at three or four of the parables of Jesus, the teaching passages. One of the parables was the Prodigal Son, the guy who wasted all his money and had to feed pigs before going home to his father. I invited the girls to write a letter for him after he got home, back to his old employer. Here's Kate's response to that exercise:

"Hi there Rob,

"I hope this letter reaches you well and your pigs are good.

"I just wanted to send you a letter regarding myself and thanking you for the opportunity to work for you and your pigs. I would really be a lost cause by now and probably died of starvation. I have returned home now to my father; as scary as it was I needed to do it. Surprisingly, it went a lot better than I anticipated and he was so overjoyed to see me, I am still in shock with his reaction. He thought I died, I mean fair enough I was gone for a long time and hadn't been in contact with him. My older brother has really given me the cold shoulder and is not happy to see me at all which is what I expected but not this badly.

"Thank you for the opportunity to work for you and helping me get back on my feet. I will forever be eternally grateful for what you have provided me with, although it wasn't where I thought I would end up. But I believe it provided me with a reality check of what is important and how I need to be more cautious, respectful and responsible. If you ever need anything please don't hesitate to ask as I believe I owe you a favour for what you've done for me.

"Kind Regards"

To help you remember the story, here it is from Luke chapter 11.

Jesus continued: "There was a man who had two sons. The younger one said to his father, 'Father, give me my share of the estate.' So he divided his property between them.

"Not long after that, the younger son got together all he had, set off for a distant country and there squandered his wealth in wild living. After he had spent everything, there was a severe famine in that whole country, and he began to be in need. So he went and hired himself out to a citizen of that country, who sent him to his fields to feed pigs. He longed to fill his stomach with the pods that the pigs were eating, but no one gave him anything.

"When he came to his senses, he said, 'How many of my father's hired servants have food to spare, and here I am starving to death! I will set out and go back to my father and say to him: Father, I have sinned against heaven and against you. I am no longer worthy to be called your son; make me like one of your hired servants.' So he got up and went to his father.

"But while he was still a long way off, his father saw him and was filled with compassion for him; he ran to his son, threw his arms around him and kissed him.

"The son said to him, 'Father, I have sinned against heaven and against you. I am no longer worthy to be called your son.'

"But the father said to his servants, 'Quick! Bring the best robe and put it on him. Put a ring on his finger and sandals on his feet. Bring the fattened calf and kill it. Let's have a feast and celebrate. For this son of mine was dead and is alive again; he was lost and is found.' So they began to celebrate.

"Meanwhile, the older son was in the field. When he came near the house, he heard music and dancing. So he called one of the servants and asked him what was going on. 'Your brother has come,' he replied, 'and your father has killed the fattened calf because he has him back safe and sound.'

"The older brother became angry and refused to go in. So his father went out and pleaded with him. But he answered his father, 'Look! All these years I've been slaving for you and never disobeyed your orders. Yet you never gave me even a young goat so I could celebrate with my friends. But when this son of yours who has squandered your property with prostitutes comes home, you kill the fattened calf for him!'

"'My son,' the father said, 'you are always with me, and everything I have is yours. But we had to celebrate and be glad, because this brother of yours was dead and is alive again; he was lost and is found.'"

The parable forms half of Jesus' central teaching. We talked online about four questions: What does the younger son assume when he demands his share of the wealth? What is he guilty of? What would it cost him to go home? What characteristics does the father show in the course of the story? We saved the older son for later.

And they went quickly to the kernel of it — the young man was presumptuous and greedy, he was guilty of base ingratitude and it would require a sacrifice of pride before he would go home, and the father demonstrated generosity and tolerant forgiveness.

Then, on their own, I invited them to choose from one of three tasks. One was the young son's letter to his old employer, which gave us Kate's letter. The other two were the next 100 words of the conversation between the father and the older brother, or a paragraph saying which of the two sons might have upset his father more. No one chose to explore the father's conversation with the older brother, but we had a couple of other letters to the pig man. These lines came from Emily:

"Dear Pig Farmers,

"Working for you has very much been a low point in my life. I was too prideful to admit my wrongs to those who could provide for me. So, I worked for you, rather than facing all the damage I had caused my family, caused my father. Yet in a strange way I am indebted to you. Because without you, the lack of food, the pitiful pay for a work that went so against everything I believe, I never would have returned home. Because once I humbled myself before those I so carelessly cast aside I found splendours I thought I could never see again. I have a father who loves me, despite all the pain I am sure I caused him. I have realised the errors of my way. But I could not have done that without you. You made it so that putting aside my pride for my father was so much less painful, for I had put aside so much for you. And because of you, I have had the most decadent party for a long time."

And these from Ella:

"I am writing this letter to acknowledge the great service you have done me. You gave me work when I had nothing to my name, and while I was not treated well during my time there, it is this that became my revelation. It was your lack of suitable working conditions that allowed me to realise how selfish I had been regarding my own family; I took advantage of my father's kindness and squandered his love. However, thanks to you, I now live with my father, who has graciously forgiven me. And so, in my father's spirit, I forgive you for how I was treated, and wish you all the best."

And then, as he always must in any consideration of this parable, the older son entered the discussion, as the girls engaged with the question of which of the sons was more of a problem to his father. Opinions were divided. Not much ground was left uncovered.

Hannah picked up on the older brother's niggardly spirit, when she wrote: "I think that the father may have been more upset by the son who stayed with him and reacted negatively to his brother, than the son who left. It seems as though he expected that one of his sons would want to leave and be on his own for some time, but wasn't upset by the idea, because he believed that he would come home to him, or God would look after him. It appeared that the father was confused and surprised by his other son's reaction to his celebrations and would have been disappointed that his son was jealous or thought that he didn't love and appreciate him as much."

Zoe was inclined to agree: "I believe that the older son upset his father more because the older son didn't uphold the father's beliefs of forgiveness and repenting. Despite the younger son's actions, the father admired his ability to come back and beg for his forgiveness and admit his wrongdoings. The father showed the younger son mercy, and the father's actions mirror God who 'forgives us our sins'. The older son is disappointed that he never received the treatment the younger son is receiving when the younger son's actions didn't warrant his treatment and rewards i.e. robes and a ring. Yet the purpose of the parable is to show how God is always forgiveful and shows mercy which the older brother should have done. I believe the older brother's actions, not welcoming back his brother despite what he had done, upset the father more."

Grace thought so too: "I think that the younger son would've upset him more originally as he was a disappointment and had terrible morals ruining other lives so that he could live a fun one, which ended up not really working out. But as he came home and wanted to be forgiven by his father, he was, yet the oldest son would not forgive him. I think that God is very forgiving and that is a key characteristic of Him, so when the oldest brother could not find it in his heart to forgive and instead became overcome with jealousy, the father was upset by this more than from the recklessness of the youngest son.

There were those with the opposite view. Annika said: "I think that the younger son would have upset him more. Even though the father is really happy that he has been found and has come home, he would have caused him a lot of worrying and sadness while he was 'lost.'"

Gabrielle considered they were both disappointing, before deciding the younger one was more so: "I think the younger son deciding to abandon his responsibilities of helping his family around the farm would have been most disappointing because it shows a lack of caring. However, I feel that the older son not being happy about the return of his brother must have made the father feel a little upset. Because they're a family and the older brother doesn't regard them as a family anymore since the brother left and this has broken the connection between all of them. But I think the father would be more upset with the son who left, rather than the son who stayed and felt jealous because his loyalties went unrewarded."

Beatrice worked the pair of them over too, before coming down with the older: "I think that while the younger son would have initially upset the father more, in the end, the father would be more disappointed in the older son. When the younger son left and squandered the money, it was clearly upsetting to the father, who lost not only the property but also his son, both literally in that he left but also in that he likely lost belief in the younger son's integrity when he left. Upon the son's return, however, his owning up to his actions and taking responsibility will have regained his father's goodwill. The older son would have initially not upset the father, working responsibly and taking up his duties on the farm, but in showing his jealousy for the younger son, the father has now lost his belief in the integrity of his older son."

Jesus' stories are among the oldest and most enduring that we have. Because of Covid lockdown, I asked the girls to say less, write more, and email it to me. Some of them, of course, responded by not doing it, but the thinking I received was perceptive and subtle. As well as the Prodigal Son, we also considered The Pearl of Great Price and The Parable of the Yeast. The Good Samaritan just may have got a mention in there, too.

I have never been too sure why the pearl and the yeast are graced by the name of "parables" but they are, and who am I to argue with the scholars of the ages? But they're metaphors really — or more correctly, similes — and they don't take too long to cover. Here's the parable of the pearl, in its entirety:

> "The kingdom of heaven is like a merchant looking for
> fine pearls. When he found one of great value, he went
> away and sold everything he had, and bought it."

I asked the girls: What is meant here by "the kingdom of heaven"?

Jade's opening line showed appreciation for a normal classroom ("I got a bit stumped for some of them as I didn't have the in-class discussion") but she went on to say "it was good that I had to think for myself." It probably was too, for everyone. Here are some extracts from their responses.

The Kingdom of Heaven:

- is an extension of God. It may not refer to a physical space, but the holy and righteous space that is occupied by those of great faith and virtue

- is essentially the place where God reigns alone without external influences
- is worth selling everything you have for, because it's more valuable then all your items and clothes and stuff put together
- is the main content of Jesus' preaching in the gospel of Matthew ... a process or a course of events whereby God begins to govern or to act as King or Lord
- is used in this story to describe how our relationship with God is the most important thing on Earth and is what we should prioritise over everything else. The merchant in the story has treated the pearl like we should be treating our belief in God. We should treat the value of our relationship with God as a priority, as something different from our material possessions. The relationship we have with God cannot be quantified, which is unique and expresses the impact that God's presence has on us. By describing "the kingdom of heaven" as a pearl that is worth all of an individual's possessions, it helps us to realise that there is more to life than the value of what we can buy and being rich or powerful isn't everything to life. It is nice to be these things, but it doesn't mean that it is fulfilling and will make us happy. Like the merchant in the story, there are sometimes more important things in life than material possessions – such as having a relationship with God.
- When Jesus talks about "The kingdom of heaven" being worth more than the cost of all his possessions he is encouraging us to explore the real value of his kingdom. He is suggesting that if we want to follow Jesus, we need to be prepared to make sacrifices.

Well, there's enough in there to gladden an RE teacher's life, or even an English teacher's life, if it comes to that. But then they went on to the yeast:

> "He told them still another parable: 'The kingdom of heaven is like yeast that a woman took and mixed into about sixty pounds of flour until it worked all through the dough.'"

My question about the yeast was: "In a single line, say what Jesus' main point is here." Their incoming comments included (with a profligate disregard for the concept of "one line"):

- When yeast is first added to dough, it is in one place, but will eventually spread throughout the dough. This is likened to the kingdom of heaven, because the spirituality of the kingdom has spread through the world, having started in one place.
- The yeast is like the kingdom of heaven because only a small amount of yeast is needed for the sixty pounds of flour and as the yeast works through the dough this allows it to rise and grow. This yeast is just like the word of God, which allows people to grow and become better people. In a similar way when Jesus arrived on earth to spread this message, there were people who were defiant and didn't want to listen, yet he had his small group of disciples. Now Christianity is a large global faith who will ultimately reach the kingdom of heaven which is just like the yeast which has worked itself through the large amounts of dough.
- The kingdom of heaven is alive and always growing, similar to how the yeast in the bread is growing. The kingdom of heaven is everywhere, just as the yeast is all through the dough, so we are surrounded by the kingdom of heaven which is always growing,

rising and revolving as we are on earth. When you take even a little bit of yeast and mix it through sixty pounds of flour, the yeast still helps it to rise and grow. It's similar to how when we learn to understand the Kingdom of Heaven it will help us grow personally. Even if we only understand a little part of it and it only starts as a small part of our life it will continue to grow to impact all areas of our lives. Another observation in the similarities is that making bread is quite a long process, you have to be careful, patient and it takes a lot of time. It is similar to understanding the Kingdom of Heaven, it can be a long process to see it and learn how it works and the similarities to the earth but when you are careful and patient you will receive a reward similar to how when you make the dough you end up with bread.

- The kingdom of heaven is everywhere, incorporated into every aspect of the world. In the same way yeast causes dough to rise from within, small acts of goodness and kindness spread and influence others, causing our society to thrive and flourish.
- The kingdom of heaven exists within everyone.
- The flour is the people and the yeast is like the Holy Spirit or the goodness of God which creates the bread which is the kingdom of heaven.

In the last lesson of lockdown, we were ready for a change from the parables. I found it in a book called *God, a Biography*, written by Jack Miles, an American author who won the Pulitzer Prize for it in 1996.

Miles does not treat his biblical subjects as either transcendent deities, like God, or historical figures, like Abraham Lincoln. Rather, he considers them as literary protagonists, as one might discuss, say, Hamlet. So in

Miles's book, God becomes the central character in the work of literature that we call the Bible. We looked at some of Miles's opening paragraphs.

He begins by saying, "That God created mankind, male and female, in his own image is a matter of faith. That our forebears strove for centuries to perfect themselves in the image of their God, is a matter of historical fact." For centuries, he reminds us, the people who forged the basis of Western civilisation consciously sought to model themselves on God. Both Jews and Christians aimed to mould themselves in the image of the God who occupied their sacred writings. Elsewhere in the world, the shaping of culture came from different sources. The result, Miles claims, is a difference of DNA between Western culture and any other, and this remains true whether the faith remains dominant or not.

To illustrate this claim he suggests that a young man raised in wealth who gives away his fortune in adulthood and chooses to live in poverty would have changed his present circumstances, but not his history. He would still be a man whose character was raised in wealth. So with Western culture, whose ideal of human character remains in the image of those who forged it. Other cultures differ because those who forged them looked into a different "religio-cultural mirror."

"Knowledge of God as a literary character neither precludes nor requires belief in God," says Miles. And he says that the literature where God is found has been successful beyond all comparison with Western literature, and probably in any literature, because although it is true that literary characters have an influence on their readers, no character has ever had the reception that God has had. Whether Western individuals like it or not everyone, *everyone,* can tell you something about him.

And however the ancient writers perceived God, their work has been, in literary terms, a staggering success. It has been read aloud every week for two thousand years to audiences who have received it with utmost seriousness and consciously sought to maximise its influence upon themselves. That being so, it has shaped the values of the West in a way that most of us can only dimly appreciate.

I gave the class a page or so of these thoughts, with the requirement to ponder it for 10 minutes and the opportunity to voluntarily respond. Beatrice did.

She wrote: "I appreciated the excerpt, as I have thought before about the importance of the Bible as a literary text regardless of if one holds faith. I think many people are too quick to dismiss the Bible's importance just because they don't believe in God. I find this a little hasty, especially as a student of history. So much of our society has been shaped by religious teaching and in western society, Christian teaching, and to ignore the Bible means that you lose a lot of this context.

"Thank you for sharing the extract and quotations. I found them an interesting way to spend my Tuesday afternoon."

Conclusion

Good People to Be Around

When I left Queen Margaret College at the end of 2021, I said in my farewell speech to the staff that the years there had included some of the best times of my teaching career, and that they had come from my dealings with the student body. It was true. As a standard characteristic, girls through the years expressed goodwill, good work and good humour, and there was a positive tenor that created a wonderful teacher/student relationship.

I remember getting to the end of the course with a Year 9 class in 2015 and having someone say to me, "Mr Edgecombe, look at this." "This" was the back page of her friend Olivia's RE book, upon which Olivia had drawn, with precision and class, a small facsimile of every tie I had worn during her lessons in the course of the year. There were 31 of them, in full colour. I asked her to sign me a copy and let me have it, which she did. It's on my study wall.

I mentioned it to Robyn Brader, my colleague in the Maths Department, who asked, "Did she not have enough to do in your classes?" It's the obvious question, but the less than obvious answer was, "Well, I think she did." Because Olivia had been one of those people who had been attentive and present throughout, and engaged in the theme of the day. Just busy in parallel, that's all, recording my ties. And showing me.

The girls took a keen interest in the things you wore. Not infrequently, and sometimes in the most inopportune moments, someone was likely to comment on your shirt, or shoes or, most commonly, tie. I recall a girl once looking at my tie, which featured an assemblage of very red raspberries, and saying, "Yum!" She looked a bit disconcerted when I said, "Well, thank you, Hayley. It's a long time since a young woman looked at me and said that."

I was also given a few ties over the years. There was one with a large picture of Noah's Ark, and a red one with Chinese dragons brought all the way home from a school visit to Hong Kong. One had hand-drawn Easter chickens, another, white, was colourfully signed by the class who gave it to me. One had a Christmas motif, one featured the Beatitudes, one was a very natty patterned blue item. One year the prefects asked me over to the Common Room to conduct a session in knotting their ties — following on, I think, from a day in their Year 10 year when I had paused to knot for someone a tie she had taken off in Phys Ed and whose father, not being present at the school, couldn't re-do it for her that afternoon.

Comments on ties became commonplace, but of course some things were new. Some were even unique. There was a day when, straight after lunch and with the girls arriving in the room in clumps, one of them asked me thoughtfully, "Mr Edgecombe, are those Julius Marlowe shoes?"

"Strike, I don't know," I said. I was more than a tad flabbergasted. But I took one off to have a look and sure enough, there on the inside sole and not yet worn completely off — "Julius Marlow." "Well done," I said. I looked at her with a new respect. She likely looked at me with a new contempt.

There was another unique question another day, on a completely different tangent. It was straight after lunch, again, with glorious sunshine streaming through the windows. We were just about to start, waiting for the last class members to arrive, and while there was a friendly sort of informality going on, one girl said to me, "Mr Edgecombe, can you remember when you liked girls?"

I blinked. This was fraught, if you like. If I'd heard her right. Did I look like a frizzled relic? Or maybe like I hated everyone? Hurry slowly.

"What?" I said.

"You know," she looked a bit bashful, but she stayed on course. "When you ..." she tailed off, with an expressive gesture.

I grinned at her. "Hang on Jess," I said. "I'm only old. I'm not dead." She laughed with me, but she clung to her theme. "You know ..."

"Listen, where are you going with this?" I asked her. It turned out that she had noticed a young man at her sports club, and what she really wanted to know was, had he noticed her? I was the nearest male whose opinion might reflect the species in general. She was a nice girl, and he certainly ought to have noticed her, but you can't really say that. What I said was, "Jess, if he hasn't noticed you, he's not worth wasting your time over."

This opinion went down well among the assembled onlookers, though I never was sure if it brought Jess any comfort or not. But some years later in another context I retold the story for another class, and at the end of it they applauded me. Clearly it aligned with some of their prejudices, and you couldn't always guarantee that.

All this is not to say that everything always went as well in the classroom as you would want it to, even on the best of days. For one thing, I kept on forgetting their names. I was inclined to excuse myself for that — I mean, the timetable allowed for one lesson per week per class in RE, and it was therefore a week and 400-plus girls between drinks for any individual. But excusable or not, it was still embarrassing, not to say a hindrance. Sometimes you got a name in the first lesson and it stayed with you for the next five years, and sometimes the five years just seemed to have ingrained the problem. The girls were very forgiving. They suffered, though, from the same malaise that affected the whole of the education system, in that they couldn't tell the difference between teaching and assessing. Instead of saying, "My name's Hannah and here's how you can remember it," they would typically say "What's my name?" and be glad if I knew it and no help at all if I didn't. Shaped by the system they'd had modelled to them, I suppose. Throughout my time at the school it never ceased to mildly irritate me that, whenever anyone wanted to take a class out of school for some excellent reason, the major grounds for not doing so were always "Unless they have an assessment to be done." If they only had a lesson to be done, it could wait.

It's fair to say that QMC was no different from anyone else in this regard. But it remained a fact that education was too often driven by assessment, and not the other way around. I was thankful to the end that no formal assessment applied in Religious Education, with the exception of one class in my final year. It meant that we could get on with the learning, and the thinking, and even though it put the spotlight firmly on the teacher to make it all real, it also protected me as an assessor from the charge that I was only awarding grades to people who agreed with me. In passing, the effect on the one class we did assess seemed to be that they took more notes in that time, and offered fewer comments. Busier; less engaged.

Going briefly back to the names, it was always a pleasure to reach the point where you did actually know everyone in the room, and could even show off a bit. I recall the day I was teaching the youngest of three sisters in the school, about Year 9, with her sisters in Year 12 and 13. I knew them all, but on this day I absent-mindedly addressed the youngest by the name of one of the others — in the same way, I have no doubt at all, that her own parents did twice a day. But she looked at me with sweet patience and said, "Mr Edgecombe, I do get tired of being called by my sisters' names." "I'm sorry, Phoebe," I said. And I was.

So, later in the day when I met her Year 13 sister in the corridor, I said to her, "Hello Phoebe." Ruby looked mildly surprised, smiled and corrected me. "I'm sorry," I said. "Of course." Later that afternoon I met Charlotte, and we went through the same routine. The next day Phoebe said to me, "Thank you for calling my sisters by my name." It was a teaching moment — a pity I knew her name already. I'd have remembered it after that.

The girls' feedback at the end of a class or the end of the year was also very personable, and often very helpful. Sometimes it was challenging. There was always a range of Christmas cards with a variety of friendly comment — one year an entire Year 10 class signed a card remarking, "Basically, you're everyone at QMC's third grandfather." It was an observation to which I could choose my reaction: I chose the warmth of intent above any commentary related to calendars.

But as well as the personal greetings, there were very often little reflections about the lessons, and things appreciated. One girl presented me, at the end of Year 10, with a hand-drawn picture of Mary and Joseph, with

Jesus, on the legendary donkey mounted as a sliding feature with a close resemblance to the famous Year 7 sliding camel of Abraham. Another commented "You're always careful not to preach at us, but we trust you enough. You could probably do it more." I regarded it as good advice to not follow.

More collectively, the Year 11 group of 2012 produced their own memorable moment. On the day of their last dean's assembly Natasha Selkirk, who was dean of Year 11, asked me if I would attend her assembly to pray for the girls before they went off to their exams. They had made this request, and I was delighted to respond to it. "You don't need to come to the whole assembly," Natasha said. "I'll stop whenever you arrive, and you can pray for them then."

So that's what we did, but when I had finished, Natasha assumed an uncharacteristically shifty expression and said, "Actually, that's not the only reason they wanted you to come today." And at a prearranged signal, two girls came forward carrying some object wrapped, if I recall, in a school cardigan. It looked a bit unwieldy, and when they arrived at where I was standing, they removed the cardigan and revealed a picture that had been painted by one of their number. It depicted two girls in Queen Margaret College uniform walking into heaven, with a suitable text from Matthew's Gospel inscribed in the background. The frame had been signed by the entire complement of Year 11, who were now sitting in front of me in expectation of some appropriately flowing rhetoric. It was some moments before I could muster up the self-control to deliver it. I have cherished that picture ever since, even if I had been inveigled into receiving it under, if not exactly false pretences, certainly a degree of mixed motivation.

More formally, it was fairly standard practice through the school for a teacher to conduct a review of the year past with a class or two, with the aim of adjusting details. I always kept my questions brief and hopefully manageable — "What's been good about the year? What hasn't? One thing you've learned? One thing to do differently next year?" Responses were variable, but I always read them carefully and tried to implement the best of the advice, remembering that even if things were OK you don't have to be sick to get better. There were many thoughtful comments, and the responses to "One thing you've learned?" were an index to basic effectiveness.

And some of them were fundamental, going to the core of the exercise. Comments like "Makes you really think about your views and makes you question your first thoughts on something" or "Looking at people for who they are, not what they have done" are little windows into the whole point of the course. One girl wrote: "I didn't use to believe all this about God, but now I do. It's true." Another recalled a story in which a needy person met, by totally random chance, Mrs Harris, who helped her. I had asked, "If she hadn't prayed, would Mrs Harris have been there?" and Rebecca's response was "I don't think *she'd* have been there." Someone else said, "Starting something is better than not doing anything at all": surely a lesson in life for the teacher as well as the pupil.

Because, of course, we were all in it together. As a teacher who professed a faith, I was always aware that I needed to be clear and unapologetic about it, while giving space to those who did not share it. Some pursued another faith: some acknowledged none — although, as I have suggested, I would personally contest any claim to "none". But even as I sought to make my faith transparent, it too was evolving, in no small part because of the honesty of the questions I was constantly being asked. At best, so was theirs.

And as a believer in truth, I'll take that. Once the questions come, there is usually an answer, and Jesus himself said that the person who seeks will ultimately find.

It was a mark of the girls I taught that they tended to be appreciative. At the end of a lesson, as they left the room, a steady stream of them would say, simply: "Thank you." Sometimes it was humbling: you might have just finished a lesson you'd have to be charitable to call ordinary, and there they were saying thank you. It kept you up to it. If there was going to be all that thanking, you needed to be worthy of it. But the thanks was a two-way thing, too. A good lesson is made by good pupils, and so is a good teacher. Like faith, it's a gloriously woven fabric of the varied materials of life. No wonder I was grateful to be there.

A QM Sort of Place

Queen Margaret College celebrated its centenary in 2019. Obviously, that anniversary signifies a lot of things — one being that, when it was founded, there were already well-established places where a girl in Wellington could get a very good high school education. Wellington Girls' College is about a three-minute walk from Queen Margaret's front gate.

So we might fairly ask, "Why start a new, private, girls' school – then, or any time in the last hundred years?" And a second question is also fair, "Has it been worth it?"

It's simpler to essay a shot at the first answer than it is at the second. The twin clues are that state education in New Zealand has been legally secular since 1877 and that Queen Margaret College's founders were Presbyterians. So, applying their rights in a democratic society, they founded a school where a full education included reference to God.

That meant several things. Symbolically, the Presbyterians named their school after a Scottish queen who was later recognised as a saint, the monogram included a lamp, and the motto, Luce Veritatis, reflected the Bible's teaching that God is both light and truth. More substantively, a chaplain was appointed as part of the school's staffing, the school's state occasions were marked by Christian observances and by prayer, the curriculum included Religious Education and the Presbyterian Church was represented on the College Board. More subtly, the school aimed to produce a tone in keeping with its Christian character, although tone is a difficult thing to put your finger on and, of course, any decent school attempts to foster selfless values that some people are fond of calling "Christian".

Addressing the question of whether it has been worth it would probably be easier if we allowed a two-word addition: "Has it been worth it *for me*?" We could then consider a variety of individual points of view. But I hope the founders of 1919 would be able to look at the school in 2019 — and later — and recognise enough of their original vision to give their hundred-year endorsement. Since they are not able to do that, we can only table selected facts and subjective opinions and leave it to inference.

Some things are true. My first-day experience with blazers left in classrooms and no thought given by their owners about theft, is true. I have taught in places where you dared not leave your keys on a desk while you closed a window in case you lost them and created insecurity throughout the school and caused an immediate, and expensive, change of locks. At Queen Margaret, I don't think I ever locked a door, be it cupboard, classroom or car, at times when the place was populated only by its student body. There were occasions of theft in the school, but they were genuinely uncharacteristic and always something of a shock.

It is likely, of course, that this tendency to honesty might be explained by a lot of factors less subtle than a Christian ideal among the school's founders. Nonetheless it is real, and the founders would have wished for it.

Also real was a deliberate intention to strive for a sense of worked-out charity. Every year, each class level in the school selected and raised funds for a charitable cause — Wellington City Mission, incoming refugees, Amnesty International, World Vision, Free Ambulance all come readily to mind, and there were many others. Again, such efforts were less than specifically Christian, but they were certainly in the ballpark, and there were times when Year 9 solemnly knitted Peggy squares all the way through an RE lesson to help kit out needy people, and such activity seemed totally in keeping with the nature of the classes.

Specific Christian events, apart from the weekly chaplain's assembly, came and went a bit over the years. There was an annual Sunday night Founders' Service at St John's Presbyterian Church, but attendance from the school body was less than overwhelming, apart from the parents of choir members, especially the junior ones. In my early years at the school there was an annual midweek church service at St Andrews on The Terrace, one each for Junior, Middle and Senior School, but it had fallen away by the time I left. Easter services took the entire school to the Wellington Cathedral, and the school Christmas service was an authentically big deal. Also, special events such as the opening of a new building were generally marked by prayer, so the character of a Christian private school was certainly addressed. Yet there is a distinction between doing special things on the one hand, and seeing spontaneous expressions of ingrained character on the other. Something of it was caught for me one day by an informal comment that was intended to be companionable, but that underlined distance.

We had a whole-school outdoor activity planned, to open a building or something similar, and the day of it dawned sunny and pleasant. We were relieved. As we stood outside for the ceremony to begin, the Chairman of the Board said to me, "You must have some influence up there, Ken." I would have hoped that the Board Chairman's influence "up there", and that of the school's officers in general, would not be less than mine. There was another day when the principal, introducing me to a visitor to the school, said, "Ken's responsible for the spiritual values of the school."

All right, I had my responsibilities, and I certainly had no wish to avoid them. But — on my own? Ideally you would hope for a climate within which, if the chaplain fell off the bus tomorrow, no one would realistically notice for the rest of the year. Apart from the individual gap in the seating plan, of course. Being a focal voice for group unity is different from being a spokesman for a group of uncertain identity. Any Christian school requires constant self-auditing to ensure they are still true to the rock from which they were hewn. Even better, additional auditing from outside is often helpful, to check that small changes here and there, over time, do not result in a distortion of original aims. I know that Waikanae Christian Holiday Park, for years, added an external spiritual audit to their normal, required financial audits. Jack Miles's contention in *God, a Biography,* that the DNA remains through many changes is true, but deliberate practices are a more than helpful honing of it.

Because any institution that grows out of a vision has to manage two risks. For the school, the collective, there is a natural wish to accept anyone who wants to come, in the admirable name of inclusivity. All good. But the accompanying temptation is to swallow the bait of pluralism and attempt to meet the grounds of a diverse membership by settling for an unidentified "spirituality", deemed to be big enough to include

Christianity and everything else but actually vague enough to clarify very little. It's a trap, and a school has to be vigilant in guarding against it. The second risk is for the individual. It is to absorb the bland apathy of the world around us together with an unconsidered aversion to anything resembling spiritual rigour, calling it tolerance and vaguely aspiring to perhaps "science", itself a usually unconsidered entity.

The origin and special character of QMC, the raison d'être, is tied to an expression of Christian identity that is neither compromised nor apologised for, while accepting willing participants of any stripe and treating them with unaffected respect. That respect includes a clear and unwavering expression of its own undiluted character. From that basis comes an automatic and unstriven-for acknowledgement that other people are different. When Christian schools own who they are and were founded to be, they are at their best, and the members of a different outlook are clear about what to expect.

There were times when the school was called involuntarily to express its Christian character. When I became the chaplain, a friend of mine said to me, "You'll be conducting their weddings in a couple of years." At the time I left, I had conducted no weddings of old girls, though I had performed the service for six or eight staff members. But, sadly, I had participated in funeral or remembrance services for no fewer than six immediate old girls, none of whom had been gone from the school for more than four years. In two cases I conducted the funeral service. In 2011 Penelope Lake died suddenly from meningitis at the age of 19, and in 2019 Sophia Crestani, also 19, was the victim of an accident at a student party in Dunedin. On both occasions the school stepped up to its broader responsibilities, most visibly for Sophia whose funeral was at the school during school hours. They had also sent the head of the senior school, Jacqui Brown, and me to Dunedin for two days, to lend support to the large number of Queen Margaret old girls who were Sophia's contemporaries. Respect, care and spiritual support in times of singular need.

The school's custom of filing into assemblies in silence twice a week, once for the principal and once for the chaplain, were less dramatic examples of the principle of group identity, as well as allowing a quick and seemly beginning for the person conducting the assembly. The school fostered a number of customs aimed at demonstrating the importance of corporate identity in an age of individualism. You saw the upside of it at the end of Term 2 every year, when a complete day was given in a darkened hall to the heaving, screaming, impossibly-costumed mass that were the participants in and the audience for house music, the culmination of weeks of disciplined and creative rehearsals and obeisance to the honour of the house. Wonderful, cathartic, unifying: "I am part of a larger whole." Also competitive.

In passing, there was an annual chaplains' and RE teachers' conference that did a lot for collegiality among those charged with "the spiritual values of the school". I attended my first one in 2002, mildly unsure of what to expect, and found among my colleagues in the Presbyterian and Anglican schools of New Zealand a rich bond of like-mindedness, and also of open-mindedness. Every year, in Term 3, the members of what someone without poetry in their soul had named NZARETSC (you work it out!) administered to one another a generous shot of inspiration and renewed vision, both spiritual and practical.

So there was time and effort given to fostering the school's special character. There was also a genuine climate of goodwill. How "Christian" some of it was is debatable, but it was certainly part of the school's identity. And if the reason for the school's founding was to create a special ability to add understanding to a girl's world view, you would want to see it in daily outlook as much as in academic understanding. Outlook and understanding, ideally, are the two sides of a single face.

And that's where you could be dismayed and cheered in any given moment. I asked a senior class in my last year at the school to write down their ideas of what God should be like, and they did. Their list included: fair, loyal, kind, patient, loving, sympathetic, understanding, good, knowing, empathetic. Terrific list: not a cliché in sight, and wouldn't we all want to follow a God like that?

Yet many of them didn't. Not infrequently, someone whose comment was about to include a Christian insight would precede it with the disclaimer so prevalent among the social commentators of our day, "I'm not religious but …" They may not always have been as irreligious as they thought they were, but they were a very present challenge to the school to remain clear about its century-old responsibility to be Christian in its fibre and its ways, and to equip its students to face a community of confusion and disillusionment.

In a world of diversity, there is of course a delicacy in this. There is always a voice that seeks the line of greatest conformity, so as not to confront anyone whose views might be different. The opposite view is to be so visibly true to yourself that those who differ may see what they are differing from, and relate accordingly.

If you err at the extreme of the first outlook, you become a non-distinctive blob. If you err at the extreme of the second, you become a strident shrew. So the trick is not to err at either extreme. It requires constant attention to what you stand for, and why you do, and how it is best addressed.

Would the Founders of 1919 be satisfied with the school of 2020? I don't know. But their goals remain current: to include awareness of God as part of a good education. Certainly, times have changed. We live in a world of climate change, of Black Lives Matter demonstrations, of diverse gender identity, widely different political and social views, the internet with all its potential to enrich and destroy, dictators in unlikely places. Those who founded the school, of course, had just finished World War 1. Either way, the need is clear for a set of cohesive moral and philosophical values. Given that everything, *everything,* is based on some version of such values, we do well to identify clearly where our own come from.

Which I think spotlights the essence of RE or EPR in a Christian school. It is a time to look at the school's acknowledged values, and at those of others, and also at our own. It is why I was so dismayed to see RE disappear from the senior course in 2011, and so pleased to be part of its re-emergence in 2019. Times to step off the treadmill and reflect on life are not plentiful in our day, and it is good for a Christian school to make them conscious. Spiritual values may not always be easy to grasp: the more reason to address them deliberately, and to refuse to allow a tension between faith and science.

World War 1 was a check on the evils of science ungrounded. Climate change is too. And the godless regimes of Soviet Russia and Nazi Germany that filled much of the space in between them give us little encouragement that studied irreligion offers any hope at all. The school's reason for being is as great now as it was a hundred-and-few years ago. The challenge remains constant to keep checking that it is worth it. A friend of mine, former state school principal, remarked to me years ago that a leader without a clear philosophy of life would end up "cunningly leading the school nowhere."

Over 125 years ago, the emergence of the modern Olympics stated the dream that amateur athletes from all lands might create a unity not found anywhere else. The games have evolved almost beyond recognition, and some would say that they are a world away from their founding goals. Some would say they work against them. But the goals remain good goals. Queen Margaret's challenge is not dissimilar: to keep pursuing the goals even through change, and to not be so changed that our relevance is doubtful.

Through my years at the school, the encouragement came through the insights given, often unconsciously, that those goals were being addressed. The dismay came through other insights, similarly given, that they were not — that "all this" was unimportant, or even worse, when viewed alongside the "real world" of material gain.

The whole world lives in the tension between the material and the spiritual, between love and money. Queen Margaret's deliberate acknowledgement of it is not just a fashion accessory for a nice girls' school: it covers ground that is critical to life. It is not facetious to speculate that it may be the reason that the school has outlasted the Soviet Union. When the chips go down, this is where people turn. It is not common to hear people at a funeral taking genuine comfort from such thoughts as "He made a lot of money." This *is* the point.

The aim of the school, of any school, is to produce lifelong learners. Its leaders articulate that. This is the field for it. Grounding of leaders — and indeed also of followers — needs to occur in the big things of life. Those doing the grounding have a responsibility to not ignore it. Gandhi and Mandela, Moses and Gideon: all looked above themselves. Even the "Be kind" of Prime Minister Jacinda Ardern is very close to Jesus, who is more than a mere example to the whole lot of us. "Remember your creator in the days of your youth" is neither a platitude nor a command. It is an inspiration to strive for wholeness. The school has a house prayer that acknowledges that. It is the Sarum prayer, sung on state occasions:

"God be in my head and in my understanding
God be in my eyes and in my looking

God be in my mouth and in my speaking
God be in my heart and in my thinking
God be at mine end and at my departing."

It's quite a delicate thing and tricky to sing and I don't think I ever heard it done compellingly, but it articulates a profound aspiration.

How much of it all went home, and made a difference? No one knows, except God alone. But the girls sometimes said things that gave glimpses. I can think of three of them who specifically thanked me for reinforcing their own Christian faith. I was gratified by that, because most of my awareness was shaped by the need to engage with those who professed none. Another one wrote to me as she left school to say that her faith outlook had developed over her years at Queen Margaret and was still doing so. This was a girl whose mother had once sent me an email to say that her family appreciated the mealtime conversations that came out of our classroom discussions. What delighted me was the evidence, not of a fixed point of religious outlook, but of fluidity and life. Another girl wrote of being led to question her decisive answers to life's big questions.

The comments were not all of a kind. Another girl talked of how school gave her mixed messages. "RE strongly shows me to value others' faiths and to protect my own, (not let others taint or confuse it), but school presents a lot that is not in line with Jesus, eg that you have to be academic to have a good life, or to value worldly things or to put yourself before others and studies before a distraught friend. RE counters this with love. But the way you live your life speaks louder than words and relations and your actions are stronger than you realise. Wisdom is important and you can't leave a bad or an OK situation as it is, you have to do something to make it better."

I closed my teaching career when I left Queen Margaret College. It was a career both typical and singular: early years finding my way as a teacher of English, promotion to deputy principal, then 10 years outside the profession, working for Scripture Union while many of my contemporaries were promoted to top jobs. When I came to teach Religious Education, all of those experiences came together for the final years: not a traditional career outcome, but incredibly fulfilling. It was a calling, and a real privilege, and it required all of my skills, knowledge and experience. There was a feeling of helping to shape and express the school's identity and ethos, and of holding RE on a higher plane than it might be allowed to slip away from, and of trying to open girls' horizons to their widest possible extent. On their last day in the school in 2021, Emma and Bella came to see me and to say they were sorry I was leaving, and in the course of the conversation Emma said, "My friend said she could believe more in God after your last assembly," and Bella said, "You always linked faith to real life." That would be because faith *is* real life, and how exhilarating to hear it offered back.

So, there it was. Twenty-one years teaching RE at Queen Margaret College, about 20 percent of the life of the school and no one needs to wonder what percentage of the life of me. And someone out there will be asking me, "Was it worth it?"

Well, briefly, it was for me. But the bigger answer is, "Right now, you can't know." I can say I enjoyed it, all the way up to full time. On balance, it looked as if the girls also mostly enjoyed it, although of course I am a long way from being the best judge of that. I can say I learned a huge amount. I met some wonderful people.

But the school does not exist for me to enjoy myself, or learn a lot, or meet wonderful people. It exists as a place of education with awareness of God, and its RE programme was established to meet the founders' goal of an awareness of God in the day-to-day life of a Presbyterian school.

That's why it's too soon yet to know if it was worth it. Certainly a lot of them suggested progress, and many told me they had developed their spiritual awareness in ways they had not expected to. But God is not a philosophy, and an academic "awareness" of him is an insufficient outcome, especially if he is then to be reduced to the level of a political fashion or a social trend.

If God is the fulfilment of the yearning of the human heart for honesty, truth and justice, for decency, trust and love, then an awareness of him can be developed only by personal commitment to him and to all his ways. And a commitment can be followed only through the years. If any of my pupils were following more closely at the end of the course than they were at the beginning, and if that following laid the foundation for better following in the years ahead, then it was worth it. But I don't know that, and, appropriately, I mostly won't.

I do know that knowing about God is shallow without a commitment to letting him move me forward. I do know that I tried to awaken understandings that might encourage knowing God better. I do know that there was much to encourage, and there was some that did not.

I spent 21 years in the company of many, many wonderful people for whom my love and respect deepened as time passed. I developed my own faith further in conversation with them and in reaction to their questions, and their mysterious female powers became both an apprenticeship and a finishing school for being a grandfather to my own seven beautiful granddaughters. Maybe you can't "prove" God, but the beauty and dignity of the young women with whom I worked, and their thoughtful insights and approach to matters of morality and faith were surely hints of his existence.

So, "worth it"? I can only pray that the Great Arbiter himself may deem it worth it, in the lives of many, a long time from now.

And there is a school prayer. It was published in 1860, written by William Chatterton Dix. Few of the girls of Queen Margaret would have heard of William Chatterton Dix, but they sang his prayer every year. It referenced the magi, the wise men who made their way to where the new-born Jesus was, and it linked their journey to ours. The college had adopted it as their school hymn, and its singing was the last act of the formal prizegiving which occurred annually just before Christmas. It's a good note to end a prizegiving, or a school year, or indeed a book. Forever may they sing …

"As with gladness men of old
Did the guiding star behold
As with joy they hailed its light
Leading onward, beaming bright
So, most gracious Lord, may we
Evermore be led to thee.

"As with joyful steps they sped
Saviour to thy lowly bed
There to bend the knee before
Thee whom heaven and earth adore
So may we with willing feet
Ever seek thy mercy seat.

"As they offered gifts most rare
At thy cradle rude and bare
So may we with holy joy
Pure and free from sin's alloy

All our costliest treasures bring
Christ to thee our heavenly king.

"Holy Jesus every day
Keep us in the narrow way
And when earthly things are past
Bring our ransomed souls at last
Where they need no star to guide
Where no clouds thy glory hide.

"In the heavenly country bright
Need they no created light
Thou its light its joy its crown
Thou its sun which goes not down
There forever may we sing
Alleluias to our king."

Notes: Sources and Quotes

Chapter 1: Scripture Union, an interdenominational Christian organisation dedicated to promoting Bible reading and represented since 1867 in over 135 countries throughout the world, with a presence in New Zealand since 1880.

The allegory of the long spoons is attributed to Rabbi Haim of Rumšiškės, Lithuania, as well as other sources. One commentator on it has said, "It's hard to know who wrote it."

Chapter 2: Jerry Seinfeld is an American stand-up comedian, actor, writer, and producer.

The story featuring Mrs Nat King Cole is a long-standing urban legend.

"The Cab Ride I'll Never Forget" is by Kent Nerburn, originally written as part of a chapter in his book, *Make Me an Instrument of Your Peace: Living in the Spirit of the Prayer of St Francis* (pp. 57–64), published by Harper, San Francisco, 1999. Various versions of the story have been circulated on the internet. The author says: "The story is real, my friends. It was a gift of a moment to me, and I hope that by passing it along it is a gift to you, as well." It happened in Minneapolis, Minnesota in the early

1980s, when Nerburn was working as a driver for the Yellow Cab company on what he called "the dog shift" overnight. It can be found in its full form at: https://zenmoments.org/the-cab-ride-ill-never-forget/

Lumsden does indeed have a fire brigade, volunteer. I have no idea whether they have a social group or not, with or without a band.

Chapter 3: Henri Charrière, 1906-73, was a Frenchman convicted of murder in 1931. He wrote the semi-autobiographical novel *Papillon* and its sequel *Banco*, memoirs of his incarceration in and escape from Devil's Island, a penal colony in French Guiana. The source acknowledged here is *Banco*, published in Great Britain by Hart-Davis, MacGibbon Ltd in 1973.

Rev Dr Tony Campolo, born 1935, is an American sociologist, pastor, author, public speaker and former US Presidential spiritual advisor. A PhD from Temple University and an ordained Baptist minister, he is Professor Emeritus of Sociology at Eastern University in Pennsylvania and has been a leader of progressive thought and reform within the evangelical community. The references in this chapter were taken from a video of addresses he gave at the Waikanae Easter Convention at Waikanae Christian Holiday Park, in 1993.

Chapter 5: Andrew Lloyd Webber, Baron Lloyd Webber Kt, is an English composer of stage musicals, including *Joseph and his Amazing Technicolour Dreamcoat.*

Chapter 6: Ian Grant QSO has been an advocate for youth and parenting in New Zealand for many years. In 1993 he and his wife Mary established Parenting with Confidence Inc (now The Parenting Place).

Terry Eagleton: see notes on Chapter 9.

T S Eliot OM, 1888-1965, was an essayist, publisher, playwright, literary critic and editor, and one of the 20th century's major poets. This line comes from his poem "The Love Song of J Alfred Prufrock".

Karl Barth, 1886-1968, was a Swiss Calvinist theologian. His line about the snake has been often repeated, in many contexts.

J K Rowling's words taken from an interview of J K Rowling CH OBE HonFRSE FRCPE FRSL by Max Wyman, in *The Vancouver Sun,* a division of Postmedia Network Inc, October 26, 2000.

Abigail BeauSeigneur wrote an article called "Is Harry Potter the Son of God?" in *Mugglenet,* "The #1 Wizarding World Resource since 1999", published July 13, 2007.

Chapter 7: Caroline Hill is not today a corporate lawyer.

No Country for Old Men, a novel published by Random House in 2005 and a Coen Brothers/Scott Rudin film in 2007, written by the American writer Cormac McCarthy.

Chapter 8: An article in *The Dominion Post*, date lost, in which a police officer assisted someone who was walking over the Remutakas in inclement weather.

Stuart Townend is an English Christian worship leader and a writer of hymns and contemporary worship music.

Chapter 9: "Nothing comes from Nothing" is a song in the musical *The Sound of Music,* which made its premiere in 1965, with Julie Andrews singing the song that I chose not to replicate in the classroom.

Richard Dawkins FRS FRSL is a British evolutionary biologist. He is an Emeritus Fellow of New College, Oxford, and was Professor for Public Understanding of Science in the University of Oxford from 1995 to 2008.

An often-quoted atheist, he is well known for his criticism of creationism and intelligent design.

Terry Eagleton FBA, English literary theorist, critic, and public intellectual, and Distinguished Professor of English Literature at Lancaster University, published a review of Richard Dawkins' book *The God Delusion* in *The London Review* of *Books*, in October 2006, in which he questioned Dawkins' methodology and understanding. He is quoted here with permission from *The London Review of Books*.

Editorial in *North and South* magazine in 2019, specific date lost.

Rabbi Lord Jonathan Sacks, Baron Sacks, (1948-2020) was a British Orthodox rabbi, philosopher, theologian, author, peer and public figure, who served as the Chief Rabbi of the United Hebrew Congregations of the Commonwealth from 1991 to 2013. He sums the issue up in his book *The Great Partnership: Science, Religion, and the Search for Meaning*, published by Penguin Random House in 2012, by saying that science seeks to tell us how things work, and theology seeks to tell us why they should.

Cormac McCarthy's *No Country for Old Men*.

Chapter 10: From a 2020 headline in Stuff, "Paid content" section, that said, "A scientist released a painting of Jesus." By Lammie, in *Opera News*, Nigeria.

Boris Johnson, Prime Minister of the United Kingdom from 2019-22 and a former Mayor of London, was a solid-looking man with a conspicuous crop of very fair hair.

Yuri Gagarin (1934-1968), Soviet pilot, became the first man to journey into outer space, completing one orbit of Earth on 12 April 1961.

Nikita Khrushchev was the First Secretary of the Communist Party of the Soviet Union from 1953 to 1964.

Clive Staples Lewis was a British academic don, writer, and lay theologian. He held academic positions in English literature at both Oxford University and Cambridge University. He published an essay in 1963 exploring a number of topics related to space-travel, including the idea of finding God in space, in *The Seeing Eye*, republished in *Christian Reflections*, edited by Walter Hooper, Grand Rapids, MI, USA.

James Edward Lesslie Newbigin, 1909-1998, was a British theologian, missionary and author. He spent much of his life in India.

Noel Fellowes served in the Lancashire police force, left them at age 22, was convicted of the murder of a man he had never met, and jailed in 1970. During nearly five years in prison, he suffered intimidation and violence as an ex-policeman. Upon release, he entered a life of substance abuse, hoping to escape the years of pain, bitterness and hatred resulting from his sense of injustice until, ten years after his release, new evidence came to light and he was completely vindicated. His 1996 autobiography, *Killing Time*, published by Lion Publishing PLC, became a best-selling book.

Captain Edward Vernon Rickenbacker MOH, 1890-1973, was an American airman, racing car driver and automotive designer, military consultant to the government and air transport pioneer, notably with Eastern Air Lines. The seagull story is referenced by Max Lucado in *In the Eye of the Storm*, published by Thomas Nelson, 1991, pp221, 225-226.

Mount Everest account of Frank Smythe, 1900-1949, English mountaineer, author, photographer and botanist; this story included in *Adventures of a Mountaineer*, published by J M Dent Ltd (London) in 1940.

Rob Harley, New Zealand documentary film maker, spent more than 26 years working in TV news and current affairs before moving into the world of communications consultancy because he found he was becoming cynical with the media. He has made many documentaries, often focusing on inspiring lives.

Chapter 11: Pontius Pilate was the Roman governor of Palestine whom history placed in the intolerable position of being the man to hear the Jewish charges against Jesus.

Story of a London minister who spent Sunday evening preaching up a storm about the virtues of honesty: attributed to Lou Nicholes (1933-2021), in *Family Times* website. https://www.family-times.net/-

Chapter 12: John Ernst Steinbeck (1902-68), was an American author and the 1962 Nobel Prize winner in Literature. The opening paragraph of his classic short novel, *Cannery Row*, published by William Heinemann in 1947, gives an insight into the universal flaws and grandness of human nature.

Tom Slater, former National Director of the Australian Evangelical Alliance, was State Director of Scripture Union Victoria, Australia, in the 1990s.

In July of 2011, terrorist attacks in Oslo and Utøya, in Norway, left 77 people dead.

Chapter 13: King Caractacus was a character in a children's song released in 1980 by Rolf Harris, before he became discredited. The character is probably derived from Caratacus, a leader of assorted tribes who resisted the Roman invasion of Britain in AD 43. The original Caratacus would have had no harem, in the official sense of the term.

Gary Edward "Garrison" Keillor, born 1942, is an American author, storyteller, humourist, voice actor, and radio personality, best known as the creator of the Minnesota Public Radio show *A Prairie Home*

Companion, which he hosted from 1974 to 2016. "Ronnie and the Winnebago" first appeared on the Highbridge Label HBP 56790 in Mother Father Uncle Aunt, in 1997.

Count Leo Tolstoy (1828-1910) was a Russian writer who received nominations for the Nobel Prize in Literature every year from 1902 to 1906 and for the Nobel Peace Prize in 1901, 1902, and 1909.

Digby Hannah, Melbourne, Facilitator, Parenting after Separation, spent almost 20 years with Anglicare conducting camping programmes for disadvantaged families and teenagers.

Michael Jordan is a former basketball player, of whom the official NBA website laconically states, "Michael Jordan is the greatest basketball player of all time."

Ernest Lee Jahncke (1877-1960) was US Assistant Secretary of the Navy. He was the first, and until 2002 the only, person ever to have been expelled from the International Olympic Committee.

Rev Canon Rebecca Totterdell became the rector at St Mary's Church, Hemyock, England, in 2019. She had previously been on the staff at Exeter Cathedral.

John Cleese (born 1939), English actor, comedian, screenwriter, and producer, and star of *Fawlty Towers* and *Monty Python* comedy series.

Thomas A Harris (1910-1995) was an American psychiatrist who became famous for his 1969 self-help book *I'm OK, You're OK*, published by Harper & Row. It sold over 15 million copies in 20 languages. Its name became a byword during the 1970s.

Chapter 14: The story of a desperate woman in Auckland who, abandoned by her husband when her youngest child was a few months old and providentially rescued from killing herself and all three of her children, came to me years ago from a source I have since regrettably misplaced.

Founded in 1961, Amnesty International is an international non-governmental organisation focused on human rights and interceding for political prisoners. It claims more than seven million members and supporters around the world.

Chapter 15: Westboro Baptist Church was established in 1931 as a branch of the East Side Baptist Church in Topeka, Kansas. It is now independent of any Baptist denomination, having been denounced by a number of Baptist alliances and other mainstream Christian denominations. It is known for its vigorous and litigious opposition to atheists, Jews, Muslims, transgender people and numerous Christian denominations.

Chapter 16: New Zealand's 2013 suicide statistics were provided by the New Zealand Ministry of Health in July, 2016.

Mary Therese Hansen (1966–2002; apples/bananas poem) was an Australian guitarist and singer.

Dr Francis S Collins ForMemRS, born 1950, is an American physician-geneticist who led the Human Genome Project. He has written several books on science, medicine, and religion, including in 2006 *The Language of God: A Scientist Presents the Evidence for Belief*, published by Free Press, subsidiary of Simon and Schuster. It topped the *New York Times* bestseller list.

John Steinbeck's *East of Eden* was first published by William Heinemann Ltd in 1952.

Chapter 17: Macbeth was King of the Scots from 1040 until his death in 1057. His successor, Malcolm III, was married to Queen Margaret. In

1606 Macbeth was the subject of a less than flattering play loosely based on him, written by William Shakespeare.

Asia Bibi was imprisoned for blasphemy in Pakistan in 2009 and sentenced to death. The sentence was commuted in 2018, and she was released in 2019, arriving in Canada the next day. During her 10 years in prison, two politicians who spoke on her behalf — Shahbaz Bhatti and Salman Taseer — were murdered. Taseer, a Muslim, was the governor of Punjab province; Bhatti, a Christian, was the federal Minister for Minorities.

Meriam Yehya Ibrahim Ishag is a Sudanese woman who was arrested for apostasy during her second pregnancy and who gave birth in prison, in chains, on 27 May 2014. On 24 June she was released by a Sudanese appeal court, re-arrested the following day as she and her family were about to board a plane to the United States, and freed again the day after. She took refuge in the United States embassy, and finally arrived in Rome on 24 July 2014.

Amina Lawal Kurami is a Nigerian woman. On 22 March 2002, an Islamic Sharia court in the northern state of Katsina sentenced her to death by stoning for adultery and for conceiving an illegitimate child. The man she identified as the father of the child was not prosecuted for lack of evidence and was deemed innocent by the court. Lawal's conviction, which coincided with plans to hold the Miss Universe contest in Nigeria and which sparked an international controversy, was overturned by a Sharia Court of Appeals which ruled that it violated Islamic law, and she later remarried. In their successful defence of Amina Lawal, lawyers used the notion of "extended pregnancy" (dormant foetus), arguing that under Sharia law, a five-year interval is possible between human conception and birth, and noting that two years before her daughter's birth, Lawal was still married to her husband.

C S Lewis wrote the seven titles of *The Chronicles of Narnia* between 1950 and 1956, a series of fantasy novels for children. The series, in continuous reprint (in 47 languages) ever since publication, has been adapted for radio, television, the stage, film and computer games. *The Lion, the Witch and the Wardrobe* was first published by Geoffrey Bles in October 1950.

Chapter 18: Gregory King, who died in 2012, was a highly regarded New Zealand criminal defence lawyer and broadcaster.

Lewis's claim that his children's book was not an allegory was outlined in a letter among his correspondence in 1958 and has been numerously quoted since.

Chapter 20: The Beatitudes of Jesus as quoted here are from the New International Version of the Bible (first published 1973), whose copyright is held by Biblica worldwide, Zondervan in the US and Hodder & Stoughton in the UK.

Joyeux Noel is a 2005 film, directed by Christian Carion and based on a World War I temporary and unofficial Christmas truce of December 1914.

"Information Please", internet viral story whose historicity is unknown, by Paul Villard and originally published in the June, 1966 *Readers Digest*; about a little boy who kept ringing up the local telephone exchange and both gave and received encouragement to and from the operator.

Amazing Grace is a 2006 film directed by Michael Apted CMG about the political campaign to abolish the slave trade in the British Empire, and showing the personal and political life of William Wilberforce, leading anti-slavery political activist over many years. The title is a reference to the 1772 hymn "Amazing Grace" written by John Newton, who was a former slave trader before becoming an Anglican clergyman and a mentor of Wilberforce.

Robert Nesta Marley OM, (1945-1981), aka Bob Marley, was a Jamaican singer, songwriter, and musician, a pioneer of reggae who became a global figure in popular culture and a Rastafarian symbol. "Buffalo Soldier", written by Marley and Noel "King Sporty" Williams, was recorded by Tuff Gong Island Records in 1978 but not released until 1983, posthumously for Marley.

Emperor Haile Selassie I was Emperor of Ethiopia from 1930 to 1974 and an international voice in the forum of African rights. Full name Ras Tafari Makonnen, he became a symbol of Rastafarian idealism and saviourhood.

Chapter 21: "A Poor Rich Family", by Eddie Ogan, original publication details lost, although the article first appeared in a denominational newsletter. In 2019, Ogan was in Colville, Washington, where she died that year aged 88. References to Eddie Ogan and the story may be found at https://dickstannard.com/my-world-as-i-see-it/2019/04/05/catching-up-with-eddie-ogan/

There is a strong suggestion that the line "Some people are so poor that all they have is money," is attributable to Bob Marley.

Mr Holland's Opus is a 1995 American film directed by Stephen Herek. The title character, Glenn Holland, is a dedicated high-school music teacher who attempts to compose his own music while struggling to balance his job and life with his wife and profoundly deaf son.

The story of Quique, a young man escaping the drug cartels of Central America and in desperate but illegal flight into the USA, is featured in *To Obama: With Love, Joy, Anger, and Hope*, by Jeanne Marie Laskas, published by Bloomsbury in 2018 and telling the story of the correspondence room of President Obama to the end of 2016.

John Steinbeck, in *Sweet Thursday*, published by Wm Heinemann Ltd in 1954 as a sequel to *Cannery Row*.

Mike Starkey, English television and Greenbelt poet: first collection of poems published in 1987. "Mary He Said" included in *Stand Up Poetry, Performance Poems with Teeth* edited by Fraser Grace and published by Frameworks in 1991. Starkey's lines are used here with permission granted in February 2022 by IVP UK, parent company of Frameworks.

Chapter 22: Joseph M Stowell, graduate of Cedarville University and Dallas Theological Seminary and retired president of Cornerstone University, is the author of over 20 Christian books.

Simon Wiesenthal KBE, 1908-2005, a student of architecture living in Lwów at the outbreak of World War II, was a Jewish Austrian Holocaust survivor, Nazi hunter, and writer.

Extract from *Driving to Treblinka: A Long Search for a Lost Father* (Awa Press, 2017) courtesy of the author Diana Wichtel and Awa Press. Diana Wichtel, a New Zealand writer and critic and columnist for *New Zealand Listener*, was born in Vancouver, Canada, the daughter of a New Zealand mother and a Polish Jewish father who had escaped from the train taking his family to the extermination camp at Treblinka. In *Driving to Treblinka*, she told of her mother's bringing her to New Zealand when she was 13 with the expectation that her father would follow, but she never saw him again. Her return to Canada in search of him revealed he had died in a mental hospital with the listing "Family and friends: none."

A BBC World Service *Hardtalk* interview, posted on You Tube in 2017, featured Niklas Frank, son of the World War II Nazi Governor of Poland, Hans Frank, interviewed by Stephen Sackur.

Richard Batista, a doctor, married Dawnell in 1991. In 2001 he donated his wife a kidney in an attempt to save her life and their marriage. The marriage failed, however, and he sued to get his kidney back, or 1.5 million dollars. The court ruled against him.

In 2018 a young man was discharged without conviction on a domestic assault charge. His selection for the New Zealand national rugby team, the All Blacks, soon afterwards occasioned a deal of criticism from various quarters, including a couple of teams the All Blacks were due to play against.

A Wellington man who had once been a child molester repented of his actions over the course of years, became first a Christian and later a minister of religion, and then sought advice on whether he should try to make amends for his past actions. He was advised not to, in case he re-opened old wounds. When the woman later lodged a complaint and the police came looking for him he confessed openly, and then served a prison term.

In 2001 Rais Bhuiyan, a Muslim citizen of Texas, was shot and blinded by a white supremacist seeking revenge after the 9/11 attacks on the Twin Towers in New York. Bhuiyan sued the governor of Texas to prevent his assailant from being executed, but the sentence was carried out in 2011.

A South Auckland family whose child was killed by a drunken teen-aged driver wanted to protect the young man responsible from lasting damage in the aftermath.

Chapter 23: "Ronnie and the Winnebago" was a Garrison Keillor monologue from *Prairie Home Companion*, a weekly radio variety show created and hosted by Keillor that aired live from 1974 to 2016. "Ronnie and the Winnebago" was first broadcast in 1997.

Debbie Morris: In 1993 Sister Helen Prejean's book, *Dead Man Walking*, was published by Knopf Doubleday Publishing Group. A film based on the book was made in 1995, directed by Tim Robbins and featuring Prejean's experiences as spiritual counsellor to two death row inmates of Louisiana prisons. One of the crime victims featured in the book was Debbie Morris, and in 1998 Zondervan published *Forgiving the Dead Man Walking*, her story written with Gregg Lewis of gradual forgiveness which was later featured by Philip Yancey's video series based on his own book *What's So Amazing about Grace?*, which had been published by Zondervan in 1997.

Chapter 24: *To Kill a Mockingbird* was one, *The Power and the Glory* was another, of the novels up for study in Year 12 EPR classes. We had another unit on six films, including *Citizen Kane* and *Sully*.

Rev Dr Nouh Ag Infa Yattara, born 1954, is the senior pastor of Eglise Evangelique Baptiste, the Christian Church that he and his wife, Fati, founded in Timbuktu.

Stephen Farris Saint, born 1951 in Ecuador, is a business entrepreneur, pilot, and author. Many of the details in this story were published in the American magazine *Christianity Today*, September 1996, and in *Martyrs: Contemporary Writers on Modern Lives of Faith*, a collection of essays edited by Susan Bergman (Harper San Francisco), also as an article by Steve Saint in January 1991: "To the Ends of the Earth." Guideposts (https://www.guideposts.org/magazine-contact-us)

G K Chesterton KC*SG, 1874-1936, English writer, philosopher, lay theologian, and literary and art critic.

The Parkin Drawing Prize is New Zealand's premier award for drawing. It is sponsored by arts patron and philanthropist, Chris Parkin. The 2020 Parkin Drawing prize-winner was Poppy Lekner, who won a $25,000 cash prize for her work *Forward Slash*. Reflecting on the winning artwork, Charlotte Davy, the judge for the 2020 prize, said: "It is a delicate unrelenting work produced on a Brother typewriter. The artist has mechanically made the same mark over and over again, meshing and weaving the symbol into a single image. Far from the kind of quick digital keyboard art that can readily be morphed into emoji, this piece is a beautiful meditation created using a laborious process of pressing the character into the surface repeatedly in a line, then adjusting and realigning the paper at the end of each row before setting out again."

Robert L Short's book, *The Parables of Peanuts*, first published in 1968 by Harper and Rowe.

Rev Martin Luther King Jr was an American Baptist minister and political activist who became the most visible spokesman and leader in the American civil rights movement from 1955 until his assassination in 1968.

Chapter 25: The Auckland story of Richard, Wing Lee and Szymon, was given to me by Richard, who is a personal friend of mine. He wishes the story to remain as loosely identified as I have presented it.

C S Lewis remarked, in a radio talk on the BBC during World War II: "Aim at heaven and you will get earth thrown in. Aim at earth and you get neither." The line was later included in his book, *Mere Christianity*, published in 1952 by Geoffrey Bles.

His Honour Judge Andrew Becroft QSO was appointed a District Court Judge in 1996. In 2001, he became the Principal Youth Court Judge of New Zealand, a role that he held until 2016 when he was appointed the Children's Commissioner, until 2021.

Ghosts of Mississippi, a 1996 American civil rights film directed by Rob Reiner.

"Something for Stevie", by Dan Anderson, about a young Down Syndrome man looked after by a group of truckers, in RPM *Magazine for Truckers*, November 1998.

Chapter 26: Laura Hillebrand's book, *Unbroken*, the story of Louis Zamperini, published by Random House in 2010.

Sir Kim Workman KNZM, QSO, born 1940, New Zealand criminal justice advocate of Ngati Kahungunu ki Wairarapa affiliation.

Suzanne Aubert, 1835-1926 aka Sister Mary Joseph, who founded a home for orphans and the under-privileged on the Whanganui River, and two hospitals in Wellington.

Coca-Cola established a bottling plant in the village of Kaladera, in India, at the end of 1999. In 1998, the area's groundwater had been declared as overexploited. The plant was closed in 2016, following a degree of lobbying.

Dr Hannah Fry (born 1984), a British mathematician, author, lecturer, radio and television presenter, podcaster and public speaker and Professor in the Mathematics of Cities, occasioned an editorial in *The Guardian* on 18 August 2019 after she had commented on a possible need for a moral code for scientists and mathematicians.

Corrie ten Boom, born 15 April 1892, died 15 April 1983, was a Dutch Christian watchmaker and later a writer who worked with her father, Casper ten Boom, her sister Betsie ten Boom and other family members to help many Jewish people escape from the Nazis during World War II by hiding them in her home. In 1971 *The Hiding Place*, written by her with John and Elizabeth Sherrill, was published by Chosen Books. It became a best-seller, and World Wide Pictures released the major motion picture in 1975.

Chapter 27: Jack Miles, an American author who won the Pulitzer Prize in 1996 with *God, a Biography*, published by Alfred A Knopf, Inc, has had writings on religion, politics, and culture published in numerous national publications.

Chapter 29: Waikanae Christian Holiday Park, which calls its campus El Rancho, was established by an independent inter-denominational Christian group in 1963 and seeks to maintain and represent general Christian core values.

NZARETSC: New Zealand Association of Religious Education Teachers and School Chaplains.

The Sarum Prayer, a short song of petition for God's presence, is from the 1558 Sarum Primer, which was a collection of prayers and worship resources developed in Salisbury, England, during the 13th century. The author is unknown.

William Chatterton Dix, 1837-1898, was an English layman who lived in Scotland and became a writer of hymns and carols. His song "As With Gladness" was written as an Epiphany hymn in 1859, included in *Hymns Ancient and Modern* in 1861, and has been sung inside and outside of churches ever since. It links the pilgrimage of the Wise Men of Christmas to our contemporary life journeys. The music is by Conrad Kocher, adapted by William Henry Monk. "As With Gladness" was adopted as the Queen Margaret College hymn early in the school's history, and is sung annually at the school's prizegiving ceremony.

Acknowledgements

This is my book, and I am responsible for anything in it that you don't like. However, a lot of people helped me to get it there, variously, and I am indebted to them all.

When we talked about it early, Michael Steer first got a light in his eye and then lent moral support and critical comment, as well as administrative assistance, throughout the course. Even down to final proof-reading: no wingman could be called upon for more. Tom Slater's early enthusiasm stopped about one pace short of melodrama. He suggested Ark House as a publisher, too. Jayne-Ann Young's early encouragement and enthusiasm were pivotal when I was wondering if it was OK for Queen Margaret College to be exposed to the public when it hadn't asked to be; and she later provided a most generous endorsement of the book; Rachael Day provided a more than warmly welcoming gateway to the school after I had left the staff; Amanda Peake and Sharon Bulmer were helpfulness and good cheer personified in providing on-site assistance. Michael Keith lent invaluable editorial assistance and much shrewd observation, and Adrienne Jansen gave a slew of helpful advice, guidance, and critical encouragement, latterly assisted by Matt Gillon. Liz Hay gave some early discerning comment and so did Deborah Wilson. Mark Edgecombe added his literary critical faculty and provided a title at a time when everyone I respected was being lukewarm about mine. Or cooler. He also took the picture of the author for the cover, and such a task is never a sinecure. Anita Edgecombe gave me a second and more informed opinion on a couple of specialist issues. Shona Murray, Caroline Hollow, Caroline Hill, Phoebe van Boheemen, Siobhan Murray all provided contacts with people I needed to talk to. Erinn Aspell gave me a written endorsement, and she did so with a level of enthusiasm and goodwill that warmed the soul and half the nearby horizon. Sharon Kennedy, in the face of a degree of personal distraction, provided the illustrations, and her enthusiasm was up there with Erinn's. Ann Mildenhall, Geoff Troughton, Tim Cooper, David Dell and Peter Lineham all offered advice and encouragement, and Peter and Tim both volunteered a public comment. Hamish Galloway added the offer of a foreword to his own early comments and encouragement, and Jacqui Brown and Philip Yancey gladly gave me public endorsement. So did Wendy Strachan and Lilly Taulelei. James Newman and Nicole Danswan and the team at Ark House were not only professionally inspiring but also warm and encouraging on a personal level.

I am grateful to my wife, Felicia, for her unwavering support and assistance and for her belief in the project, and of course my deep thanks to every girl I have quoted or alluded to and the hundreds of others they represent, who made up the journey of the years. Some of them, past and present pupils, I spoke to or emailed, and they were unanimously positive and unfailingly encouraging: Jemma Balmer (Hartley), Alex King, Franziska Dobbie (Plimmer), Amy Wiltshire, Katie Bagley, Georgie Moore, Ursula Scott, Jacqui Ormsby, Shruti Iyer, Bethany Kaye-Blake, Shweta Iyer, Charlotte Lee, Ruby van Boheemen, Emma Law, Isabella Pennington, Laura Miller, Ella Monnery, Adibah Khan, Yovela Li, Jessica Teh, Caitlin Lei, Kate

Charteris, Emily Brown, Ella Briggs, Hannah McCadden, Zoe Cooper, Grace Symmans, Annika Peterson, Gabrielle Clark, Beatrice Markwell, Jade Morrison, Charlotte Gee, and if there were others whom I have overlooked, I am grateful to them as well and sorry to have omitted their names. Just like the old classes, really.

Ken Edgecombe

Lightning Source UK Ltd.
Milton Keynes UK
UKHW012145130223
416920UK00002B/530